I Made You to Find Me

I MADE YOU TO FIND ME

*The Coming of Age of the Woman Poet
and the Politics of Poetic Address*

Jane Hedley

 THE OHIO STATE UNIVERSITY PRESS | COLUMBUS

Copyright © 2009 by The Ohio State University.
All rights reserved.

Library of Congress Cataloging-in-Publication Data
Hedley, Jane.
I made you to find me : the coming of age of the woman poet and the politics of poetic address / Jane Hedley.
p. cm.
Includes bibliographical references and index.
ISBN 978-0-8142-1101-4 (cloth : alk. paper)
1. Women poets, American—20th century. 2. American poetry—Women authors—History and criticism. 3. American poetry—20th century—History and criticism. 4. American literature—Women authors—History and criticism. 5. Women and literature—United States—History—20th century. I. Title.
PS151.I25 2009
811.'54099287—dc22
2009002739

The author has received permission to quote from the following sources: *The Unabridged Journals of Sylvia Plath, 1950–1962*, edited by Karen V. Kukil (New York: Random House, 2000); Carol Muske, *Women and Poetry: Truth, Autobiography, and the Shape of the Self* (Ann Arbor: University of Michigan Press, 1997), courtesy of the University of Michigan Press; Gwendolyn Brooks, *Report from Part One* (Detroit: Broadside Press, 1972), reprinted by consent of Brooks Permissions; "The Double Image," from *To Bedlam and Part Way Back* by Anne Sexton, copyright © 1960 by Anne Sexton, renewed 1988 by Linda G. Sexton, reprinted by permission of Houghton Mifflin Harcourt Publishing Company, all rights reserved; and Gwendolyn Brooks (© 1949), Poem XI from *Annie Allen*, "The Womanhood" (New York: Harper Perennial, 1999). The poem "SOS" by Imamu Amiri Baraka (LeRoi Jones) is reprinted in its entirety in chapter 4 by permission of SLL/Sterling Lord Literistic, Inc. Copyright by Amiri Baraka.

Paper (ISBN: 978-0-8142-5642-8)
Cover design by Mia Risberg
Text design by Juliet Williams
Type set in ITC Giovanni

For my colleagues and students at Bryn Mawr College

CONTENTS

List of Illustrations		ix
Acknowledgments		xi
Introduction	Making "You" to Find "Me"	1
Chapter 1	Anne Sexton and the Gender of Poethood	25
Chapter 2	Adrienne Rich's Anti-Confessional Poetics	48
Chapter 3	Sylvia Plath's Ekphrastic Impulse	71
Chapter 4	Race and Rhetoric in the Poetry of Gwendolyn Brooks	103
Coda	Presence and Absence	144
Notes		151
Bibliography		179
Index		189

ILLUSTRATIONS

Figure 1 Giorgio De Chirico, *Conversation Among the Ruins*, 1927. Chester Dale Collection. Image courtesy of the Board of Trustees, National Gallery of Art, Washington. 83

Figure 2 Paul Klee, *Perseus. (Der Witz hat über das Leid gesiegt.)* 1904, 12; *Perseus (wit has triumphed over grief)*: etching, 12.6 x 14 cm. Zentrum Paul Klee, Bern. 89

Figure 3 Sylvia Plath and Ted Hughes in Paris, August 1956. Mortimer Rare Book Room, Smith College, © Warren J. Plath. 91

ACKNOWLEDGMENTS

My indebtedness to other scholars' published work will emerge in due course, and is documented in the footnotes, but I would especially like to thank a few colleagues from whom I have learned a great deal about contemporary poetry and poetics in more informal exchanges: Heather Dubrow, Roger Gilbert, Nick Halpern, Karl Kirchwey, Jeanne Minahan, and Willard Spiegelman. A wonderful group of Philadelphia-area colleagues, including Scott Black, Betsy Bolton, Claire Busse, Edmund Campos, Nora Johnson, Laura McGrane, Kristen Poole, Katherine Rowe, and Lauren Shohet, read drafts of the book's individual chapters and helped me to do yet further thinking about the issues they raise; I'm grateful for their time, their candor, and their friendship.

At The Ohio State University Press I have been fortunate indeed to work with Senior Editor Sandy Crooms and her superb editorial staff; special thanks to Copyediting Coordinator Maggie Diehl. I am grateful to two anonymous readers for the press whose suggestions helped me to make this a better book in several key ways. Bryn Thompson, our departmental secretary at Bryn Mawr, did the work of securing permission to include the images that appear in chapter 3.

Bryn Mawr College, where I have spent my whole career as a teacher, has supported my work with sabbatical leaves, research funds, and an institutional expectation that I would put both my students *and* my scholarship first; with students as good as I've had at Bryn Mawr, this has proved eminently feasible. I would especially like to thank Nancy Vickers and Robert Dostal, who were Bryn Mawr's president and provost, respectively, during most of the time I was writing this book, for increasing the frequency of sabbaticals and raising the level of funding for faculty research. My present and former colleagues in the English department have made coming to work every day a treat and an adventure. I am also grateful to those colleagues at Bryn Mawr and Haverford Colleges whose commitment to feminist and gender studies over the past thirty-plus years has made the "bi-co" a hospitable place to engage in this kind of scholarly project—among them Jane Caplan, Anne Dalke, Elaine Hansen, Carole Joffe, Raji Mohan, Judith Shapiro, and Sharon Ullman.

My colleague Joseph Kramer, now emeritus, whose wide-ranging knowledge of English and American literature includes both lyric poetry and queer studies, read an early draft of every chapter and made astute suggestions for revision. Often Joe saw where I was headed next before I did, and his belief in the project's potential to interest readers never wavered (or if it did, he never let on). Sandra Berwind, with whom I traded a course in "The Lyric" back and forth while she was my colleague in the English department, has kept me walking and talking about this book throughout the whole process of its gestation and writing; Sandra's advice and support have been important to me. My sister Barbara Turner-Vesselago, who writes and teaches writing, is a good friend to all my intellectual endeavors, and our sororal relationship has itself become part of the book in all kinds of ways.

Tony Jenkins's undergraduate honors seminar at the University of Victoria brought it home to me many years ago that I would never tire of dissecting and discussing poems. At Bryn Mawr, my own undergraduate students have been reading and discussing women's poetry with me since the 1970s. This book is dedicated to them and to my faculty colleagues, with heartfelt thanks for their intellectual companionship.

Steve Salkever, with whom I have been privileged to share domestic arrangements for more than twenty years, has been my professional colleague for even longer. In both capacities I couldn't live without him, for too many reasons to list here.

INTRODUCTION

MAKING "YOU" TO FIND "ME"

Arrogant, I think I have written lines which qualify me to be The Poetess of America (as Ted will be The Poet of England and her dominions).

—The Unabridged Journals of Sylvia Plath, *entry for March 29, 1958*

The prototypical woman poets of the twentieth century are, of course, Sylvia Plath and Adrienne Rich. . . . They were (along with Anne Sexton) the beginning of an era. Prior to this era the categories were set well apart. Women and poets. Of course, there was the Uber-frau-ish "poetess," a dread diminutive with an arched eyebrow over every syllable.

—Carol Muske, Women and Poetry:
Truth, Autobiography, and the Shape of the Self

My father provided me with . . . an old desk . . . with . . . a removable glass-protected shelf at the top, for books. Certainly up there, holding special delights for a writing-girl, were the Emily books, L. M. Montgomery's books about a Canadian girl who wrote . . . dreamed, reached. . . . Certainly there, also, to look down at me whenever I sat at the desk, was Paul Laurence Dunbar. "You," my mother had early announced, "are going to be the lady Paul Laurence Dunbar."

—Gwendolyn Brooks, Report from Part One

In the first of these three passages, the status of "poetess" is invoked in a spirit of playful grandiosity by an aspirant to poethood who has just produced—to her own amazement—eight poems in as many days. Four years later, on the verge of writing the poems that would lay claim posthumously to the status she craved, this same poet would align herself with "the poetess Anne Sexton," telling a radio interviewer that she found Sexton's willingness to engage with certain "private and taboo subjects" "quite new, quite exciting."[1] Meanwhile, however, on the back cover of her first published volume, *The Colossus*, poetry critic A[lfred] Alvarez was assuring potential readers that "Miss Plath . . . steers clear of feminine charm, deliciousness, gentility, super-sensitivity, and the act of being a poetess: she simply writes good poetry."[2] According to Alvarez, furnishing book jacket copy in 1961, "poetess" was indeed a "dread diminutive" whose connotations needed fending off in the interest of garnering the widest possible readership for a woman poet's work.

Implicit in Alvarez's praise for Plath's début volume is the conviction that good poems are not acts of self-expression, but of making—acts to which gender, a category of social identity, is or should be irrelevant. The stereotype of the poetess stands in for the difficulty women are supposed to have in rising above or "steering clear" of their social identity on the way to poethood. Plath's use of the term "poetess" suggests, however, that it helped her find a way to make poems that would explode the stereotype invoked by Muske and Alvarez. Sexton, Plath, and Rich all found ways to speak as women in their poems without being limited *to* or *by* the "Uber-frau-ish" stance of "poetess": that is presumably what Muske has in mind in suggesting that together these three poets represent "the beginning of an era."[3]

"Who rivals?" Plath goes on to ask in the journal entry cited above, and answers her own question with a summary checklist of other poetesses: "Well, in history—Sappho, Elizabeth Barrett Browning, Christina Rossetti, Amy Lowell, Emily Dickinson, Edna St. Vincent Millay—all dead." Still living: "Edith Sitwell & Marianne Moore, the ageing giantesses & poetic godmothers." In her own generation: "Adrienne Cecile Rich," who, she assures herself, "will soon be eclipsed by these eight poems."[4] By the time Plath wrote this journal entry, Adrienne Rich had already published two books of poems, winning the Yale Younger Poets prize in 1951 for her début volume, *A Change of World*. But Rich aspired to poethood on terms that emphatically did *not* allow for conceiving of her as a poetess: the stance she crafted for her first two published volumes was intended to give her readers as little incentive as possible to hear a woman's voice speak from their pages.

In 1949 Gwendolyn Brooks won the Pulitzer Prize for *Annie Allen*, her second book of poems. Neither Plath, in 1958, nor for that matter Carol Muske, in 1997, saw fit to include the poet of "Bronzeville" among the prototypical women poets of the twentieth century, and yet this is a status Brooks was not loath to claim for herself. "Weeps out of western country something new," is how she announced the "birth in a narrow room" of an American girl child whose difficult coming of age is the organizing trajectory of the *Annie Allen* volume as a whole.

"The birth in a narrow room," which is the title of the volume's leadoff poem,[5] evokes not only the home of Annie's parents in the black belt of inner-city Chicago but also the location of the poet who is her true begetter, a writing-girl whose role models are female and male, "Negro" and "Gentile," and who seeks to extend the purview of "western" poetry. For Brooks, race proved to be a more salient identity marker than gender in determining what kinds of poems she would want to write and would be able to publish.[6] Throughout her long career it was the politics of race that gave her the work she most needed, as a poet, to do. And yet this work was strongly inflected by a woman's perspective and experiences. Like Plath, and unlike Rich, Brooks early aspired to a niche in the canon of American poetry that awaited her *because* she was female: "a *lady* Paul Laurence Dunbar" would indeed be "something new."

These four poets, who were near-contemporaries, all had their gender working both for and against them. Being female may indeed have worked for them by working against them, in that it brought each of them inescapably to grips with the question of who she would be speaking *as* in her poems and where she would be speaking *from*.[7] Rich explained in her Foreword to *The Fact of a Doorframe*, in 1984, that the nineteen- or twenty-year-old poet who wrote the earliest poems collected in that volume had not yet realized "that she was neither unique nor universal, but a person in history, a woman and not a man, a white and also Jewish inheritor of a particular Western consciousness. . . ."[8] According to the "Western" tradition of the lyric she and her contemporaries inherited, the poet is a unique individual who leaves "his" individuality behind to some extent in order to be able to speak both to and from "our" shared humanity.[9] This was a status only poets who were white and male could easily claim. In 1950 a woman who aspired to poethood had to learn by trial and error what kinds of authority *she* could lay claim to: "the learning of poetic craft," Rich recalls, "was much easier than knowing what to do with it. . . ." How each of these poets crafted a viable poetic stance for herself as "a woman and not a man" is the story I have written this book to tell.[10] Inasmuch as each turned a potential liability into an opportunity, the notion that gender should or could be transcended in the interest of universality no longer has much currency among us—which means that not only women but also men who are poets no longer aspire to poethood on the same terms as before.

Crafting a viable poetic stance involved coming to grips not only with the problem of the "I," of how to write from the perspective of a woman's experience and yet be taken seriously as a poet, but also with the problem of the "you"—of constructing poetically and politically viable figures of address. "I made you to find me": Sexton was ostensibly confessing to maternal malfeasance when she said this to her youngest daughter in "The Double Image," but it's a statement that also speaks to the rhetorical challenge she faced as a maker of poems. The question of whom the poem's speaker supposes herself to be addressing is not, in the first instance, a question of who will actually be reading the poem. In the first instance, it goes to the always implicitly and often explicitly vocative character of lyric discourse.

What does it mean to say that lyric discourse is "vocative"? Poems often purport to be addressed to a significant other, be it another human being, a divinity, a force of nature, or a personified work of art; at the same time, however, when Richard Wilbur insists that a poem is "not a message from one person to another," we know what he means.[11] A poem's deictic pronouns, its "I's" and its "you's," are components of a verbal construct that is both "self-focused" and, as a linguist might put it, contextually underspecified.[12] Thus even if the poet is *ostensibly* addressing his daughter, as Wilbur himself does in one of his poems, we do not take such vocative gestures at face value: they are figures of address. Does their addressee stand in for the reader? Very often it seems such gestures are being used to *turn away* from the reader, producing a structure of address that is ambiguous and complex.[13]

The term for this rhetorical tactic is "apostrophe," which Jonathan Culler has suggested we think of as lyric poetry's founding trope. Its purpose, Culler suggests, is to claim for oneself the power and prestige of poethood—as in "Make me thy lyre," Percy Shelley's High Romantic apostrophe to the autumn wind. But American poets who came of age in the middle decades of the twentieth century were the inheritors of at least three different ways of conceiving of the lyric, and of the vocative force of lyric utterance. According to the first, of which Culler is a persuasive exponent, poems are "overheard" by their readers, but according to the second, proposed by Helen Vendler, poems are scripts for performance *by* their readers, and according to the third, espoused by W. R. Johnson and more recently William Waters, it is the "you" rather than the "I" that is the reader's proxy inside the poem.

It will be worthwhile to look briefly at each of these ways of conceiving of lyric utterance, not only because each still has adherents in our own historical moment but also because Brooks, Sexton, Rich, and Plath each found her voice as a poet in the presence of all three ways of understanding what kind of speaker it was that poethood "called" or enabled or required her to be. When Rich declares in her Foreword to *The Fact of a Doorframe* that "the impulse behind writing poems" for her has always been "the desire . . . to be heard, to resound in another's soul," she is speaking as the inheritor of a Shelleyan, High Romantic conception of poethood; when she adds that "increasingly this has meant hearing and listening to others, taking into myself the language of experience different from my own," she is reaching for an "I-you" stance that is more dialogic and conversational. Plath, on the other hand, writing ecstatically in a 1958 journal entry that she "[feels] great works which may begin to speak from me . . . beginning cadences and rhythms of speech to set world-fabrics in motion," is in the grip of a creative impulse that seems oblivious of others' potential responsiveness. Plath's conception of lyric utterance is consistent with Helen Vendler's approach to the lyric; Brooks's and Sexton's poetic orientation is better captured by Johnson's insistence that the lyric was originally and is properly an "I-you" poem. It is this interlocutory conception of the lyric that is gaining ascendancy in our own historical moment, but since a poem *is* finally a monologue, even a radically interlocutory stance also harbors an "apostrophic" conception of lyric discourse.

Literary theorists and critics for whom the Greater Ode is the quintessential lyric utterance are fond of citing J. S. Mill's dictum that whereas eloquence is "heard," poetry is "overheard." In Shelley's "Defence of Poetry" the poet is figured as a nightingale "who sits in darkness and sings to cheer its own solitude with sweet sounds." Mill's often-cited characterization of the lyric dispenses with the figure of the nightingale to make the same point more explicitly: "Poetry is feeling confessing itself to itself, in moments of solitude." "The peculiarity of poetry," for Mill, "appears . . . to lie in the poet's utter unconsciousness of a listener"; the poet is thus as different as possible from the orator, whose eloquence "supposes an audience."[14] T. S. Eliot espoused this conception of the lyric in *The Three Voices of Poetry*, where he aligned himself with Valéry, Rilke, and the German poet-critic Gottfried Benn in giving special primacy to the "first" voice, the voice of "the poet talking to himself—or to nobody," and suggested that "part of our enjoyment of great poetry is the enjoyment of *overhearing* words which are not addressed to us."[15]

Northrop Frye's taxonomy of literary genres codified Mill's and Eliot's insistence on the lyric poet's stance of solitary self-communion, but with a subtle shift of emphasis that brings the audience back into play: "the lyric," according to Frye, "is the genre in which the poet . . . *turns his back on his audience*" to commune with himself, or with an interlocutor he conjures up through an act of poetic imagination (my emphasis). It is in Frye's account of the lyric that the rhetorical figure of apostrophe takes on special importance as the means by which its "radical of presentation" is established. Frye's lyric poet is not unconscious of having an audience, but turns away from them by having recourse to a device that was, according to Cicero and Quintilian, part of the orator's stock in trade. In Frye's account of the lyric its speaker is playing a role: he "*pretends* to be talking to himself or to someone else: a spirit of nature, a Muse . . . a personal friend, a lover, a god, a personified abstraction, or a natural object" (my emphasis).[16]

Why would he do this? If we think of the poet as a special kind of orator, what is this gesture's intended impact on its audience? Jonathan Culler has encouraged us to think of apostrophe as "the pure embodiment of poetic pretension":

> If asking winds to blow or seasons to stay their coming or mountains to hear one's cries is a ritualistic, practically gratuitous action, [its very gratuitousness] emphasizes that voice calls to be calling, to dramatize its calling, to summon images of its power so as to establish its identity as poetical and prophetic voice.[17]

Charles Altieri takes a different view of Romantic apostrophe, arguing that it was not an exercise in narcissistic self-inflation but the exercise of a calling whose strongest imperatives were ethical and social. Apostrophe and related devices broached the possibility of a "countereloquence" that "in place of mere efforts to persuade an audience"—efforts that were "bound to the rules of the marketplace"—could open up "alternative ethical vistas," affording its readers or listeners "new possible identities in which to participate."[18] According to this way of understanding the function of apostrophe, as Ann Keniston explains, it is a figure which, by turning the poet's face away from us, paradoxically "compels [us] toward and into the poem."[19]

Even though his account of lyric poetry's radical of presentation is more dramatistic than Mill's and Eliot's, Frye does attempt to capture some of what is at stake in the claim that poetry is "overheard" when he remarks that the word "audience" won't quite do for the readers of a lyric poem. What is wanted instead, Frye suggests, "is something analogous to 'chorus' which does not suggest simultaneous presence or dramatic context" (*Anatomy of Criticism*, 249). As when a priest or preacher prays aloud with his back to the congregation, the lyric comes to us with an implicit invitation to "repeat after me"; the difference is that each reader is in a condition of solitude that corresponds to the condition of solitary self-communion in which the poem was "uttered" in the first place. As Virginia Jackson explains, glossing Shelley's and Mill's depiction of the lyric poet, "this structure is one . . . in which the poet's solitude stands in for the solitude of the individual reader—a self-address so absolute that every self can identify it as his own."[20] "Let us go then, you and I, / When the evening is spread out against the sky, / Like a patient etherized upon a table": the opening lines of "The Love Song of J. Alfred Prufrock" make this structure of self-address explicit, putting the reader in a position to overhear and identify with a lyric speaker whose own self is the only interlocutor for whom he might even begin to broach what he feels, or say just what he means.

In *Poems, Poets, Poetry,* an anthology she published for students and teachers of poetry in 1997, Helen Vendler takes this way of understanding the reader's position a step further, insisting that "a lyric is meant to be spoken by the reader as if the reader were the one uttering the words."[21] Vendler rejects the notion that we "overhear" the lyric speaker's utterance, on the grounds that overhearing would put us in a position of voyeuristic detachment,[22] whereas the lyric's gift to us is just the opposite—an invitation to dwell, for the duration of the poem, in "the innermost chamber of another person's mind." "Lyric is the genre of private life," she explains: "it is what we say to ourselves when we are alone." Lyrics therefore do not have an audience in the usual sense: "I do not, as a disinterested spectator, overhear the lyric speaker: rather, the words of the speaker become my own words. This imaginative transformation of self is what is offered to us by the lyric" (*Poems, Poets, Poetry,* x–xi).[23] It is at once "the most intimate of genres" and the most universal, since it "presumes that the reader resembles the writer enough to step into the writer's shoes and speak the lines the writer has written as though they were the reader's own." When we are reading the poem successfully, "the speaker's past is our past; his motivations are ours, his emotions ours, his excuses ours, his predictions ours" (*Poems, Poets, Poetry,* 177). Vendler's readings of particular poems are astutely attentive to structures of address, but figures of address do not play the generically constitutive role in her account of the lyric that Frye and Culler have assigned to them. If it is by way of the "I" that the reader gains access to the poem, even though some "you" may also be specified no such gesture will be needed for reader orientation, or to establish what kind of discourse the "I" has undertaken.

According to all the theorists whose efforts to specify its generic distinctiveness have thus far been summarized, the lyric is preeminently the genre of "the poet talking to himself—or to nobody."[24] Whereas a "you" may be conjured up to secure the lyric speaker's authority, privacy, and/or solitude, any such interlocutor is a figment of the speaker's imagination, unproblematically subject to his or her intentions. But according to W. R. Johnson, this way of understanding lyric utterance misrepresents its origins in Greek and Roman poetry and describes a post-Romantic trajectory for the lyric that has proven to be a dead end. For the poets who invented the western lyric it was preeminently an "I-you" poem—addressed to readers either directly, or by way of a human interlocutor who serves as "symbolic mediator . . . between the poet and each of his readers and listeners." The Greek lyricists often built particular human interlocutors into their poems because, Johnson argues, they were attempting "to incarnate, in the songs themselves, the reciprocity which must govern any genuine act of discourse." The addressee their poems envisaged was not a figment of the speaker's imagination, brought to life and made responsive to his utterance by an act of poetic imagination, but a social being like him- or herself, whose responsiveness she or he hoped to enlist but whose differences from her- or himself must be reckoned with, and were indeed a significant incentive for the translation of private thoughts and feelings into public speech.[25]

According to Johnson, T. S. Eliot's "first voice"—that of the meditative speaker who apostrophizes "nonhuman entities, abstractions, or the dead" to help him focus his meditation—is scarcely to be found in the lyrics of Sappho, Catullus, and Horace, nor in English Renaissance poetry until Henry Vaughan, who was an early harbinger of the meditative lyric's subsequent efflorescence. Meditative verse gained ascendancy with the "greater Romantic lyric" and reached a kind of negative apotheosis in the poetry of Mallarmé, whose intuition of the human condition as one of utter loneliness strongly influenced the Modernist poets of the early twentieth century.[26] Johnson argues that as the lyric "forgot how to say 'you'" in our own century it also became ashamed and/or terrified "by the idea of saying 'I,'" except insofar as a few poets, including Yeats and William Carlos Williams, "tried to continue the old pronominal forms" (*The Idea of Lyric*, 15). According to Johnson it is important to conceive of the lyric in "I-you" terms because it is only in an interlocutory context that the poet-speaker has the incentive to shape a discourse that can "[make] visible the invisible forms and rhythms of personality" (31). The lyric self or subject only exists, it can only be brought to life, in words, insofar as the poem specifies or presupposes an interlocutor for those words and a dialectic of engagement between them. Noting the important role that deictic words play in lyric poems, not only the deictic pronouns "I" and "you" but also the deictic adverbs "here" and "now," Johnson argues that it is because lyrics have particular occasions, occasions which are implicitly social, that they manage to capture "the universal" in a meaningful, powerful way:

> By focusing on what he has to say, on why he is saying it, and on the person *for* whom—not so much *to* whom—he is saying it, the speaker discovers the exact, the proper, form for his own character as speaker on this particular occasion, in this particular discourse; and in fact, the purpose of discourse and the presence of the hearer furnish the speaker with enormous power and vitality. (Johnson, 31)

Remarking that it used to be fashionable to credit the Greek lyricists with having invented the self as we know it, Johnson argues that what they did invent was a literary genre in which selfhood can be made manifest:

> A self without another self or selves to aggress or to admire or to solace might not—I doubt it—be truly a self; but, without a doubt, when two or more selves come together, their near likenesses and their absolute distinctions combine to promote *knowledge* of identity, even as they engender the sense of community. (75, Johnson's emphasis)

That lyric poetry is preeminently the genre of "overheard" speech; that lyric poems are scripts for performance by the reader; that lyrics are always implicitly if not explicitly addressed *to* the reader: none of these ways of describing the lyric is mistaken, even though they make conflicting claims. Each gives priority to a different moment in the history of European poetry, or else to different poets within a single historical moment. Neither Johnson, who privileges the Greek and Roman lyric poets, nor Culler, for whom Romantic apostrophe is the lyric's constitutive gesture, has much to say about the possible versions of "you" that Vendler cites to insist that while "there may be an addressee in lyric (*God, or a beloved*) . . . the addressee is always absent" (Vendler, x, emphasis mine). If Shelley's west wind and Keats's nightingale are lineally descended from the Christian deity who is addressed in the religious lyrics of the Renaissance, then Romantic apostrophe is not only—and perhaps not primarily—a device for turning one's back on the reader. Instead it does begin to look like a device for bringing the reader into the poem, to partake of what prayer also promises: a "transformation of self" (Vendler, xi). As for the beloved, who is also ubiquitous in Renaissance poetry, Vendler appears to be thinking of Shakespeare's *Sonnets* rather than Philip Sidney's contemporaneous

Astrophil and Stella sequence, where the beloved is more fully realized as a social presence and the poems often seem to be scripting not an inner meditation but a conversational gambit. Among the poets I take up here, Vendler's emphasis on the lyric "I" as the reader's lifeline to the poem works well for Plath, whose poems aspire to a condition of vatic self-sufficiency, but gives less of a purchase on Sexton, whose speakers are more socially embedded, on Rich, who often worries out loud about the ethical implications of her own vocative gestures, and on Brooks, whose mixture of first- with second- and third-person voicing keeps a strongly self-centered "I" from emerging in her poems. Even where Plath's poems are concerned, the very absence of a viable "I-you" relationship is of considerable interest: in several of her late poems an interlocutor is conjured up only to be emphatically, hysterically repudiated ("Off, off, eely tentacle! / There is nothing between us!"). Meanwhile, however, as Johnson points out, in poems of Plath's that have no designated interlocutor the "I"-position also gets emptied out, so that the voice that speaks from the page seems eerily devoid of agency, of feelings—in short, of selfhood.[27]

What is particularly valuable in Johnson's account of the lyric is his insistence that hypothetical readers are always implicated in its structures of address. In poems where an "I-you" relationship is made explicit, the more socially embedded that relationship is, the more subject it must be to negotiation, the more alive to hypothetical differences in attitude or viewpoint between the "I" and the "you." But even where the "I" and the "you" share a single body they occupy different vantage points, so that even where feeling is "confessing itself to itself in moments of solitude," that confession is getting a hearing and, potentially, a reading. Johnson's approach also helps to explain what is going on when a poem's speaker has recourse to a "you"-formulation that is not, or not only, being used to summon up an interlocutor, but is a rhetorical device for generalizing from the speaker's feelings and experiences to those of others who are, or can imagine being, comparably situated. "Abortions will not let you forget" is the opening line of one of Brooks's early poems. That way of using the second-person pronoun actively constructs the possibility of stepping into another person's shoes, prompting two related inferences: first, that we don't do this easily, and second, pace Vendler, that a poem's strategies of interlocution are its means of persuading us to do so.

And yet, as Jonathan Culler's and Barbara Johnson's discussions of apostrophe have emphasized,[28] figures of address in poems are always to some degree apostrophic: always they are "turning away" from actual readers, constructing a certain "you" in order to bring a certain "I" into focus. Whether the designated interlocutor be God, the cliffs of Winander, the poet's child, or the poem's reader, the one who is speaking has always "made you to find me."

A few specific examples will give these claims some traction. In Louise Glück's poem sequence *Ararat*, we can see what Johnson means in suggesting that a poem's speaker gains "enormous power and vitality" from having an interlocutor:

> Long ago, I was wounded.
> I learned
> to exist, in reaction,
> out of touch
> with the world: I'll tell you
> what I meant to be—
> a device that listened.
> Not inert: still.
> A piece of wood. A stone.
>
> Why should I tire myself, debating, arguing?[29]

Glück's interlocutor is each of her readers: "I'll tell you" is a vocative gesture that enables her to speak from the page, so that as we read her words we seem to hear a voice talking out loud. The directness of "I'll tell you" begins to give us a sense of the person behind the voice: she won't mince words, she will tell us the unvarnished truth. Interestingly enough, the first thing she tells us is that a forthcoming, self-disclosive person is not at all who she "meant to be." A long-ago wounding set the terms of her bargain with existence: she decided to be "a device that listened," taking up an existential stance that did not oblige her to be fully human. Now, for whatever reasons, she is willing to speak about and from her "wounded"-ness, instead of letting it silence her. A slight air of truculence and irascibility bespeaks some residual unwillingness to do this, but she does appear to possess the requisite self-detachment. In the second poem of the sequence the note of irascibility becomes louder as her range of reference expands. Having made the decision to be fully human, she is prepared to hold forth not only about herself but also about the human condition more broadly considered:

> I'll tell you something: every day

> People are dying. And that's just the beginning.
> Every day, in funeral homes, new widows are born,
> new orphans.... (*Ararat*, 16)

Insofar as we don't need to be told that people are dying every day, these lines have an edge of self-parody: now that this woman has committed herself to talking as well as listening, we can expect to get an earful!

Glück's self-presentation in these passages seems to give the lie to Vendler's claim that "all the tones of a poem are the tones of an inward, not an outward, quarrel."[30] Only now that she is willing to quarrel with others is this poet-speaker in a position to speak about, and thus make poetry out of, the quarrel with herself. Throughout the entire sequence, "I'll tell you something" is strongly implicit in her stance and tone of voice, in her syntax and the rhythms of her speech.[31] "In our family, everyone loves flowers," is the first line of the fifth poem in the sequence: this is information we are being given to put the poem's subsequent reflections in context ("That's why the graves are so odd: / no flowers, just padlocks of grass ..."). "To say I'm without fear— / it wouldn't be true" is how another poem begins, setting the record straight after several poems whose candor may well have struck us as courageous. In a poem that hails her readers more explicitly, Glück hearkens back to the sequence's opening lines to proffer an etiological explanation of the condition of woundedness that had been broached there without explanation:

> ... Like Adam,
> I was the firstborn.
> Believe me, you never heal,
> you never forget the ache in your side,
> the place where something was taken away
> to make another person. (*Ararat*, 55)

"Believe me," a more emphatic version of "I'll tell you," is accompanied here by a way of using the "you" pronoun that not only gestures toward an interlocutor but also, as in the Brooks poem I have already cited in passing, posits common ground between "us." "You never heal" and "you never forget the ache in your side" are formulations which insist that the predicament in question is generic: it belongs to the existential condition of being "the first-born."

Many of the *Ararat* poems include "you"-formulations of this kind. It is a rhetorical strategy with characterological implications: these poems' speaker is a woman who has chosen to think of herself as predestined toward certain habits of feeling by family dynamics that are ruthlessly predictable. It also participates, however, in constructing a "radical of presentation" that is not the self-communing stance of the meditative lyric, but of a poet-speaker who is addressing her readers directly, making interlocutors of us. That way of using second-person address was identified by poet-critic Jonathan Holden in 1980 as "one of the most salient conventions to gather momentum in American poetry today." In keeping with Frye's definition of the lyric as "an intensely personal song [that is] designed to be overheard," Holden argues that because it "acknowledges the presence of an audience" this way of using the "you"-pronoun is "inappropriate to the lyric mode."[32] But if W. R. Johnson's history of the lyric is persuasive, Glück and other poets of her generation have found their way back to a rhetorical stance that was occluded by the meditative lyric, but rediscovered and reasserted by the Confessional poets during the 1950s and '60s.

"Don't listen to me; my heart's been broken. I don't see anything objectively" is how another of Glück's poems begins, whose title is "The Untrustworthy Speaker." As Ann Keniston points out in calling attention to this poem's strategy of address, "its initial negative command is disingenuous, even devious," since "the ferocity of its disclaimer makes us want to read further" and its speaker, presupposing that we have done so, continues to instruct us to discount her perspective.[33] "If you want the truth," she insists, "you have to close yourself / to the older daughter, block her out." But do we want the truth on these terms? Are we not likely to find a first-person account more powerful, untrustworthy as it may be, than the more "objective" account she gestures toward by referring to herself as "the older daughter"? Glück's use of reader-address in this poem raises questions that fall within the ambit of "confessional" poetry, psychological and epistemological questions about the authority and validity of speaking from personal experience whose crucible is family life. My first chapter focuses on the poets who began to raise such questions during the 1950s: Anne Sexton and Robert Lowell. Like Glück, Sexton and Lowell were speaking from a position of having been "wounded"; like hers, it was a gendered position, and one whose trustworthiness is open to question. My contention will be that their interlocutory projects were not, however, symmetrical: in order to get a hearing for a *woman* speaker's untrustworthiness, Sexton was constrained to lead with her gender in a particular way.

In Adrienne Rich's poems, strategies of address are more often used to raise ethical and political questions: Rich makes "you" to find "we," and this has impelled her toward an anti-confessional stance. In a poem entitled "In Those Years," dated 1991,[34] she gives that stance a bleakly definitive assertion:

> In those years, people will say, we lost track
> of the meaning of *we*, of *you*
> we found ourselves
> reduced to *I*
> and the whole thing became
> silly, ironic, terrible:

The people who will say this will be looking back to a span of years that includes, presumably, the year in which this poem was written, but the poem has nothing to tell us about how the world they inhabit then will be different. Its purpose is not to foretell the future, but to create a sense of prophetic foreboding about the hypertrophy of the personal that afflicts us in the present.[35] The interrelatedness of the deictic pronouns "I," "you," and "we" is crucial to its grimly abstract calculus: without elaborating on how it is that the meanings of *"we"* and *"you"* are mutually implicated, the voice that speaks from the future explains that as the one was "lost track of," the other also fell into disuse. In its closing lines the poem leaves its collective protagonist trapped in a desolate place of historical irrelevancy, "where we stood, saying *I*": the "terrible" irony of modern mass society is that we unknowingly constitute a "we" by doing the very thing that keeps us from having any meaningful access to that way of conceiving of ourselves.

Interestingly, however, "we" is the only personal pronoun that has a pragmatic function for the collective speaker this poem cites in its opening line. Try to imagine that speaker saying "I'll tell you" or "Believe me," and you realize that "they" are not in a position to do so. In terms of Johnson's theory of the lyric, "In Those Years" is the exception that proves the rule. Is the poem itself aware, in the sense of intending us to notice, that a recovered capacity for saying "we" has been purchased at the expense of consigning both "you" and "I" to the dustbin of history?

"In Those Years" is addressed to potential readers with a prophetic urgency that is disturbingly impersonal, reaching a limit of abstraction from which it is hard to imagine further poems being written. The final section of "An Atlas of the Difficult World," written by Rich at around the same time,[36] apostrophizes potential readers in a way that is disturbingly personal, to make a similar point. Entitled "(Dedications)," it functions as an "envoy" for the poem as a whole:

> I know you are reading this poem

late, before leaving your office
of the one intense yellow lamp-spot and the darkening window
in the lassitude of a building faded to quiet
long after rush-hour. I know you are reading this poem
standing up in a bookstore far from the ocean
on a gray day of early spring, faint flakes driven
across the plains' enormous spaces around you.

The litany continues: two hypothetical readers are conjured up whose personal lives are in crisis, three whose condition is one of waiting helplessly for something to happen, one whose eyesight is failing, one who speaks very little English, and various others whose lives don't easily make room for the reading of poetry. The one thing these hypothetical readers have in common is a need for what poetry has to offer that some of them recognize and some do not: elsewhere, in prose, Rich appositely speaks of how poetry can "break open locked chambers of possibility, restore numbed zones to feeling, recharge desire."[37] Coming at the end of a poem that addresses its readers in their public capacity as citizens of a democracy that has failed its own ideals, her litany of dedications emphasizes that reading a poem is a private act, something we do in isolation from one another. This complicates the task of a poet whose project is to rescue her readers from anomie by speaking to our "we"-ness.[38]

Rich's engagement with the politics of the personal pronouns "I," "we," and "you" will be the focus of my second chapter. Her commitment to dialogue has led her to test the rhetorical force of reader-address, apostrophe, and second-person voice in poems that often are strikingly transgressive of the usual conventions of reader-address. Her interlocutory strategy in the passage I have just quoted from "(Dedications)" is a good case in point:[39] I am startled to be told by the poet whose poem I am reading that she knows who I am. At the same time, however, my situation has not been captured in any of her descriptions: have I just finished reading a poem that is not addressed to me, if I am neither lonely nor bored nor afflicted nor desperate to change my life? What this reaction highlights is that "I know you are reading this poem" is an apostrophe: an address to hypothetical readers that "turns away from" the reader who is actually present. What is the force and meaning of the gesture in this context? Does it stage a poet's own wishful thinking? Is it intended to goad actual readers into active dialogue with her poem? Does it instance the necessarily ironic predicament of prophets from Cassandra onward, whose conviction of the urgency of their message is self-discrediting and gets in the way of their being believed? It is a powerful but also risky gesture, one that Rich must have undertaken with full awareness that she could not wholly foresee or control its impact.⁴⁰

In the examples I have adduced thus far, what is at stake in the deployment of the second-person pronoun is reader-address. Glück's *Ararat* sequence is addressed to the reader explicitly and, for the most part, unproblematically, except in the poem whose opening gambit calls attention to the rhetorical contrivance involved in creating a dialectic of engagement between the one who says "I" throughout the sequence and the one to whom she says "I'll tell you something" or "Don't listen to me." Glück's deployment of "you" in this sequence is minimally apostrophic; Rich, by contrast, has used apostrophe in "(Dedications)" to put her relationship with actual readers at risk and in crisis.

Let us now turn to a figure of address that is more obviously consistent with Vendler's insistence that the lyric addressee is always absent: the "you" that is used in elegies to call upon the dead. Apostrophe is one of elegy's most important resources, presupposing as it does that the dead can still hear us and hence that they are still alive, in some sense. It is used in elegies not only to address the dead but also, as in Milton's "Lycidas," to affirm the existence of a divinely created universe that is responsive to our sense of loss and can reconcile us to our mortality. Jahan Ramazani has richly demonstrated that twentieth-century elegies often reject the consolation this genre has traditionally afforded, refusing to let their dead rest in peace, displacing mourning onto the neighboring terrain of melancholia.⁴¹ Sylvia Plath is a notorious case in point: the first time she visited her father's grave, as a young adult, she wrote in her journal that she had been strongly tempted to dig him up—"To prove he existed and really was dead" (*Unabridged Journals*, 473). "The Colossus," one of a number of elegies Plath wrote for her father, is the poem Vendler singles out in *Coming of Age as a Poet* as being Plath's first "perfect" poem, the first that "wholly succeeds in embodying a coherent personal style."⁴² Its success is owing, Vendler suggests, to the poem's "daring resort to abstraction. No longer a buried corpse, [the father] is now literally what he has always been in his daughter's imagination . . . a colossus" (*Coming of Age*, 123). Apostrophe becomes a scheme as well as a trope in this poem, whose antiphonal rhythm arises from an alternation between "I" and "you," "my" and "your" that occurs both within and between successive sentences:

> *I* shall never get *you* put together entirely,
> Pieced, glued, and properly jointed.
> Mule-bray, pig-grunt, and bawdy cackles

Proceed from *your* great lips.
. . .
Perhaps *you* consider yourself an oracle,
Mouthpiece of the dead, or of some god or other.
Thirty years now *I* have labored
To dredge the silt from *your* throat.
. . .
The sun rises under the pillar of *your* tongue.
My hours are married to shadow.[43]

This poem's speaker is strikingly self-sufficient and self-enclosed: she has turned away not only from the reader, but from every conceivable interlocutor who is not her dead father. To put this more carefully, she has turned away from every conceivable interlocutor who is not the colossus, a figment of her own imagination that stands in for her father's inaccessibility. She addresses it/him unhurriedly, without discernible affect, speaking of a project of reconstruction that is hopeless, never-ending, and utterly lonely. Her one-sided colloquy removes her from the ordinary world in which each of us is socially embedded, answerable to others, subject to growth and change. The place to which she has removed herself corresponds to the condition of her psyche, where the mythic structure of the Electra complex implacably holds sway. It is a weatherless, time-indifferent, wholly literary realm:

A blue sky out of the Oresteia
Arches above us. O father, all by yourself
You are pithy and historical as the Roman Forum.

This is apostrophe at its most ceremonious, but with an edge of self-mockery: we are more than halfway through an account of this daughter's labors of restoration that depicts them as the prosaic drudgery of a Lilliputian housewife or prisoner.

The key to the poem's success, according to Vendler, is explicitly present in the lines just quoted, which herald the subsumption of "Plath's filial anguish into the complex dialectic of Greek drama." It is a complex dialectic because it includes the "barnyard grunts" of the satyr play as well as "the tragedy of ritual obligation," thereby enabling "the contradictory emotions of anger and love to cross and fuse in a single lyric" (*Coming of Age*, 132–33). The criterion of poetic success that Vendler's reading invokes is New Critical, which is consistent with what we know of Plath's poetic beginnings: she read the New Critics at an early age and found their precepts thoroughly congenial. Leonard

Scigaj has suggested that her early poetry "offers us as lucid a retrospect of the end of American New Critical poetry as Marvell did of the end of English metaphysical poetry."[44] In my third chapter I will argue that the analogy with Marvell is even more appropriate for late poems such as "Medusa," "Daddy," and "Lady Lazarus," which explode the "well wrought urn" of New Critical poetics. But my present reason for citing "The Colossus" is that it exemplifies Plath's use of apostrophe to build poems that are self-contained sites of utterance. You'll not get these poems' speaker to meet you at eye level; she knows too much, and knows it too absolutely, for there to be any question of dialogue. Where she uses figures of address to apostrophize the living in her poems, she seems bent on asserting a "Medusan" prerogative: these are "I-you" structures that kill their interlocutors into art.

Anne Sexton wrote an elegy for Plath soon after receiving the news of her suicide in February of 1963. What had drawn the two poets together in the first place, as students in Robert Lowell's poetry workshop at Boston University, was not only their admiration for each other's poetry but also their shared obsession with suicide. And yet Sexton's last letter from Plath had emphasized how contentedly alive she was, with her children in Devon, "keeping bees and raising potatoes and doing broadcasts off and on for the BBC."[45] Sexton felt blindsided, and also betrayed. "Sylvia Plath's death disturbs me," she explained to her psychiatrist. "She took something that was mine, *that* death was mine! Of course it was hers too. But we both swore off it, the way you swear off smoking." As Diane Middlebrook, Sexton's biographer, points out, "this rivalrous attitude made its way into" Sexton's elegy. Middlebrook concurs with Jahan Ramazani and a number of other critics that "Sylvia's Death" is not a good poem: she finds it to have "a spurious tone, saturated with self-pity posing as grief."[46] And yet Middlebrook reports that Sexton "liked the poem and defended it to critics." She sent it to George Starbuck, who had often joined the two of them for martinis after Lowell's poetry class, saying, "It's really good. You may paste it on your wall" (ctd. in Middlebrook, 200).

Sexton was hard on her own poems, and so her liking for "Sylvia's Death" is worth paying attention to. Perhaps she liked this poem because it is a different kind of elegy than Plath herself would have written—just as unconventional, but in a different register. She may also have liked it because it captured the complexity of her own attitude toward suicide. Even while acknowledging "a terrible taste for it, like salt," the poem's speaker resists her friend's death with all the rhetorical and emotional resources their friendship puts at her disposal. Using apostrophe much too often, she creates a sense of unfinished business between the two women that is ugly and poignant and, above all, full of the vitality her friend has (traitorously) renounced:

> O Sylvia, Sylvia,
> with a dead box of stones and spoons,
>
> with two children, two meteors
> wandering loose in the tiny playroom,
>
> with your mouth into the sheet,
> into the roofbeam, into the dumb prayer,
>
> (Sylvia. Sylvia,
> where did you go
> after you wrote me
> from Devonshire
> about raising potatoes
> and keeping bees?)
>
> what did you stand by,
> just how did you lie down into?
>
> Thief!—
> how did you crawl into,
>
> crawl down alone
> into the death I wanted so badly and for so long. . . .[47]

In "The Colossus," apostrophe keeps the daughter-speaker's attention firmly focused on her otherworldly task. Sexton's hectic spate of exclamations seems, in contrast, defiantly this-worldly: Plath's death has not changed the terms of a friendship that was dishonest, impure, and socially embedded, between women who were always in one way or another competing for a man's attention.

The poem recalls a cab ride home with "*our boy*," "the one we talked of" while downing extra-dry martinis: "Sylvia," it seems, has run off with him while the poem's speaker wasn't looking. Sexton had been having an affair with George Starbuck behind her friend's back, but in the present context "our boy" alludes to an even more seductive escort who'd been a powerfully absent presence at their boozy trysts. Sexton's interest in "Sylvia's" relationship with "our boy" is compulsively prurient; her resentment is mingled with envy: "O tiny mother, / you too!

/ O funny duchess! / O blonde thing!" If a woman in a 1950s Hollywood movie (call her "Persey") had been found to be secretly dating a fascinating stranger, this is how her girlfriends might have greeted the news of her conquest. "Sylvia's Death" overcompensates for its addressee's abruptly chosen silence with an out-of-control barrage of gossipy questions, bitchy vituperation, and excited admiration—as if in a desperate attempt to bring their friendship back to life, in all of its dishonest complexity.

The poem solicits our interest and commentary by the impression it makes of not having mastered, or even fully understood, the feelings it discloses. "This is something I would never find / in a lovelier place, my dear," is Sexton's apt gloss on her own confessional stance in poems like these.[48] The "something" referred to is not only a subject matter that was, as Plath had acknowledged, "quite new" for poetry in the early 1960s but also a set of rhetorical tactics that draw "enormous power and vitality" (W. R. Johnson's phrase) from the emotional complexities of everyday personal relationships. Sexton's attempt to overcompensate for Plath's silence by talking too much, for Plath's aloofness with an assertion of intimacy that is clinging and cloying, for her self-protective secrecy with a self-disclosive openness that holds nothing back, is ostensibly provoked by Sylvia's death rather than by her poems. I will be suggesting in my chapter on Plath, however, that Plath's stance as a poet had an analogous impact—not only on Sexton, but also on her husband and fellow poet, Ted Hughes.

"When you have forgotten Sunday: the love story" is the most openly autobiographical poem in Gwendolyn Brooks's first published volume, *A Street in Bronzeville*. At poetry readings during the 1990s she would introduce it by recalling the series of kitchenette apartments she and her husband rented as a young married couple in the "Bronzeville" section of Chicago's south side. And yet the poem's strategy of address is highly stylized, its use of apostrophe more conventional than in any of the poems we have looked at thus far. Love poems are typically addressed to the beloved, while being "overheard," as this one is, by an audience of readers the poet-lover pretends to ignore. "Only in you my song begins and endeth," said "Astrophil" to "Stella" in 1591, succinctly explicating the logic of a love poem's apostrophic mode of address. The young wife in Brooks's poem is an unlikely heir to that tradition in several respects. Along with the husband she addresses, she is a black, working-class resident of inner-city Chicago. She speaks in free verse, and her love story is full of the small change of domestic married life. But the poem is out to show its readers that the more things may seem to be different, the more they remain the same. It consists of a single "when-then" sentence, recommenced at irregular intervals by subtly varied renewals of its proleptic "when" clause. Many of Shakespeare's sonnets use "when-then" constructions to similar effect, capitalizing, as this poem does, on their capacity to adumbrate both chronological succession and logical entailment.

Here, as there, a poet goes to war with Time on behalf of Love. But the rhetorical device this young wife uses to render her "love story" unforgettable is as un-Shakespearean as the rhythms of her discourse. The poem begins as if it were picking up the thread of an ongoing connubial exchange:

>—And when you have forgotten the bright bedclothes
>   on a Wednesday and a Saturday,
> And most especially when you have forgotten Sunday—
> When you have forgotten Sunday halves in bed,
> Or me sitting on the front-room radiator in the limping afternoon
> Looking off down the long street
> To nowhere,
> Hugged by my plain old wrapper of no-expectation
> And nothing-I-have-to-do and I'm-happy-why?
> And if-Monday-never-had-to-come—
> When you have forgotten that, I say . . .

After a leisurely catalogue of details that trace the arc of this couple's typical Sunday, from the time they get up in the morning to the moment when they have "gently folded into each other" among "the week-end / Bright bedclothes," the young wife completes both her sentence and her poem by playfully suggesting that when her husband has "forgotten all that . . . / Then I may believe / You have forgotten me well."[49] Her prolepsis is a witty device to fend off sentimentality while giving sentiment a space in which to flourish. On the one hand, the details of how she and her husband spend their Sundays are not in themselves memorable; on the other hand, how could he forget "all that," with her love for him and their pleasure in each other so skillfully woven into her story?

The poem's unstated purpose—Brooks's purpose, as distinct from that of her poem's speaker—is to depict for an "overhearing" audience, who in 1945 are probably white and therefore probably not from Bronzeville, a working-class Negro couple whose values, appetites, and pleasures are very little different from their own. In the context of that purpose, and of the *Street in Bronzeville* volume as a whole, the wife's proleptic apostrophe is doing work that is easy to miss, but crucial. Not only does it enable her to discover, in Johnson's words, "the exact, the proper, form for [her] own character as speaker" in the context of her relationship with her husband; it also gives the poem a means of staging that relationship for the poem's readers, to whom her discourse is not directly addressed but "*for* whom" it is intended.

Because her interlocutor is inside their relationship, he takes it for granted. She tells him what he already knows, reframing the all-too-familiar contours of their domestic life from the more distanced perspective of a time when they will no longer be young and relatively carefree and convinced of their own good fortune ("When you have forgotten my little presentiment / That the war would be over before they got to you . . ."). They will look back one day on this time in their lives as if it were some other couple's idyll of domestic *otium*—unless, of course, *he* has by then forgotten it all. In order to coach him into remembering, *she* must practice self-detachment—as she does, for example, by giving the "plain old wrapper" she wears around the house an allegorical reading and by using her mind's eye to place their dining table "in the southwest corner" of the room, "inkspotted" to hint at its secondary function as a writing-surface. And thus the angle of vision she constructs, ostensibly for herself and her husband, is one that also serves to put their life in perspective for readers whose outsider vantage point is a function not (or not only) of the passage of time, but of segregated housing patterns and racist assumptions about black people's difference from themselves.

In this poem Brooks is making "you" to find "me," or to find "we," on two different levels. Using apostrophe to turn away from her poem's readers, she has built a poem whose unstated purpose is to bridge the distance that keeps them from getting to know their Bronzeville neighbors. Part of that bridging is done by subtly alluding to a poetic genre whose conventions are well known and whose "western" pedigree is well established. This particular love poem is not a sonnet, but the *Bronzeville* volume also includes a sequence of war sonnets that give the traditional sonnet sequence a new lease on life.

Over the course of her long career as a poet, Brooks developed a repertory of strategies for voicing both lyric and epic poems that were at once more innovative and more tradition-conscious than any of the other three poets with whom this study is concerned. Early on, her stance as a poet was constructed with an eye to the special challenges involved in writing simultaneously for both black and white readers, both "Negroes" and "Gentiles." She sought to represent black people's lives and perspectives in a way that would be compelling for both sets of readers, heightening their awareness of interests and values they had in common as human beings and as American citizens. Midway through her career, Brooks turned away from white readers not figuratively, as in this instance, but by attempting to fashion a poetic vernacular that would no longer reference the conventions of "western" poetry. She became committed to setting an agenda for poetry "by Blacks, about Blacks, to Blacks" without regard to white readers' interests, expectations, or canonical reference points.[50] Zofia Burr has recently argued that this shift carried Brooks in the direction of oral performance; I will argue that Brooks did not turn her back on literariness to the extent that Burr and others have suggested. What she did was give her poems a different kind of work to do: work that is epideictic in its orientation and quasi-ekphrastic in its approach. In her late poems people's actions begin to do the talking, and actions have a certain taciturnity. In this context, apostrophe is reborn as a device for en-voicing "Blackness" and enhancing its legibility, while at the same time calling attention to the inadequacy and/or bankruptcy of earlier modes of call and response.

CHAPTER 1

ANNE SEXTON AND THE GENDER OF POETHOOD

> *And this was my worst guilt; you could not cure nor soothe it. I made you to find me.*
>
> —Anne Sexton, "The Double Image"

"I made you to find me," ostensibly a confession of maternal narcissism, could equally serve as a motto for Anne Sexton's practice of the confessional mode. In the poems that created her reputation as a Confessional poet she is almost always confessing *to* someone: she has an interlocutor within the poem itself. "The Double Image," from which this chapter's epigraph is taken, is addressed to her three-year-old daughter, Joyce;[1] more typically, the "you" Sexton conjures up is adult and male, a father-doctor-mentor figure whose authority the poem's speaker both covets and is seeking to undermine. In such poems there is a difference not only of gender but also of status or power between the speaker and her confessor—a difference that is taken for granted by the society at large, but that Sexton's poem highlights, troubles, and destabilizes. More than any other device, it is this strategy of subversive apostrophe that gives *To Bedlam and Part Way Back*, Sexton's first published volume of poetry, its distinctive voice. In subsequent volumes Sexton also found her way to a persona whose effectiveness derives in a different way from the social power dynamic to which it calls attention: the persona of a "middle-aged witch," an outlaw storyteller who is mockingly inward with her own society's myths of gender.[2]

Both the middle-aged witch and the seductively vulnerable subject of Sexton's confessional poems are inescapably, transgressively female—and indeed when Sexton first began to write poetry in the late 1950s, her confessional persona was doubly transgressive. For poets who came of age during the 1950s, the decision to speak as a woman in poems was one that could not be taken lightly. Looking back with feminist hindsight from the 1970s, Adrienne Rich explained that in her first two published volumes she "tried very much not to identify [herself] as a female poet" because she "had been taught that poetry should be 'universal,' which meant, of course, nonfemale."[3] The lesson Rich had learned from teachers and mentors was that a woman poet who called attention to her gender would be relegated to "minor" status and patronized by the critics. This had been the fate not only of Amy Lowell and Edna St. Vincent Millay, but also of Emily Dickinson, who was epitomized for generations of students by John Crowe Ransom and R. P. Blackmur as "a little home-keeping person" who "wrote indefatigably, as some women cook or knit."[4] Marianne Moore and Elizabeth Bishop resisted this stereotype by writing poems that kept their speakers' gender more or less out of play.

If "universal" meant nonfemale, it also meant transpersonal: the consensus of Eliot and Auden's generation was that poets should not traffic in merely personal experience. In his introduction to *A Change of World*, the volume that won Rich the Yale Younger Poets Prize in 1951, Auden noted approvingly that "the emotions which motivate [these poems] . . . are not peculiar to Miss Rich but are among the typical experiences of our time. . . ."[5] What was riding on this criterion was poetic authority—the authority to speak to and for one's audience about matters of abiding human concern. The authority of poets—and of poetry as an institution—was predicated on their citation of generically human feelings and experiences: those of "a heart in unison with his time and country" is how Ralph Waldo Emerson put it in one of his essays.[6] And a woman's experiences and feelings did not count as generically human if they were those of a woman in any obvious way.

But how could poets keep from trafficking in personal experience, and how could they avoid "the gender of things," at a time when Americans were preoccupied as never before with family life and with a vision of the family that assigned men and women radically different tasks and roles?[7] During the 1950s the middle-class family was the central focus of a peacetime renewal of democratic capitalism; in the political rhetoric of the Cold War period, the single-breadwinner household became the linchpin of a distinctively American way of life. The popular media helped that vision take hold: according to Betty Friedan, in the 1950s the leading women's magazines ceased to give their middle-class readership any horizon of aspiration beyond the family and the home.⁸ But the roles of breadwinner-husband and homemaker-wife were vulnerable constructs, both economically and psychically: a high level of what we have subsequently learned to call "gender anxiety" was generated by the society's commitment to heterosexual monogamy and to an account of gender difference that justified the sharpest possible division of labor within the middle-class household. "Can This Marriage Be Saved," a regular feature of *The Ladies' Home Journal*, told a story that was always different in its particulars, but in structure and outcome always the same: the marriage in question, which had come to seem unworkable to both partners, *could* be saved by a confessional process that brought each partner's disappointments and frustrations out in the open for a professional counselor to help them face together. These scenes from a marriage gave equal time to the *He says* and the *She says*, for an exclusively female audience. Middle-class men subscribed in large numbers to *Playboy*, whose popularity during the 1950s Barbara Ehrenreich attributes not to any real intention on the part of its readers of embracing a bachelor playboy lifestyle, but to a need for reassurance that their masculinity had not been sacrificed on the altar of middle-class marriage.⁹

The surest way for a poet, male or female, to hold on to what Robert von Hallberg calls the "tone of the center" in poems with a domestic focus was to speak not from the gendered perspective of a husband or wife, but as a sympathetic onlooker of the marriages of others. That's the position from which John Hollander speaks in a 1958 poem von Hallberg cites as especially successful in this mode: "For Both of You, The Divorce Being Final." On behalf of the divorced couple's friends, Hollander laments not only that "your" marriage has ended but that, ironically, "our" very civility keeps us from responding to the breakup in a fully humane way.¹⁰ Alternatively, a dramatic monologue or persona poem could expose the fault lines in a domestic situation that was obviously not the poet's own: one of Rich's early poems takes on the perspective of a woman in her fifties, the childless wife of a distinguished Harvard professor, whose adult life has been so circumscribed as to leave her only partly able to fathom her own unhappiness. Like Hollander's, Rich's poem raises questions about marriage as a social institution—this time, by getting inside a marriage whose bargain has been scrupulously kept but has failed both partners in important ways.¹¹

When Robert Lowell began to write poems about marriage in the late 1950s he decided to move directly, by way of the "He says" and the

"She says," onto the embattled terrain of middle-class domestic life. In doing this he put both his poetic authority and his masculinity at risk. In the first place, he committed himself to speaking not transpersonally but personally—to confessing, indeed, how badly he'd behaved as a husband. In the second place, "To Speak of Woe That Is in Marriage" was a distaff prerogative: if not more authoritative on the subject of marriage, wives were at any rate well known to be more talkative than their husbands. That this was Lowell's assumption is confirmed by his choice of title for a poem in *Life Studies* (published in 1959) that ventriloquizes his second wife, Lizzie: the allusion is to Chaucer's Wife of Bath, who embarks on a garrulous confessional monologue by assuring her audience of Canterbury pilgrims that "Experience, though noon auctoritee / Were in this world, is right ynough for me / To speke of wo that is in mariage."[12] As Chaucer's Wife well knew, authority and experience—along with taciturnity and garrulity—have traditionally fought on opposite sides in the battle of the sexes. In *Life Studies* masculine authority and feminine experience, male taciturnity and female garrulity, are comparably pitted against each other on the social and psychic terrain of Cold War domesticity.

Like Sexton, Lowell is a poet who "made you to find me"; he, too, used apostrophe very tellingly to put gender anxiety at his poems' disposal and enlist it as a poetic resource. But Lowell and Sexton had different motives for making an issue of gender in their poems, and different rhetorical options available to them for doing so. Discussions of confessional writing that treat Sexton as Lowell's protégée or fellow traveler in the Confessional movement have neglected to notice this asymmetry or to gauge its rhetorical impact.

Before we begin to look at how Sexton and Lowell "found" themselves as poetic speakers by enlisting and resisting their society's gender stereotypes, let's look more closely at the stereotype of the poet they inherited and at the impact of that stereotype on women poets who came of age during the Cold War period. During the 1950s and well into the 1960s "it was difficult," remarks Judith McDaniel, "for a woman to escape the fact that poet was a masculine noun."[13] Take, for example, the case of Denise Levertov, who had never been averse to writing poems from an unmistakably female subject-position. In 1967, after more than two decades and seven published volumes of poetry, Levertov published a manifesto entitled "The Poet in the World" that puts forth an activist vision of poethood in the high Emersonian tradition. The essay begins with an elaborate birth allegory in which the poet is first a woman in labor, then a father looking on at the delivery of the child he has conceived, and finally a newborn—a man-child—who must enter the world and come to terms with it, in political as well as other ways. The purpose of this allegory, apparently, is to endow "the poet" with an androgynous creativity that transcends the limitations of conventional gender roles. It also functions, however, as McDaniel has astutely suggested, to negotiate access to generic masculinity for Levertov herself: "the female poet gives birth to a male child who becomes the poet-he, who then goes out into the world to experience it."[14]

Levertov's allegorical device betrays that although poets are sometimes women, poethood is not a gender-neutral status. Levertov unabashedly claims that status for herself throughout the essay, and yet the poet as she envisions him—a figure of mythic stature in modern dress who has "crossed in a day the great oceans his ancestors labored across in many months," who has looked up from reading of the death of Socrates while riding the New York subway to see "one man stab another and a third spring from his seat to assist the wounded one"—this Whitmanian figure of the poet is clearly a man among men.[15]

Levertov shared with other women poets a "problem of voice" (McDaniel's phrase) that had more to do with institutional stereotypes than with any particular poet's willingness to speak as a woman in her poems. Adrienne Rich, for her part, attempted to solve the problem by crafting a poetic stance that studiously avoided calling attention to her gender. Several of the poems in her first two published volumes, *A Change of World* (1951) and *The Diamond Cutters* (1955), are dramatic monologues whose speaker is a man; others have a generic protagonist who could be a woman but whose gender is given as masculine. In the Notes to her *Poems Selected and New* of 1975, Rich explains that in "The Tourist and the Town," written in 1953, she felt she could not afford to let "the tourist" be "she" even though, she confesses, "I never saw her as anything else."[16] Poems that do have a female protagonist use the voice of a coolly omniscient observer to detect the irony or pathos of her situation on the reader's behalf. Looking back at "Aunt Jennifer's Tigers" twenty years later, Rich says she was startled by its obvious reference to her own predicament as a fledgling woman artist; at the time, she explains, "it was important to me that Aunt Jennifer was a person as distinct from myself as possible—distanced by the formalism of the poem, by its objective, observant tone. . . ."[17] Also pervasive in Rich's first two published volumes is a transpersonal "we" that implicates the reader him- or herself in a humanly generic dilemma or predicament:

> Is any light so proudly thrust
> From darkness on our lifted faces
> A sign of something we can trust,
> Or is it that in starry places
> We see the things we long to see
> In fiery iconography?[18]

This is a stanza from a poem Auden singles out in his introduction to *A Change of World* as having successfully captured "the typical experiences of our time."

In "Storm Warnings," the leadoff poem in the volume and another of Auden's favorites, Rich even managed to speak *in propria persona* from within a domestic setting without calling attention to her gender. As Auden recognized, the poem is allegorical: its New England country setting is specific, but also resonant with generalized historical foreboding. "Laying my book aside," the poem's speaker gets up and walks around the house closing shutters, drawing curtains, "set[ting] a match to candles sheathed in glass / Against the keyhole draught." These precautions against the coming storm are precisely detailed, but then subsumed by a "we"-statement that distills their significance at a higher level of abstraction: "These are the things that we have learned to do / Who live in troubled regions."[19] Arguably such things belong to women's traditional domain of housekeeping, but no task is cited that strongly connotes women's work: the speaker does not interrupt the preparation of a meal, for instance, or look in on a sleeping child. Her attitude thus need not be written off as the timidity of the weaker sex, but can be taken instead for the prescience of a speaker who has divined—on behalf of "his" contemporaries—which way the wind is blowing.[20]

Yet no matter what precautions Rich took, the achievement of her early poems was bound to be refeminized—and by Auden himself, who assures us in his introduction to *A Change of World* that "the poems a reader will encounter in this book are neatly and modestly dressed, speak quietly but do not mumble, respect their elders . . . and do not tell fibs."[21] Thus, ironically, the guardedness and self-detachment Rich had enjoined on herself as the price of universality, and which made her sound middle-aged at twenty-one, were given a feminine inflection—found, indeed, to be ladylike—by the distinguished exponent of the "tone of the center" who had undertaken to sponsor her poetic début.

In the late 1950s, in "Snapshots of a Daughter-in-Law," Rich did begin to write "directly about experiencing myself as a woman"; but

"Snapshots" is far from having the naked intimacy of Lowell's or Sexton's confessional writing. Its speaker's stance is just as detached and objective as in "Aunt Jennifer's Tigers" or "The Tourist and the Town." Rich concedes that even though the poem felt like a breakthrough to her at the time, she "hadn't found the courage yet to do without authorities, or even to use the pronoun 'I.'"[22] Actually, there is some "I"-reference in "Snapshots of a Daughter-in-Law," but its function is to keep the one who has taken these "snapshots" in a position to speak as her female subjects' critic and judge:

> Two handsome women, gripped in argument,
> each proud, acute, subtle, I hear scream
> across the cut glass and majolica
> like Furies cornered from their prey:
> The argument *ad feminam*, all the old knives
> that have rusted in my back, I drive in yours,
> *ma semblable, ma soeur!*[23]

The poem's speaker knows these women better than they know themselves. She may even be one of them; if so, she is divided against herself and has become the object of her own contempt. The rhetorical strategy is reminiscent of T. S. Eliot, not only because Rich has cited a line from Baudelaire that was used to similar effect in "The Waste Land" but also because she has learned from Eliot how to savor the irony of a generic predicament that is also her own.

Claire Keyes has suggested that throughout the whole transitional volume that includes this poem, "Rich [still] cannot reconcile *what* she is (a poet) with *who* she is (a woman)";[24] and sure enough, the poems in *Snapshots of a Daughter-in Law* (1963) typically speak of women with a mixture of pity and contempt. "Readings of History" plays off the women pictured in *Life* magazines from the war years, "so poor but honest," against those depicted in women's magazines of the fifties who "sail / to shop in Europe, ignorantly freed for you, an age ago."[25] Rich was using autobiographical material more frankly than in the two earlier volumes, but always with rueful self-detachment, as when the speaker of "A Marriage in the Sixties" reminds her husband of their common vulnerability to inscrutable forces of change: "The world breathes underneath our bed. / Don't look. We're at each other's mercy too."[26] The only poem in the volume whose speaker casts her lot with the forces of change is one in which she uses a masculine persona to speak of her sense of having the wrong tools, as a poet, "for what [she has] to do": "I'm . . . a naked man fleeing across the roofs

/ who could with a shade of a difference / be sitting in the lamplight / . . . reading . . . / about a naked man / fleeing across the roofs."²⁷ The poet's nakedness comes of being ready to give up the formalism she had espoused in the title poem of *The Diamond Cutters* in favor of subjecting her poems more directly to the pressure of experience. And yet the courage (or is it recklessness?) that will enable her to do this is envisioned as a masculine prerogative.

Interestingly enough, "The Roofwalker" carries a dedication to Denise Levertov, who had already published a poem entitled "From the Roof": the speaker of Levertov's poem is taking in the washing while she waits for her husband to join her in their new home.²⁸ But the problem of voice Rich and Levertov shared in the 1950s and '60s could not be solved by an individual poet working alone; only in the context of the women's movement, from a stance no longer detached and "objective" but politically engaged and adversarial, could a generic "I" that was female begin to be produced. Rich would not succeed in making what she later described as "the mere, immense shift from male to female pronouns" until *The Dream of a Common Language* in 1978.²⁹

Anne Sexton, meanwhile, was venturing into women-only territory that both Rich and Levertov considered off-limits. At a memorial service for Sexton following her suicide in 1974, Rich reminded other feminists that Sexton had written "poems alluding to abortion, masturbation, menopause, and the painful love of a powerless mother for her daughters, long before such themes became validated by a collective consciousness of women. . . ."³⁰ Such themes were not just unmistakably, they were *unspeakably*, female: these were the things that we had learned to do—and suffer—without expecting to read or to write about them. There were no dysfunctional families on Sunday night television, and *The Ladies' Home Journal* was not in the business of saving people's marriages from incest or spousal abuse. But Sexton's transgressiveness involved not only her themes or subject matter; it also had to do with the positioning of her poems' aggressively female speakers. Whereas Rich and Levertov were both inclined to depict their poet-self as "not-a-woman" in some important sense, Sexton led with her femaleness, as if unable or unwilling to do anything else.

Many of the poems in her first volume, published in 1960, call up a masculine interlocutor right at the outset—often in the title, as in "You, Doctor Martin," "Said the Poet to the Analyst," and "For John, Who Begs Me Not to Enquire Further"—and oblige him to pay attention to what their female speaker has to say. He is obliged to do so either by the terms of a specific professional relationship (he is her therapist or teacher) or simply by virtue of social arrangements that have placed women in a dependent status relative to men. Say he's the average middle-class man in the street, and she a woman who needs his assistance: if she accosts him on that basis, how can he refuse her?

One of these early poems, set in a mental hospital, begins, "Wait Mister. Which way is home?"—a rhetorical question that is at once naïve and sophisticated, simple and complex. Strikingly inappropriate as a request for information, it is easy to recognize as an appeal for help: sane or crazy, this woman knows how to get a passing stranger's attention by flaunting her helplessness. On another level, her question is uncannily prescient: sane people do share a precious yet utterly commonplace knowledge that gives them the ability to walk out of this place, which is nobody's home but where she will have to stay. How come he knows the way home and she does not? If her interlocutor is a decent man with reasons of his own for coming to visit this "private institution on a hill," he'll still be troubled by her question as he gets back into his Ford or his Buick and drives away.[31]

Alicia Ostriker has trenchantly characterized the rhetorical strategy of Sexton's early poems as one that creates an "imperative of intimacy": "we are obliged," says Ostriker, "to experience the hot breath of the poem upon us."[32] Ostriker explains this propensity for turning poems into "personal transactions" as a particular instance of the "drive to connect" (Adrienne Rich's phrase) that Ostriker finds to be pervasive among women poets. But whether or not women share a drive to connect that is distinctive and gender-specific, Sexton's strategy was politically canny: one way for a woman to get the upper hand with a male interlocutor might be to personalize their transaction by playing the gender card. In a verbal encounter between a man and a woman, the one who calls attention to their gender difference has turned that encounter into a personal transaction whether the other one likes it or not. Taking the initiative to do this may enable her to catch her interlocutor off balance. It's a dangerous game for a woman to play, however—one reason, perhaps, why Sexton's poems are still unsettling to read.

"For John, Who Begs Me Not to Enquire Further" (*The Complete Poems*, 34–35) is an especially interesting case of this strategy because it is also a manifesto of sorts for confessional poetry. As such, it opens the second section of *To Bedlam and Part Way Back* with a frank admission that Sexton's poems will make their readers uncomfortable. She intends them to, but in a good cause. The unlovely things she has discovered by "tapp[ing] my own head"—the rage, the despair, the death wish—are also dimensions of ourselves and of our social reality: "At first it was private. / Then it was more than myself; it was you, or your house / or your kitchen." As Sexton explains it here, confessional poetry is not only or primarily a spilling of one's guts or a publicizing of one's private life; at its most powerful, it will have an uncanny transitivity: "my kitchen, your kitchen, / my face, your face." Such poetry can do us good, and yet we fear the knowledge it offers us: the poem's title alludes to Schopenhauer's observation that the philosopher "must be like Sophocles' Oedipus" but that "most of us carry in our heart the Jocasta who begs Oedipus for God's sake not to inquire further. . . ."[33] Oedipus had to learn the whole story of his relationship to Jocasta in order to lift the curse that was on his people; Sexton's claim is that her story is likewise one that an entire society needs to know. She has suffered on our behalf to gain the knowledge "that the worst of anyone / can be, finally, / an accident of hope."

This poem's "you" is not, however, just any and every reader of Sexton's poetry: its title specifies one reader in particular, as is by now well known. "John" was John Holmes, Sexton's first poetry teacher, whom, according to her friend and fellow poet Maxine Kumin, she regarded as an "academic father" but who had spoken out in the strongest possible terms against the confessional direction of her work.[34] Holmes, of all readers, was the one whose rejection would be hardest for Sexton to live with, because of the institutional authority his disapproval carried. His opposition may actually have helped her focus and clarify her poetic objectives, as Diane Middlebrook suggests;[35] but it also must have frightened her. Without Holmes's poetry workshop she would have been just a crazy housewife with no special claim on anyone's attention. And so, like Jacob wrestling with the angel, she could not let this interlocutor go without a blessing.

Sexton is rumored to have been discouraged from converting to Catholicism by an old priest who urged her instead to recognize that "God is in your typewriter." She received a version of the same advice from the psychiatrist who got her started writing poetry as a psychotherapeutic device.[36] The sacrament of confession and the relation between analyst and analysand in psychotherapy are clearly analogous to the relationship "For John" sets up between its fledgling poet, who is female, and a male representative of the academic establishment. Like the psychoanalyst in Jacques Lacan's notorious formulation, John is "the one who is supposed to know"—in this case, how to become a published poet. Just as in therapy or in the confessional, his role is to hear her story and confer upon the occasion of her telling it the institutional authority his position carries. In this kind of interlocutory setup the one who *isn't* supposed to know does all the talking, seduced into self-revelation by the authority of her confessor and the power–knowledge imbalance between them.³⁷ But by having John play Jocasta to her Oedipus, Sexton uses gender reversal to call his authority into question even as she seeks his permission to tell a certain kind of story.³⁸ What is driving her, I would argue, is a desire not so much for connection as for recognition by a fellow poet—recognition that, in validating her experience as normative, would also concede her the authority to tell him who he really is.

"For John" is just one example of Sexton's propensity throughout this first published volume for staging personal transactions that are politically loaded and complex. Most of the poems in *To Bedlam* call attention to a difference in status and authority between their female speaker and her male interlocutor that they do not challenge directly, but instead contrive in more insidious ways to unsettle or call into question. The protagonist of "The Exorcists" (*CP*, 16–17) who will "solemnly swear / . . . / that I know you not," as she is about to have an (illegal) abortion at the hands of the doctor who was also, it seems, her partner in "summer loves"; the psychiatric patient in "You, Doctor Martin" (3–4) who follows up a jaded acknowledgment that "Of course, I love you" with the observation that in the hospital dining room "There are no knives / for cutting your throat"; the crazy girl in "Music Swims Back to Me" who asks a passing stranger how to get home—these are all versions of a speaker whose attitude toward her interlocutor is disconcertingly ambiguous. Does she regard him as her potential savior, or as the one who got her into this fix? Does she think he can help her, or is she merely desperate for male attention? If she had a knife, whose throat would she use it on? These poems make such questions undecidable; that is what gives them their political edge. "A woman like that is misunderstood," as Sexton liked to remind audiences at her poetry readings by opening with the early poem "Her Kind."³⁹

In the society whose illness both Sexton and Lowell unsparingly document, so much depends upon whether you are a man or a woman: the kind of education you will get, your relationship to money and property, your role within the family and in society at large. So much depends on whether you are a husband or a wife—marriage being of all social relationships the one most entirely predicated on gender difference. And if you are a man or a woman whose "business is words" (as the poet said to the analyst in one of Sexton's early poems), your marriage is a setting in which the relationship between language and power is liable to be especially complex.⁴⁰ Adrienne Rich's early poem "An

Unsaid Word" speaks to this, arguing that a wife has power she must not use to "call her man / From that estranged intensity / Where his mind forages alone."[41] But whereas the attitude Rich assumes toward this "truth" is rueful, resigned, dispassionate, to Lowell and Sexton marriage presented itself as a more explosive setting in which to highlight the interrelationship of language, power, and gender.

Lowell broached the subject of marriage first in the persona poems of his second volume, *The Mills of the Kavanaughs*, which came out in 1951—the same year Rich was making her poetic début with *A Change of World*. And whereas Rich had done her best *not* to sound like a woman in her poems, Lowell produced poem after poem for this volume in which he ventriloquizes a woman's voice. "It is immediately noticeable," remarks Lowell's biographer Ian Hamilton, "that the book is a clamor of distraught, near-hysterical first-person speech, and that almost always the speaker is a woman."[42] These exercises in ventriloquism gained Lowell access to the domestic arena and to the political drama of domestic relationships. He would go on to do more trenchant confessional writing from the perspective of a son, husband, and father in *Life Studies*, but it was by speaking as a woman in the earlier volume that he could begin to move away from the public, prophetic stance of *Lord Weary's Castle* toward the personal, confessional intimacy of "91 Revere Street," "Man and Wife," and "My Last Afternoon with Uncle Devereux Winslow."

In both Lowell's and Sexton's marriages the wife was the more talkative, vociferous partner, but it was the husband who had the upper hand in the most literal sense. Lowell broke his first wife's nose during a domestic quarrel; Sexton's husband often hit her, though it seemed to their daughter Linda that she goaded him into it for psychological reasons of her own.[43] Such a husband knew himself to be verbally overmatched by his wife's powers of invective. The nonviolent way to hold his own in domestic disputes was to stay aloof and allow her to spend her fury verbally; so long as he would not be drawn into battle, her verbal advantage could gain her nothing. As Lowell makes clear in "91 Revere Street," the autobiographical prose piece that became Part II of *Life Studies*, this is a strategy he learned at his mother's knee. The child depicted in "91 Revere Street" is the father not only of the man Robert Lowell, but of the poet as well.

"'*Weelawaugh, we-ee-eeelawaugh, weelawaugh*,' shrilled Mother's high voice. 'But-and, but-and, but-and!' Father's low mumble would drone in answer." As a boy, Lowell confesses, he would "awake with rapture" night after night to "the rhythm of [his] parents' arguing."[44] The man of the house invariably lost these arguments, and so his son grew up self-defensively hoarding speech. The way young Bobby "saved [him]self from emotional exhaustion" in the face of his mother's "prying questions" was by sullenly refusing to give her anything at all to pry into: "'A penny for your thoughts, Schopenhauer,' my mother would say. 'I am thinking about pennies,' I'd answer. 'When *I* was a child I used to love telling Mamá everything I had done,' Mother would say. 'But you're not a child,' I would answer . . ." (*Collected Poems*, 128).

Charlotte Lowell, as she is unsparingly depicted in "91 Revere Street," poses a clear and present danger to her son's masculinity. Having forced her "unmasterful" husband to leave the Navy, the only career for which he was temperamentally suited, she sends young Bobby to a girls' school whose "regime" is an extension of hers. Both at home and at school Bobby holds on grimly to the "outlaw" status of "boy," in spite of knowing that in either setting to be a boy "was to be small, denied, and weak." The memoir furnishes plenty of evidence that he is confused and ambivalent about his gender identity: he bullies other boys and earns the nickname Buffalo Bull on the soccer field, yet confesses to having asked Santa Claus for a field hockey stick and to "[wishing] I were an older girl" (*Collected Poems*, 134).

So intriguingly does Lowell play out this personal scenario and so tellingly does he draw on it in the poems that come later in the *Life Studies* volume that it is easy to miss the larger social picture his memoir has meanwhile sketched for us. The society depicted in "91 Revere Street" is one in which men's and women's roles and prerogatives are radically different, but these differences are unstable and volatile. All the women who figure in the memoir, with the exception of Charlotte Lowell, are anomalous in relation to the man-the-breadwinner, woman-the-housewife norm that nevertheless prevails unquestioned among them. "'Eric's mother and father are *both* called Dr. Burckhard,' my mother once said, and indeed there was something endearingly repellent about Mrs. Burckhard with her doctor's degree, her long, unstylish skirts, and her dramatic, dulling blond braids" (129). Commander Billy Harkness's wife, whose husband calls her "Jimmy," is "an unpleasant rarity," "the only naval officer's wife we knew who was also a college graduate" (139). Commander Billy goes in for "tireless, tasteless harangues" against a female member of the Lowells' own family, the poet Amy Lowell—she of the black cheroot, the "loud, bossy, unladylike" free verse, the obscenely large fortune and disinclination for marriage (143). What is "repellent" or "unpleasant" about these women is not only that they don't have what properly belongs to their station in life—stylish grooming, attractive figures—but that they do have what doesn't: a Ph.D., a college education, financial independence, a taste for cigars. The one whose aberration is truly menacing, because of the position she is in to throw the next generation out of kilter, is the school principal aptly named Miss Manice, whose "pet theory was that 'women are simply not the equals of men'" but whose educational program for girls bred contempt, we're told, for "the male's two idols: career and earning power" (132).

Feminist historians tell us that middle- and upper-class women reaching adulthood between the two World Wars were considerably freer than their Cold War counterparts to envision adult lives that were not exclusively centered on home and family.[45] The success of the suffrage movement was recent history; the New Woman of the 1920s and '30s, as she is nostalgically remembered by Betty Friedan in *The Feminine Mystique*, was independent, ambitious to have a career and a life of her own, and "passionate[ly] involve[d] with the world"[46] Clearly Lowell's nostalgia for the 1930s took a different form from Friedan's, a form more consistent not only with a masculinist outlook but also with a 1950s mindset. In "91 Revere Street" the most powerful female figures are the ones who yearn to be dominated by men but whose menfolk who are simply not up to the task: "I can hear Miss Manice browbeating my white and sheepish father, 'How can we stand up to you? Where are our Archimedeses, our Wagners, our Admiral Simses?'" (*Collected Poems*, 133).

Lowell recalls this period between the wars as a "topsy-turvy era" from the Lowell family standpoint: "'people of the right sort' were no longer dominant in city elections" (124). But a more conspicuous way in which people of the right sort are no longer dominant, though Lowell never says so explicitly, is that instead of having real wars to fight, the men are all fighting a losing battle against women for their masculinity and its prerogatives. Bobby's mother loves to phone the Admiral and berate him for forcing her husband to spend his nights on the Navy base; his father ridiculously hints at important military reasons for the Admiral's arbitrary rules and "uncommunicative arrogance." Written all over this memoir is a conviction that personal identity is very much a function of gender, but that gender difference is unstable and that women are both individually and collectively to blame for this. "91 Revere Street" is a window on Lowell's childhood in the 1930s, but it is also a product of Lowell's obsession with his own masculinity as an adult in the 1950s. "[My mother] ran into my bedroom. She hugged me. She said, 'Oh Bobby, it's such a comfort to have a man in the house.' 'I am not a man,' I said, 'I am a boy'" (132).

The memoir's script for male-female and especially husband-wife relations strikingly prefigures his marriage to Elizabeth Hardwick, as depicted in the later section of the *Life Studies* volume that is itself subtitled "Life Studies." A speaker who is unmistakably Robert Lowell confesses, in "Man and Wife," to having married a woman he fell in love with because she shared his mother's gift for marital invective. As they "lie on Mother's bed," which is also the setting for the companion poem that ventriloquizes Lizzie as a latter-day Wife of Bath, Lowell tenderly hearkens back twelve years to when

> you were in your twenties, and I . . .
> . . .
> outdrank the Rahvs in the heat
> of Greenwich Village, fainting at your feet—
> too boiled and shy
> and poker-faced to make a pass,
> while the shrill verve
> of your invective scorched the traditional South.

He continues to need her capacity for invective—it has saved him over and over from "the kingdom of the mad"—and he continues to be the silent, "poker-faced" partner in the relationship.[47]

Specific references to their friends the Rahvs, to how long they have been together, to how many times he has been hospitalized, are in the poem to persuade us, as Steven Axelrod points out, that we are gaining entrance "into its author's actual life and mode of consciousness": "the reader, as Lowell later explained, 'was to believe he was getting the *real* Robert Lowell.'"[48] At the same time, however, these details are handled in such a way as to give this marriage the kind of exemplary status the poem's title implicitly claims for it. "Tamed by *Miltown*," this Man and Wife are denizens of "the tranquilized *Fifties*" and of "Boston's 'hardly passionate Marlborough Street'"—a classic address, though less fashionable now than it used to be.[49] Their "gilded bed-posts shine, / abandoned, almost Dionysian": the mythic resonance strengthens the Oedipal overtones of the *mise-en-scène* to suggest that their predicament is also classic in psychological terms. The wife delivers herself of an "*old-fashioned* tirade" (my emphasis) while her husband devises a love poem that extends the emotional reach of the traditional aubade: literarily also, there is subtle encouragement to recognize that where love and sexual intimacy between men and women are concerned, the more things change the more they remain the same.

Lowell uses apostrophe strategically partway through the poem to emphasize that the wife he is addressing is both absent and present, real and imaginary. She is there in bed with him, but has turned her back; she is "my *Petite,* / clearest of all God's creatures, still all air and nerve," but this characterization is a figment of his need and nostalgia rather than an overture toward present-tense dialogue between them. Ironically, thus, his tenderness and gratitude are unavailable to mitigate her settled conviction, expressed in the monologue that immediately follows, of how "unjust" he is and of "the monotonous meanness of his lust."[50]

Her monologue makes it even more obvious that in both poems Lowell was trying for a generic depiction of 1950s domesticity. Richard Tillinghast notes, for example, that it was not Lizzie but Delmore Schwartz's wife who went to bed each night, as Lowell's speaker does, with ten dollars and his car key tied to her thigh.[51] The allusion to Chaucer's Wife of Bath confirms, moreover, that marital problems such as the ones this diptych exposes are perennial and somehow typical of the human species. The poem's epigraph from Schopenhauer suggests this also: *"It is the future generation that presses into being by means of these exuberant feelings and supersensible soap bubbles of ours."*[52] From one generation to the next, both title and epigraph suggest, humankind reproduces itself through the loins of "'hopped up husband[s]'" whose wives have no choice but to ride out their randiness while angrily wondering "'What makes him tick?'" These suggestions are conveyed to us over Lizzie's head, as it were, by the way in which her "tirade" is set up and introduced.

"Man and Wife" and "'To Speak of Woe That Is in Marriage'" had in earlier drafts been a single poem that gave both the husband's and the wife's perspective on their marriage.[53] Separating that poem into companion monologues made it easier to depict the married couple at cross-purposes: perhaps their perspectives can be said to be in dialogue, but they themselves clearly are not. Separating the two poems also makes room to frame the wife's monologue with a title and an epigraph that place her perspective in a particular way. Giving her a soliloquy of her own in which to deplore her husband's behavior is a gesture consistent with the unsparing self-irony that is the hallmark of Lowell's autobiographical persona in *Life Studies*. But it is an equivocal gesture, especially if the epigraph from Schopenhauer recalls "91 Revere Street" and young Bobby Lowell's successful evasion of his mother's curiosity about what makes him tick.

Lowell's poems are not, for the most part, framed as encounters with particular interlocutors; they are addressed instead, as Lawrence Kramer points out, "to a featureless interlocutor who is never represented in the text."[54] Kramer notes, however, that at strategic moments the poem's speaker *will* appeal to someone in particular: "Oh, my *Petite,*" he'll say, or "Grandpa! Have me, hold me, cherish me!"⁵⁵ These confessions of emotional neediness are rendered all the more poignant by the patent unavailability of the interlocutor who is thus apostrophized: "Grandpa" is long dead; "my *Petite*," "now twelve years later," turns her back to deliver a tirade that her husband perversely finds comforting. Such moments do not presage communication; instead they disclose the loneliness and isolation to which the poem's speaker is self-condemned by his poker-faced taciturnity. His predicament is reminiscent of the damned souls T. S. Eliot ventriloquizes in "The Waste Land," "each in his prison / Thinking of the key":⁵⁶ self-awareness only serves to exacerbate his sense of helplessness. In his need to be rescued and/or comforted he is still a little boy inside—a boy, moreover, whose gender identity is fragile and conflicted. His apostrophe to "Grandpa" amounts to a confession that his need to be held and cherished is still essentially the same as in the days of their yearly autumn trip to the family graveyard at Dunbarton, when he "cuddled like a paramour / in [his] Grandfather's bed."⁵⁷ The reader is the "featureless interlocutor" to whom such confessions are addressed; it is we who have been put in a position to figure out what makes Robert Lowell tick.

For Richard Tillinghast, a former student of Lowell's, "the biggest question to be asked about Robert Lowell is how he managed to bring such an air of authority to his poems...."⁵⁸ Elizabeth Bishop grumbled, after reading *Life Studies* in manuscript, that he managed it by being a Massachusetts Lowell: "all you have to do is put down the names," she wrote to him enviously, "and . . . it seems significant, illustrative, American, etc." Brett Millier, Bishop's biographer, observes that Lowell's poetic authority "might have had as much to do with the privileges of gender as of family background"⁵⁹—an observation Tillinghast finds reductive,⁶⁰ preferring instead to believe that Lowell possessed "an uncanny sense of timing" and of "the larger national mood."⁶¹ Another crucial factor in his poems' air of authority, as Tillinghast and others have noticed, was the way in which Lowell invoked a Freudian explanatory paradigm to lend depth, interpretability, and mythic resonance to his speaker's emotional predicament. And it was his pose of disinterestedness, a stance Lawrence Kramer has aptly characterized as one of "stylized dispassionate candor" toward his own experience,⁶² that enabled him to invoke that explanatory paradigm so effectively. In large part, Lowell's authority accrues to him from our sense that he has not spared himself, that he has fully submitted his case for study, that it interests him just as much as, and in the same way that, it interests us.

In this way, Lowell made himself heir apparent to T. S. Eliot. The speaker of *Life Studies* is a latter-day Tiresias, a man who knows too many secrets of the human heart for his own well-being and is sharing them with us at his own expense. But Lowell's version of this rhetorical posture is implicated more insistently than Eliot's in a characterological posture of beset masculinity. Gender is crucial to his poetic authority not only because "poet" is a masculine noun—the point Millier was presumably making—but also, paradoxically, because the self-intimacy Lowell dramatizes in these poems has effeminized him in an unsettling but interesting way. He achieves a kind of reverse androgyny that extends his poetic purview at the expense of his manhood by taking him onto emotional terrain that a "real man" stereotypically seeks to avoid—humiliations, experiences of dependency, feelings of tenderness and ambivalence.

It is important to recognize, with Lawrence Kramer, that the confessional force of Lowell's poems lies "not . . . in their subject matter *per se* but in how and to whom they present it."[63] That goes for Sexton's poems also: for both poets gender is a key determinant not only of subject matter but also of rhetorical posture or poetic stance. In their self-dramatization as confessional speakers both Lowell and Sexton were adepts of vulnerability. But a man's vulnerability differs from a woman's in its relationship to other attributes of personality and of self-presentation: emotional neediness, capacity for self-irony, need for approval. A male poet's access to and performance of his vulnerability is thus also in a different relationship to his poetic authority than a woman poet's is.

After Sexton had been in Lowell's poetry writing class for a few months, in 1958, she wrote to W. D. Snodgrass that she was "learning more than you could imagine from Lowell. I am learning what I am not. . . . also a fear of writing as a woman writes."[64] Five years later she produced a poem that alludes directly to Lowell's marital diptych in both its title, "Man and Wife," and its epigraph, *"To speke of wo that is in mariage . . . ."*[65] But this poem shows that Sexton may have learned less from Lowell than she imagined—less that could help her with her own rhetorical posture in her poems. In "Man and Wife" she seems to have been trying not to write as a woman writes but instead to cultivate the tone of the center. The poem begins with a series of "we"-statements that epitomize the emotional sterility of a suburban marriage; then it builds an extended simile that surreally anthropomorphizes a pair of city pigeons who "came to the suburbs / by mistake. . . ." Not until near the end of the poem, coming out the other side of this simile, does the poem's speaker address her husband directly, in an apostrophe that calls attention to their mutual helplessness to overcome their emotional estrangement from each other: "Like them / we neither talk nor clear our throats, / Oh Darling, / we gasp in unison beside our window pane, / drunk on the drunkard's dream" (*CP*, 118). In the same way as Lowell's "Oh my *Petite*," Sexton's apostrophe follows a description of the couple that highlights their physical proximity in order to heighten the pathos of their emotional estrangement: the pigeons "would pierce our heart," this wife finally tells her husband, "if they could only fly the distance."

Sexton's "Man and Wife" is not a very good poem for several reasons, but the one I want to highlight is that its use of apostrophe is banal and uninteresting. As a term of endearment, "Oh Darling" does not bear the imprint of a particular couple's intimacy; nor does it take the poem's speaker to a new level of self-disclosure, as Lowell does by using "Oh my *Petite*" to call up a specific vignette from the past. In context, "Oh Darling" merely whines: it makes the poem's pathos too easy, sounding a note that belongs to a stereotypically female range of emotional expression. When Rich used a version of this interlocutory strategy, in "A Marriage in the Sixties," she handled it more wittily and with a more firmly crafted poetic line.[66]

Thus whereas Lowell's confessional stance gave generic poethood a change of venue and a new lease on life, for Sexton generic poethood proved even more unworkable and uncongenial than it had for Rich. Sexton's best confessional poems, as we have seen, play the gender card right from the outset, in their first lines or even in their titles. Their speaker is aggressively, importunately female, and her speech acts have a relentless *ad hominem* urgency. It was in this speaker's complex, fraught relationship to a masculine figure of authority that Sexton found both the pretext and the resources for her most successful dramatization of self.

②

And yet the poem in which Sexton most openly confesses to having "made you to find me" is addressed not to a doctor or teacher or father figure, but to her three-year-old daughter. This poem's ostensible purpose is to confess to little Joy that because her mother "would rather die than love," she has not been able to be with her daughter for the first three-plus years of the child's life. "The Double Image" tells the story of those years, spent partly in a mental hospital, partly living with her own mother (whom she uncannily resembles) and having companion portraits painted (the "double image" to which her title refers). The poet-mother finally puts her "worst guilt" into words in the poem's final lines, where she brings out a second meaning for her title by confessing that she brought her daughter into the world in the first place to assuage her own gender anxiety.

> I, who was never quite sure
> about being a girl, needed another
> life, another image to remind me.
> And this was my worst guilt, you could not cure
> nor soothe it. I made you to find me.[67]

As in the poems Sexton addressed to male authority figures, but here in reverse, the power-knowledge imbalance between the poem's speaker and her interlocutor is conspicuous; and here again, her intentions with respect to this interlocutor are problematic once we begin to unpack them. Neither the disclosure of "my worst guilt" nor the parenthetical observation that "you could not cure / nor soothe it" is an appropriate thing to say to a three-year-old: who, in this context, is supposed to be mothering whom?[68]

According to Linda Gray Sexton, Anne Sexton did make a habit of asking her daughters to meet her need to be mothered at the expense of their own.[69] But of course when a *poet* makes "you" to find "me," she or he has resorted to a rhetorical device that is perhaps as old as the lyric itself. Apostrophe is the device poets use to conjure up "an absent or imaginary person"; it is "always addressed," as Lawrence Kramer reminds us, "to someone who cannot listen to it."[70] Paul De Man, Jonathan Culler, and Barbara Johnson have all suggested (thinking primarily of the Romantic lyric) that apostrophe is lyric poetry's foundational trope, insofar as it asserts a poet's special prerogative to speak with the dead or commune with extrahuman powers and sources of being.[71] Perhaps, then, the admission that "I made you to find me" is not so much a mother's as a poet's confession, exposing the logic whereby we conjure up an imagined interlocutor to find the poet in us. On this understanding of Sexton's rhetorical gesture and its motive, three-year-old Joy, like the sleeping child in Coleridge's "Frost at Midnight" or the beloved sister of Wordsworth's "Tintern Abbey," is the figment of a process of autobiographical reflection that is not literally intended for her, but is provoked and enabled by conjuring her up to speak with.

Sexton's friend and fellow poet W. D. Snodgrass had movingly apostrophized a three-year-old child in his award-winning "Heart's Needle" sequence, published in 1959. Like "The Double Image," the

"Heart's Needle" sequence discloses the guilt as well as grief of a parent who cannot be with his daughter to help her grow up. "Though you are only three, / you are already growing / strange to me," the poet-father confesses to his daughter in "Heart's Needle 5": "You chatter about new playmates, sing strange songs. . . ."[72] But Snodgrass's way of constructing his daughter as a poetic interlocutor is subtly different from Sexton's. His daughter figures vividly in the sequence, chattering or whining or singing, at one point suggesting that they pull a star out of the sky and cook it for dinner; clearly, however, she does not and cannot share his perspective on their relationship. The pathos of his predicament lies, indeed, in the distance or difference between the daughter he describes and the daughter he addresses. The poetic device of apostrophe enables him to say things, as if to another adult, that he could not possibly say to the child she really is. "I write you only the bitter poems / that you can't read," he confesses in the ninth poem of the sequence. In this way, her three-year-old innocence becomes a foil for his adult knowledge of loss and estrangement.

In "The Double Image," by contrast, a parent is speaking who cannot afford or cannot manage to honor the difference between her daughter's level of awareness and her own. Her story takes its departure from a brief verbal exchange that could plausibly have taken place between them, on a rainy November day as they stand "watching the yellow leaves go queer": "You ask me where they go. I say today believed / in itself, or else it fell." Sexton has constructed the interlocutory relation between mother and daughter differently from Snodgrass: the three-year-old is more of a conversation partner for her mother in Sexton's poem. Indeed, the child's language and perspective are so blended with her mother's that the mental conversation the mother is having with her daughter is hard to distinguish from the one that is actually occurring between them. What she would like to teach her daughter, she goes on to explain, is a lesson she herself failed to learn: "Today, my small child, Joyce, / love your self's self where it lives." Insofar as her failure to be there for her daughter has convinced her that "there is no special God to refer to," this is the best parental advice she can manage. But Sexton's allegory of the leaves, though it passes for a lesson at the level of a child's understanding in the importance of loving yourself or believing in yourself, is effectively a counsel of despair: leaves fall in the autumn whether they have believed in themselves or not. Implicitly, then, both the substance and the interpersonal dynamics of the mother-daughter exchange disclose a confessional imperative that is not only suicidal, but murderous. "I had to learn," says the mother, "why I would rather / die than love, how your innocence would hurt and how I gather / guilt like a young intern / . . . his certain evidence." The poem itself is evidence of her inability not only to protect but even to tolerate her daughter's innocence: her worst guilt is that she finds herself offering the child a poet's bitter wisdom in place of a mother's love.

"The Double Image" is the confession of a woman who, in becoming a poet, has transgressed against motherhood. The poem's interlocutory strategy puts being a poet and being a mother in tension and finally at odds with each other; it creates an unmistakable dissonance between these two roles and their prerogatives. Like the "middle-aged witch" of Sexton's fifth published volume, *Transformations* (1971), whose designated interlocutor is her teenage daughter Linda but also the child in each of us, the speaker-protagonist of "The Double Image" is a poet and an unconventional, outlaw mother, both at once. And like the mental patient in "You, Doctor Martin" and "Music Swims Back to Me" and the would-be poet of "Said the Poet to the Analyst" and "For John, Who Begs Me Not to Enquire Further," she writes as a woman writes: that is her strength and her weakness, both.

It is surprising to find Sexton confessing in "The Double Image" that she was "never quite sure / about being a girl": how could she doubt what her interlocutors and equally her readers are never allowed to forget? But that, of course, is the paradox of female masquerade and perhaps, as theorists of masquerade have urged us to recognize, of "femininity" as such.[73] Three years later, in the 1963 poem "Consorting with Angels," Sexton would declare herself "tired of the gender of things" and recount a dream she'd had of leaving it all behind for a celestial city where "the nature of the angels went unexplained, / no two made in the same species, / . . . each one like a poem obeying itself, / performing God's functions, / a people apart" (*CP*, 111). The transcendent beings Sexton here dreams of joining are *sui generis,* and they have a hermetic self-sufficiency that is strikingly antithetical to her own poetic *modus vivendi*—her need for an interlocutor, her penchant for self-exposure and for courting societal judgment and censure. The interlocutor she envisions for herself in this poem is the dream itself of transcendent androgyny, which seems to offer salvation from the hall of mirrors in which she is caught: "and I said to it . . . / 'You are the answer. / You will outlive my husband and my father.'"

For better or for worse, however, the confessional mode both Sexton and Lowell practiced was utterly steeped in the gender of things. With hindsight, the paradigms of male-female interaction their poems depict as immemorial and inevitable can be seen to have been produced by a particular set of economic pressures and ideological investments. From where we sit, what seems inevitable is that those paradigms of male-female interaction could and would be displaced. But from the perspective of a white middle-class denizen of the 1950s and early '60s, they were paramount: you could outlive your mother or father and divorce your wife or husband, but the family romance would continue to reassert itself in your life and in your poems. The scenario both Sexton and Lowell were wedded to—"*that* story," to borrow an apposite phrase from one of Sexton's recycled fairy tales[74]—was a 1950s version of the suicide pact of Adam and Eve. The man and the woman need each other, they destroy one another, their marriage cannot be saved.

Like Sexton, Sylvia Plath was attracted to the kind of story that makes the suffering we do in intimate relationships seem intelligible, yet inescapable. When the speaker of "The Colossus" says to her father that "A blue sky out of the Oresteia arches above us," she is acknowledging the "Electra" complex that makes her "every-daughter," in keeping with the psychotherapeutic paradigms of the day.[75] "I borrow the stilts of an old tragedy," says the daughter-speaker of another of Plath's Electra poems:[76] the story of her life is the high cultural counterpart of the fairy tales Sexton re-worked in *Transformations*. But the authority Plath's poems confer on such stories is differently conceived of and, in rhetorical terms, differently purchased. Sexton plays the role of storyteller in a mode of everyday gossipy inwardness with both the stories themselves and the audience to whom she is retelling them. Her frequent asides to that audience affirm these stories' relevance to contemporary social arrangements but also mock the society that harbors such arrangements. Plath was not a storyteller; instead, as we shall see in chapter 3, she uses "that story" to lift her relationships with significant others onto "that stage," a timeless a-social realm where "stony actors" strike immemorial poses.[77]

"The story of our lives becomes our lives," as Adrienne Rich observed in another context;[78] her story changed in the 1970s, whereas Sexton's and Plath's did not. My next chapter begins with Rich's reading of Sexton's suicide in 1974. For Rich, this sister poet's self-inflicted death was an object lesson in the pitfalls and inadequacies of a "Confessional" poetics.

CHAPTER 2

ADRIENNE RICH'S ANTI-CONFESSIONAL POETICS

Confession is a self-centered exercise. At the same time, however, it presupposes a "significant other": someone to whom the confessant expects his or her story to matter, in whose name it is told—as in St. Augustine's *Confessions*—or to whom it must be told, as Anne Sexton insists in "For John, Who Begs Me Not to Enquire Further." The confessant's relationship to a designated interlocutor is reciprocal: intertwined, indeed, with the confessant's desire to tell her or his own story is the desire to tell the story of the other, or a story that in some sense belongs to them both. In a secular context, this relationship can easily become a power struggle: if "I" am female and "you" are male I may feel myself to be in danger from you, but you might also be in danger from me, or from my story. Cast as the one "who begs me not to enquire further," "John" is invited by Sexton's poem to see himself as an effeminate coward who would call off her quest for self-knowledge because he cannot face the truth about himself. Cast as Jocasta vis-à-vis Sexton's Oedipus, John is not just a figment of the confessional process; he is its hostage, like the three-year-old daughter to whom Sexton addresses her confession of maternal inadequacy in "The Double Image."

I have given Sexton's confessional project a distinctly unfriendly reading in the immediately foregoing paragraph to call attention to how—and how much—Adrienne Rich's stance as a poet has differed from hers. "Making you to find me" is a strategy Rich has always found troubling, in both its political and its ethical dimension. Her resistance to this strategy is of a piece with her aversion to the confessional mode; in explaining the one, I will also be exploring the other.[1]

Making "you" to find "me" is of course what lyric poets are very often up to: Shakespeare in his sonnets, urging that "My glass shall not persuade me I am old, / As long as youth and thou are of one date";[2] Wordsworth conjuring up his sister to be his alter ego and soulmate in "Tintern Abbey"; Keats in colloquy with a nightingale or a Grecian urn. Indeed, the figure of apostrophe is one of the most obvious ways for a lyric poet to establish his or her orientation or stance, vis-à-vis both an audience of contemporaries and a prior tradition of poetic discourse. Apostrophizing his beloved as "Stella" in a love sonnet sequence at the end of the sixteenth century, Sir Philip Sidney signals to his readers that in spite of his claim to be a thoroughly modern lover, he and the lady will be found to be playing predictable roles. Apostrophizing the "wild west wind," Percy Bysshe Shelley lays claim to the traditional role of poet as prophet, but with a difference that has become a canonical marker of British Romanticism: his designated interlocutor is a force of nature rather than God or a god. Apostrophizing a sea rose, "harsh and with stint of petals," H. D. makes her poetic début early in the twentieth century by speaking as only poets speak while adding an exotic new species to the traditional garden of poetic flowers.

The Confessional poets reinvigorated this quintessentially poetic figure by using it to suture their poems to their own personal lives. By calling on specific real people, dead or living, they abrogated the distinction between poet and speaker that had become a fixed canon of both Modernist poetics and the New Criticism.[3] You would learn from Lowell's *Life Studies* what private endearments he used with his wife; from Sexton's poems, the names of her two young daughters. Throughout her career, Rich has also sought to place herself in dialogue with others, "not somewhere else but here."[4] And yet she has always worried about the potential for misusing the other that this kind of interlocutory setup carries. From Rich's perspective, misuse of the other is a misuse of the power a poet wields in the world, which includes the prerogative of bearing witness for others.[5]

In Sexton's poems an aggressively vulnerable female speaker is ready to disclose more about herself than her interlocutor, often a man, has bargained for or can handle. Rich, from the beginning of her career, has striven for a different kind of interlocutory relationship both to the reader of her poems and to significant others within them. She has avoided the scandalous intimacy of the confessional, trying instead for an interlocutory relationship that is more truly a dialogue, an exercise in "trying to talk with" someone else.[6] If Sexton is a poet of intimacy, Rich has been and remains a poet of reciprocity: instead of making "you" to find "me" in her poems, she has always been interested in making "you" to find "we."

But this too is risky business, both politically and rhetorically. If, for instance, I were to tell "your" story for you, as Rich tried to do in an anti-Confessional poem that notoriously misfired, I might replicate and reinforce your experience of disempowerment. "And so," as Rich would ruefully acknowledge in 1984 in her "Notes toward a Politics of Location," "even ordinary pronouns become a political problem": to assert that the personal is political is not to solve the problem of what your experience has to do with me, or mine with you.[7]

After Sexton committed suicide in 1974, Rich delivered a memorial tribute at City College in New York whose purpose was only partly to honor a sister poet's memory; the occasion also presented itself as an opportunity for damage control. "I wanted," she explains in the headnote she subsequently published with this piece, "to speak to the question of identification which a suicide always arouses."[8] Sylvia Plath's suicide a decade earlier had produced what Rich describes as "an imaginative obsession with victimization and death" on the part of other young women poets. Sexton, who had been Plath's friend and a fellow student in Robert Lowell's poetry class, could almost be said to have sponsored that obsession. In "Sylvia's Death," her unconventional elegy for Plath, she speaks as a frustrated rival who has experienced, "at the news of your death / a terrible taste for it, like salt."[9] Rich's memorial for Sexton had a twofold purpose: to bear witness, in Sexton's name but in spite of her example, for life against death; and to put Sexton's equivocal legacy into perspective for a women's community she describes in this headnote as having been "still-tenuous" in 1974. Rich had published *Diving into the Wreck* the previous year, and her tribute to Sexton is thematically and rhetorically akin to the poems in that volume. "I think of Anne Sexton," she says to her protofeminist audience, "as a sister whose work tells us what we have to fight, in ourselves and in the images patriarchy has held up to us. Her poetry is a guide to the ruins, from which we learn what women have lived and what we must refuse to live any longer" (*OLSS*, 123).

Would Sexton have agreed with this characterization of her work? Many of her poems suggest that she would have. In "Her Kind," which she often used to begin poetry readings, she takes on the persona of a condemned witch on her way to be tortured and burned at the stake.[10] In a satiric epigram entitled "Housewife" she distills the gist of *The Feminine Mystique*, a book we know she had read and discussed with Tillie Olsen and other women colleagues at the Radcliffe Institute.[11] A more sustained instance of "tell[ing] us what we have to fight" is her 1971 *Transformations* sequence, a volume of poems that recast Grimm's fairy tales with what Maxine Kumin describes as a "a society-mocking overlay."[12]

Even in that sequence, however, Sexton's confessional imperative resists assimilation into the agenda of the satirist and social critic. In quasi-autobiographical forewords that frame each tale, the voice of the storyteller, a "middle-aged witch" who is a canny satirist of contemporary social mores, keeps giving way to the vulnerable, self-involved confessional speaker more familiar from Sexton's first published volume, who suffers from reminiscences and can tell us what's on her mind but not what it means. In the last of these "transformed" tales, the distinction between the storyteller and the story's protagonist also breaks down. After her story is officially over and she is supposed to be living happily ever after with a handsome prince, we hear Briar Rose—or is it Anne Sexton—speaking as if from the psychiatrist's couch, confessing that she was sexually molested by her father as a child.[13] The voice of the storyteller as middle-aged witch does not return at that point to close the book she had opened in the first poem of the sequence.[14] The sequence as a whole thus contrives to leave us with the thought that it *is* the poet's task to "enquire further" without attempting a self-diagnosis. "If we understood ourselves we might stop writing poems and become critics," is how Sexton justified the open-endedness of her confessional strategy for an audience of academic critics in 1962.[15]

Confessional poetry puts the onus on its readers to spell out the larger implications of its autobiographical disclosures. That is one of the ways this poetry draws us in, by inducing us to derive a fuller or at least a different meaning from the poet-speaker's experience than she or he is in a position to do. This was also Robert Lowell's premise, but Lowell contrived to have it both ways, rejoining his readers on the other side of the confessional relationship he himself had crafted. The poems in *Life Studies*, even as they tell us with disarming candor what it is like to be Robert Lowell, are always also contriving to remind us that they are poems. Their language is shot through with subtle allusions to earlier poetry: Lowell will shift into the cadence of a poem by Donne or Marvell or Shakespeare and then back into a contemporary vernacular register within a single sentence or line.[16] As confessant he is thus so apparently also a poet that readers are likely to credit him with having precisely calculated the implications and consequences of "Robert Lowell's" psychic vagaries. For a poet who did not have Lowell's public stature, or who was not as well versed in the canonical tradition of Anglo-American poetry, this sleight of craft was both harder to manage and less certain to be credited. Coming from a woman poet, confessional writing was more likely to be construed as a compulsion to be talking about herself or a simple inability to keep her own psychological house in order. One reason Rich found the confessional mode uncongenial, even at the height of its popularity, is that she was unwilling to put her readers in a position to understand her better than she understood herself.

Rich was also unwilling to cater to readers' voyeuristic avidity for access to unlovely places in her own life and psyche. In projects of intimate self-disclosure such as the Confessional poets had undertaken, you run the risk of having sensationalized the personal instead of politicizing it. If you are a woman, you will scarcely avoid playing into the conventional expectation that this is just what you meant to do. Both Sexton's poetry and her way of performing her poems gave her the reputation of an audience junkie, a woman who exposes herself compulsively to get the public attention she both fears and craves. Sylvia Plath produced an angry parody of "a woman like that" in "Lady Lazarus," whose speaker contemptuously performs the ultimate striptease for a "peanut-crunching crowd."[17]

At the City College memorial for Sexton, Rich refers directly to only one of Sexton's poems, and she has chosen it carefully. "Little Girl, My Stringbean, My Lovely Woman" is a poem in which Sexton greets her own daughter's newly emerging womanhood, urging her to embrace her body's capacity for giving and taking sexual pleasure. Sexton had written the poem as a birthday present for her elder daughter on Linda's eleventh birthday, and she often performed it at readings.[18] Rich recalls not only the poem but also the occasion on which she and many other poets heard it first, a "read-in" at Harvard against the Vietnam War. Rich credits Sexton with having precisely calculated the political impact of her own performance on that occasion in 1966. "Famous male poets and novelists were there," she remembers, "reading their diatribes against McNamara, their napalm poems, their ego-poetry.

Anne read [her poem] in a very quiet, vulnerable voice . . . setting the image of a mother's affirmation of her daughter against [these] second-hand images of death and violence. . . ." (*OLSS*, 121). In an interview with Sexton's biographer Diane Middlebrook several years later, Rich would recall that Sexton's reading "made people rather uncomfortable, but she was completely self-possessed."[19]

We know from Sexton herself that she chose "Little Girl, My String-bean" for the Harvard reading *faute de mieux*: protest poetry, as far as she knew, was beyond her. She was opposed to the Vietnam War, but "caring," as she said to Lois Ames in 1968, was not "the same as good writing."[20] To another interlocutor cited in Middlebrook's biography she observed that she was "not a political poet . . . not even a very social one. I just do my thing and it's very personal."[21] What Rich is suggesting, however, is that she often contrived to make the personal political. In her tribute Rich credits Sexton with having broken the silence concerning much that was difficult and painful in women's experience "long before such themes became validated by a collective consciousness of women, and while writing and publishing under the scrutiny of the male literary establishment" (*OLSS*, 121). What she depicts her doing at Harvard is braving that establishment to assert the power and priority of a woman's words and to insist that even (or perhaps especially) in a time of war, women need to be minding their *own* business, that of helping one another to flourish. By transposing that business from the domestic to the political arena, Sexton created a space for the personal that was within but at odds with the public sphere. Her performance was "so out of kilter with the occasion in one sense," as Rich would recall for Diane Middlebrook, "and in another sense so completely the right thing" (Middlebrook, 296).

The woman who speaks in "Little Girl, My Stringbean" is very conspicuously not "trying to talk with a man."[22] The poem stages an intimate mother-to-daughter conversation about "the facts of life": its "you" is reaching out toward a protofeminist "we." Remembering how it felt to be her daughter's age, the poem's speaker hears, "as in a dream / the conversation of the old wives / speaking of *womanhood*." They are not speaking to her, or including her in their conversation: "I was alone. / I waited like a target" (*The Complete Poems*, 146). As her daughter enters this danger zone, she is committed to helping her cross over into womanhood with greater knowledge and confidence. At "high noon," she tells eleven-year-old Linda, "men bare to the waist, young Romans," will arrive to lay siege to her body; in anticipation of that moment, she asserts the temporal and ontological priority of their relationship to each other:

> But before they enter
> I will have said,
> *Your bones are lovely,*
> and before their strange hands
> there was always this hand that formed. (*CP,* 147)

In this context the power to shape a woman's identity belongs to another woman—specifically, to her *words.* "Women," the poem's speaker tells her daughter, "are born twice": the poem becomes in effect a second womb, where the mother-poet can keep her daughter safe from being manhandled until she has become sufficiently *self*-possessed.

"Little Girl, My Stringbean" is not a confessional poem in the usual sense. Middlebrook does, however, find traces in the poem's rhetoric of erotic feelings for Linda that were a legacy of Sexton's own troubled adolescence. Outside the poem, according to Linda's recollections, her mother had not managed to resolve those feelings: she was still coming to Linda's bed to "cuddle" when she couldn't sleep. Certain "odd emphases" in the poem seem to Middlebrook to be "hold[ing] at bay the shame of incest that occupied neighboring circuitry in the poet's brain. . . ." Middlebrook avers that many readers have nevertheless found the poem "touching and successful, partly because of its theme of a mother's protective pride in her daughter's sexual budding" (Middlebrook, 223). Perhaps the poem is touching and successful precisely insofar as its work of sublimation has not been fully achieved. Its mother-speaker is close kin to the destructively possessive Mother Gothel, a malign but finally pathetic figure in Sexton's tale of Rapunzel, as well as to the wicked queen in her version of "Snow White." Is "Little Girl, My Stringbean" a memorable poem because it betrays the inseparability of maternal protective pride from feelings of rivalry and sexual possessiveness? Such a question is in the spirit of Sexton's insistence in "For John, Who Begs Me Not to Enquire Further" that "this is something I would never find / in a lovelier place, my dear," and that "the worst of anyone / can be, finally, / an accident of hope" (*The Complete Poems,* 34–35).

Rich herself was beginning at the time of the Sexton memorial to explore the "incestuous" bond between mothers and daughters from a self-consciously feminist perspective. Both in poems and in her polemical prose between 1975 and 1985 she would undertake to re-present that bond as the basis of a woman-identified female eroticism. In "Sibling Mysteries" in 1976 she would argue that "the daughters were to begin with / brides of the mother" and would ask her own sister, in a strikingly transgressive apostrophe, to "hold me, remind me / of how her woman's flesh was made taboo to us."²³ But as empathetic as she may have been with Sexton's effort to engage with taboo feelings and make, as it were, a gift of them to her daughter, Rich was acutely conscious in the wake of Sexton's suicide that the traditionally female virtue of empathy could also be a trap. She exhorts her audience of women not to empathize with Sexton's death wish—or at least not to do so uncritically. "Her death is an arrest," she tells them: "in its moment we have all been held, momentarily, in the grip of a policeman who tells us we are guilty of being female, and powerless" (*OLSS*, 123).

Rich's play on two different meanings of the word "arrest," as well as her invocation of "a policeman who tells us we are guilty of being female," recalls her 1972 poem "Rape," in which "a cop who is both prowler and father" compounds the victimization of the woman who has to "confess" to him that she has been raped. In this poem Rich made an interesting but not wholly successful attempt to construct a stance of identification or of empathy that would represent a feminist alternative to the confessional mode:

> There is a cop you call both prowler and father:
> he comes from your block, grew up with your brothers,
> had certain ideals.
> You hardly know him in his boots and silver badge,
> on horseback, one hand touching his gun.
>
> You hardly know him but you have to get to know him:
> he has access to machinery that could kill you.
> . . .
> And so, when the time comes, you have to turn to him,
> the maniac's sperm still greasing your thighs,
> your mind whirling like crazy. You have to confess
> to him, you are guilty of the crime
> of having been forced.²⁴

This poem achieved a certain notoriety through getting roundly denounced by influential critics. Helen Vendler, in 1980, deplored its "incrimination of all men . . . in the portrait of this rapist supercop." Cary Nelson, in *Our Last First Poets*, was more sympathetic with Rich's feminist project but agreed with Vendler that the poem is "one-dimensionally didactic" and fails to speak to its historical moment in a compelling way.²⁵ For Nelson, "Rape" became an object lesson in how difficult it is to write successful poems that are politically engaged; his discussion includes an attempt to figure out how a better poem on this subject might have been written.

It would have been more convincing, Nelson suggests, "[h]ad Rich been able imaginatively to enter the experience of her protagonist"; but he doubts "that she really wanted to share the consciousness" of the woman whose experience her poem so unsparingly narrates in second-person voice (*Our Last First Poets*, 152). His most important piece of internal evidence for this is the poem's strategy of address. Third person, he suggests, would have given the poet-speaker room to explore her own thoughts and feelings and make them part of the poem; second-person voice has the effect of "distancing [her] from her subject." "This remains true," Nelson insists, "whether we view the 'you' of the poem as addressed to another woman or to Rich's uncertainty about what her own reactions might be in similar circumstances." The poem ends with what Nelson characterizes as a "harsh interrogation" of its protagonist: "The poet also has access to machinery—" he drily observes, "rhetorical machinery—and she is not willing to abjure its use" (ibid., 151). From this perspective other rhetorical strategies can also be seen to have turned against the woman whose terror and helplessness they were presumably intended to dramatize. Thus, for example, Nelson finds the repetitions deployed in the poem's last two stanzas to convey that "an inexorable fascist bureaucracy [is] closing in on the woman" becoming, ironically enough, its poetic equivalent or counterpart: "He knows, or thinks he knows, how much you imagined; / he knows, or thinks he knows, what you secretly wanted."

The critic thinks he knows what the poet secretly wanted: to think of rape as the kind of thing that happens to *other* women. If that is the case, then her attitude toward the poem's protagonist is more complicated than her rhetorical posture has allowed her to acknowledge. Nelson would like there to be an "I" in the poem who would make "more conscious use of the full range of feelings present in the writing situation"²⁶ so that her own fears and desires could be acknowledged and figured into her treatment of the other woman's predicament. Uncertainty about what her reactions might be in similar circumstances could then become part of the poem's fabric, unsettling its rhetorical "complacency."

For the author of *Our Last First Poets*—and he is by no means alone in asking for this—good political poetry is thus always to some degree confessional.²⁷ In his introductory chapter, in which poetry written to protest U.S. involvement in the Vietnam War is his testing ground for the problems and possibilities of American political poetry, Nelson finds that the most successful poems are those whose speakers' relationship to their government's role in Vietnam is one of "ambiguous complicity" (ibid., 30). This, he suggests, is the most authentic relationship that can obtain between the personal and the political, because it enables the poet to bear witness to the present moment "without falsely mastering it"—without, that is, exempting him- or herself from its historical pressures (ibid., 25). But Nelson's reading of this poem underestimates Rich's determination to find alternatives to the kind of empathy that confessional writing both elicits and deploys. A confessional stance would put the poem's speaker at her reader's mercy, authorizing "him" to know her better than she knows herself. In this poem Rich was experimenting with an interlocutory strategy that would instead achieve some of the detachment and inclusiveness of "we"-writing, but in a vernacular register that is often, outside of poems, a marker of both intimacy and solidarity.

Second-person voice implies that you and your conversation partner share a common vantage point. Like the first-person plural, it has the potential to open up a poem's narrative subject-position to the reader—but only to readers who are eligible to be in "your" situation or willing to walk a mile in "your" shoes. It would be difficult for a reader who is male to project himself either into this poem's narrative subject-position or into that of its addressee; second-person voice creates a subjective standpoint that is specifically female for a poem whose subject is the political implications of women's subjective experience. In speeches and polemical essays during the 1970s Rich often spoke about how hard it is for women to put themselves at the center of their own experience, given the history we have learned and the language in which we are immersed, with its pseudogeneric "he" and its supposedly gender-indifferent concepts like "spokesman" and "my fellow Americans."[28] In "Rape" she was using second-person voice to foster unaccustomed habits of group identification among women, so that a feminist "we," a "collective consciousness of women," could begin to be forged.

In the Sexton memorial we find Rich cautioning her female audience against a self-destructive tendency she calls "misplaced compassion," citing "a woman I know [who] was recently raped" and whose "first—and typical—instinct was to feel sorry for the rapist." Only when our first impulse is one of "compassion for ourselves and each other," she admonishes her female audience, will we "begin to be immune to suicide" (*OLSS*, 122). In "Rape" she has ensured that there be no question of feeling sorry for the rapist, who has been kept out of the poem except for its reference to "the maniac's sperm still greasing your thighs." But compassion for ourselves and each other could also be counterproductive: what if it only served to exacerbate our collective sense of helplessness? Rich was trying in "Rape" for a stance of compassion that would not be misplaced in the sense of spending itself in fellow feeling or complicity:

> and if, in the sickening light of the precinct,
> and if, in the sickening light of the precinct,
> your details sound like a portrait of your confessor,
> will you swallow, will you deny them, will you lie your way home?

The rhetorical strategy Nelson thinks is enabling her to talk down to her poem's protagonist is one that aimed to achieve both empathy and detachment—empathy with a rape victim's paralyzing terror, detachment enough to draw out its larger political implications. It was a strategy that promised to open up for women a space of identification with one another's experience in which something like consciousness-raising could occur.[29]

The poem's rhetorical strategy is, however, flawed by a crucial miscalculation, as Rich herself would come to realize. The premise of its use of second-person voice is that every woman's vulnerability to rape affords a common vantage point from which to grasp the social and political ramifications of having it happen to "you." But would not factors such as class, ethnicity, and sexual orientation also shape a woman's experience of turning to the police for help in such a crisis? Nelson detects, in the condescension toward her protagonist he imputes to the poem's speaker, "a patronizing sense of class difference" (153); the poem has laid itself open to this charge by implying that the "cop" and the woman who has been raped are from the same Boston Irish neighborhood. If the speaker of the poem is Adrienne Rich, she doesn't come from the same part of town; the only thing she has in common with her protagonist is their gender. Perhaps that was precisely her point: a victim of rape could be any one of us. But what are the political implications of speaking for as well as to your exemplary victim, putting yourself in a position to see the predicament she exemplifies more clearly than she can see it for herself?

Rich's involvement with the women's movement during the 1970s brought her up against these very questions, causing her to become aware in a whole new way of her own "location." In her "Foreword" to *Blood, Bread and Poetry*, in 1985, she recalls that in the early 1970s the consciousness-raising session, "with its emphasis on each woman's individual testimony," was what had enabled "the naming as political of women's personal experiences" (*BBP*, viii). But the passage from individual testimony to feminist consensus, from "I" to "we," turned out to be problematic in ways this model could not address. Rich and other white feminists soon found themselves in dialogue with black feminists who challenged their understanding of both women's oppression and the goals of feminist politics. "To believe that it was right to identify with all women, to wish deeply and sincerely to do so, was not enough" (*BBP*, x). In the early 1980s Rich therefore began to dissociate herself from both the radical feminist claim that "patriarchy" is the primary form of human oppression and the corollary claim that false consciousness is the chief obstacle to feminist consensus. The radical feminist obsession with "male evil and female victimization" was itself, she began to think, a characteristically North American form of false consciousness, fostered by the antihistorical bias of the Cold War period.[30] It was also a product of white women's failure to notice their own race and class privilege.

In "Notes toward a Politics of Location," a set of reflections she delivered as a talk several times in Europe and the United States during 1984, Rich faced up to a new set of questions about the bearing of the personal upon the political:

> *The difficulty of saying I*—a phrase from the East German novelist Christa Wolf. But once having said it, as we realize the necessity to go further, isn't there a difficulty of saying "we"? *You cannot speak for me. I cannot speak for us.* Two thoughts: there is no liberation that only knows how to say "I"; there is no collective movement that speaks for each of us all the way through. (*BBP*, 224)

From this perspective, the mistake she had made in "Rape" was in assuming too easily that she, her female protagonist, and her women readers could share a common vantage point. Her use of second-person voice had entailed a too-simple vision of feminist solidarity.

In a 1980 poem entitled "Frame," Rich did find a way to speak out on another woman's behalf without speaking "for" her in a too-simple way.[31] Once again this poem accuses the Boston police of misusing their powers of law enforcement, but this time the racial status of their victim is at issue along with her gender. The poem was inspired by what actually happened in 1979 to a black student at Boston University who went inside a university building in bad weather to wait for her bus, and ended up in jail.³² By the end of Rich's poem its protagonist has been "framed" in several senses: by a building custodian who calls the police to arrest her for trespassing; by the police whose harsh treatment goads her into behavior that gets her charged with assault and battery; by the university teachers she is thinking about as the poem begins, who seem unable to see her in the light of her own ambitions and talents; and last but not least, by the poem's camera eye and the poet's act of witness.

This time the police force has not been personified in a single, typical "cop," nor is the poem's central episode an instance of "male evil and female victimization": it is an instance of law enforcement officers behaving as if any black person were a potentially dangerous criminal. The poem's feminist intervention is in the spirit of Rich's reminder in "Blood, Bread and Poetry" that "most women in the world must fight for their lives on many fronts at once" (*BBP*, 218). The issue it raises is not "what are a woman's choices under these circumstances?" or "will you finally acquiesce in your own oppression?" This protagonist's impulse to *resist* oppression is what gets her into trouble, both when a building watchman orders her to "move on" and when she sinks her teeth into the hand of a policeman who has sprayed her in the eyes with Mace.

The poem's narrative is in the third person, but not as a way for Rich to discover and project her own inwardness, the advantage Cary Nelson gave to third-person over second-person writing. Instead, this poem uses third-person voice to tell another woman's story from the other woman's perspective. The narrator filters everything that happens through her protagonist's consciousness: instead of telling us she is black, for example, she identifies everyone else as white. Meanwhile, however, she keeps interrupting her own third-person narrative with italicized first-person passages that call attention to her own location "just outside the frame." "*I don't know her,*" reads the first of these passages; "*I am standing though somewhere just outside the frame / of all this, trying to see*" (*FD* 2002, 188). These "I"-voiced passages serve both to locate the narrative vantage point and to insist on its limitations. In this way the poem's rhetorical strategy is self-problematizing: the poet-narrator acknowledges repeatedly that she is describing events she could not possibly have witnessed.³³ Indeed, her claim is that she is "*not supposed to be present*" when such things happen; for that very reason, however, she needs to be present. "This is Boston 1979": her readers need to know that in a major American city in 1979 it was still not possible for a black woman to go inside a public building for shelter from the weather without getting herself incarcerated.

To underscore the urgency, the imaginative difficulty, and the legally problematic status of this act of witness, the poem's narrator-speaker asserts repeatedly that although she can see what is happening from *"just outside the frame of this action,"* she cannot hear anything:

> . . . . the handcuffs are on her
> wrists he is throwing her down his knee has gone into her breast he is
> dragging her down the stairs *I am unable*
> *to hear a sound of all this all that I know is what*
> *I can see from this position there is no soundtrack*
> *to go with this and I understand at once*
> *it is meant to be in silence that this happens* (FD 2002, 188–99)

The poem's last three lines play off the past tense of ordinary narrative against the present tense that is a poet's special prerogative, calling attention to a difference that cuts both ways between literal and figurative witness, ordinary watching and poetic vision:

> . . . . . *What I am telling you*
> *is told by a white woman who they will say*
> *was never there. I say I am there.* (FD 2002, 189)

Rich deploys the pronoun "you" only once in the entire poem, to emphasize that her readers share her privileged status relative to the events it documents. It is as if we had been watching a soundless newsreel with a super-added soundtrack that calls attention to our collective status as a viewing public. In a revisionary echo of Walt Whitman's "I am the man, I suffered, I was there," the poem associates its project with Whitman's expansive vision of a nation that draws its strength from difference. But the American poet who says "I am there" in 1979 finds it impossible to share her precursor's utopian optimism. Her way of constructing her own poetic location within the poem calls attention to both the impossibility and the necessity of "being there" for one another as fellow Americans, leaving us with a political conundrum and, on another level, a manifesto for political poetry.[34]

In the twenty-five years since this poem was published, Rich has often urged her readers to think about the political status of poems and of the institution of poetry more broadly considered. In the leadoff poem in *Dark Fields of the Republic*, a poem entitled "What Kind of Times

Are These," she presumes we think that poetry is not, or should not be, "political." This 1991 poem takes its title from a poem of Bertolt Brecht's that asks, "What kind of times are these / When it's almost a crime to talk about trees / Because it means keeping still about so many evil deeds?"[35] The opening lines of Rich's poem take us to "a place between two stands of trees," a "ghost-ridden crossroads" where "the old revolutionary road breaks off into shadows / near a meeting-house abandoned by the persecuted / who disappeared into those shadows." The poem's speaker hints at evil deeds associated with the place, both past and present, but flatly and repeatedly refuses to "tell you where it is." In the poem's final stanza she poses the question its readers may well have been goaded to ask by her truculence and air of mystery: "... so why do I tell you / anything?" and explains that it's "because in times like these / to have you listen at all, it's necessary / to talk about trees" (*FD* 2002, 253). As the first poem in the volume, "What Kind of Times are These" puts us on notice that, as Cary Nelson might have put it, Rich has access to rhetorical machinery whose use she is by no means willing to abjure. She does presume to know what we secretly or not so secretly want from a poem, and has written a poem that won't let us have it; she would rather challenge than flatter us. The relationship this poem constructs with its readers is risky, from the poet's point of view: she is willing to alienate potential readers of the volume, yet makes no secret of her desire to be heard, to be read.

In *What Is Found There* (1993), an interconnected sequence of reflections on the relationship between poetry and politics, Rich deplores the way in which we have been educated "to inspect the poem at arm's length" rather than asking what it wants of us.[36] "What Kind of Times are These" actively refuses to lend itself to such a reading. Its refusal complicates the project of making "you" to find "we," but in a way that is very much in keeping with that project, by provoking a response that unsettles readerly complacency. My immediate response to this strategy is to resent the poet's presumption that she knows who I am and what I want from a poem. On second thought, I recognize that this resentment has made me more aware of my own social and psychic "location" than I was before. Something like this happens again for a reader like me vis-à-vis the final section of "An Atlas of the Difficult World," the section entitled "Dedications," which I discussed in the introduction. "I know you are reading this poem," its speaker keeps saying, and she is right, of course, I *am* reading this poem, and yet I do not find myself among the hypothetical readers whose many different locations are mapped by its litany of reader-apostrophes. One of the most important differences between us is that I have more time to read poetry: I do it for a living. By putting readers like me on the defensive, Rich refuses to let the "verbal privilege" we have in common give us an unexamined sense of entitlement to be "the reader" to whom her poem is addressed.[37]

Making "you" to find "we" has been crucial for Rich as a poet ever since she first began to be one. In her "Foreword" to *The Fact of a Doorframe* in 1984 she explains that her "worst fear" in writing poetry has always been "that the walls cannot be broken down, that these words will fail to enter another soul" (*FD* 1984, xv). This formulation evokes a Romantic stereotype of the poet's calling: to have their words enter another soul was also Shelley's desire, and Emerson's. Rich goes on to explain, however, that she "never had much belief" in the notion of the poet as "someone of special sensitivity or spiritual insight, who rightly lives above and off from the ordinary general life." Instead, her desire to be heard has entailed "hearing and listening to others, taking into myself the language of experience different from my own . . ." (ibid., xv–xvi). And thus she disavows the Romanticist idea of the poet as lonely seer and prophet, in favor of an explicitly social and dialogical conception of poethood.[38] With this conception of the poet's calling comes another set of reasons for avoiding a confessional stance. Like Rich, the Confessional poets were committed to "hearing and listening to others" in their poems and to taking up a vantage point that was not "above and off from" the domain of ordinary domestic and social life. But Rich parted company with Sexton and especially with Lowell over the way in which Confessional poetry seemed bent on trafficking in the personal for its own sake—and in so doing, as Lowell would infamously acknowledge, "not avoiding injury to others."

Rich admired Lowell's poetry in the 1960s, both for its political engagement and for its firm purchase on a particular historical and social location. From *Life Studies* onward, Lowell's poetic vantage point was unmistakably local—strongly gendered, redolent of a particular class location, rooted in the history of the Lowell family of Boston, Massachusetts. As we have seen, in his poems he put traditional poetic devices to fresh uses; in particular, he gave the poetic device of apostrophe a new lease on life. Lowell liked to ventriloquize significant others, speaking for them in words that vividly captured their foibles and eccentricities; in a poem of Lowell's the reader was to believe he was getting not only "the real Robert Lowell" but also the real Hart Crane, the real Elizabeth Hardwick.[39] But when Lowell published *The Dolphin* in 1973, Rich found that he had purchased this capacity for dialogue at too high a price. In a sequence of love poems to his third wife, Lowell quoted verbatim from letters in which his second wife rages and pleads with him to come back to her. In her review of *The Dolphin*, Rich accused him of "one of the most vindictive and mean-spirited acts in the history of poetry" and found "the same unproportioned ego that was capable of this act [to be] damagingly at work" in his entire body of work since *For the Union Dead*.[40]

Anticipating this kind of reaction from readers of *The Dolphin*, Lowell acknowledges in the sequence's final poem that he has

> . . . plotted perhaps too freely with my life,
> not avoiding injury to others,
> not avoiding injury to myself—
> to ask compassion. . . .[41]

"I have to say," Rich wrote in response to this passage, "that I think this is bullshit eloquence . . . that it is presumptuous to balance injury done to others with injury done to oneself—and that the question remains, after all—to what purpose?"[42] Both at the time and since, other poets and critics accused her of speaking as a radical feminist rather than as a poet in passing this judgment. Diane Wakoski pointed out that whenever you address or quote someone in a poem, you are recreating them as a fictional character: this is not the real Elizabeth Hardwick, even if we admire the poet's ability to make us believe that it could be.[43] Richard Tillinghast argued, in extenuation of Lowell's cruelty to "Lizzie," that it sprang not from vindictiveness but from the "colossal thoughtlessness" of a poet who needed to bring other people into his poems to mitigate the solipsism of the confessional mode.[44]

I have already argued in chapter 1 that Lowell had a different motive for the cross-gender ventriloquism he began to engage in as early as *The Mills of the Kavanaughs*: I think it stems from his propensity to envision the domestic arena as a battleground upon which words are weapons and women do most of the talking. But what is most revealing of Rich's orientation, before as well as after she began to be a radical feminist, is that for her "the question remains, after all—to what purpose?" Implicit in this question is the belief that ethical issues cannot be bracketed to arrive at a judgment of the poetry as such. Poets should have a purpose beyond self-disclosure in seeking and claiming our attention: that assumption is a hallmark and also a limitation of Rich's anti-Confessional stance.

When Rich conjures up a significant other to speak to in a poem, her apostrophe is often accompanied by an apology or a self-reflexive critique of the gesture itself on ethical grounds. "The living, writers especially, are terrible projectionists. I hate the way they use the dead," she says to her dead husband in "Sources," explaining that for ten years since his suicide she has avoided "writing to you as if you could hear me."[45] In one of her "Twenty-One Love Poems" she wonders whether in trying to "create [her lover] in words" she is "simply using you, like a river or a war?"[46] In a more recent love poem she has her lover look over her shoulder "at this page and say / "*It's all about you None of this tells my story.*"[47] In the only poem I know of that is addressed to one of her children,[48] her explicit subject is a child's and a mother's reciprocal need to invent the other for the convenience of the self. Looking at a thirteen-year-old snapshot of her son, she confesses that

> I wanted this from you—
> laughter   a child turning
> into a boy   at ease
> in the spring light   with friends
> I wanted this for you

The difference between "for you" and "from you" catches this mother in the act of confusing her own needs with her child's. Speaking to the adult he has by now become, she speculates that his vision of her had been the need-driven obverse of hers:

> Did you think I was all-powerful
> unimpaired   unappalled?
> Yes, you needed that from me
> I wanted this from you

Her confession of maternal narcissism is akin to Sexton's at the end of "The Double Image," especially if the word "this," which is also the poem's title, refers to the poem as well as the carefree childhood its snapshot seems to capture.[49] But the difference between this poem's project and that of a typical domestic poem of Lowell's or Sexton's is even more striking. Rich has waited to speak to her son in a poem until she can engage with him as an equal in dialogue, and the poem is strongly if tacitly protective of the family history they share with one another. If we know that Rich left her marriage shortly after this snapshot was taken and that the boy's father committed suicide, it's not from the poem that we know these things.

Rich has often claimed that her poems teach her things she did not yet know about herself;[50] and yet she has been largely unwilling to publish poems that neither harvest the political implications of their autobiographical disclosures nor instruct their readers in how to do so. A good example of her unwillingness to engage in "purposeless" self-disclosure, even when that is what the poem itself seems to call for, is a 1979 poem entitled "For Memory." This poem's speaker is mentally renewing a long-distance conversation with her lover that broke off angrily some days or hours earlier. Seeking to heal the breach between them, she urges that beyond the anger and recrimination that have temporarily estranged them ("I hear your voice: *disloyalty betrayal / stinging the wires*") lies the task of continuing to explain to each other how they have come to see the world differently.

> I fell through a basement railing
> the first day of school and cut my forehead open—
> did I ever tell you? more than forty years
> and I still remember smelling my own blood
> like the smell of a new schoolbook
>
> And did you ever tell me
> how your mother called you in from play
> and from whom? To what?[51]

The ordinariness—triviality, even—of the memories she offers to exchange are what struck me my first time through this poem: for whom but oneself and one's lover would such things count as memorable? "Ah, yes," I said to myself, "what keeps our most intimate relationships going is not our allegiance to abstract ethical notions like 'trust' or 'fidelity' but the sense of a shared past we create for each other by recalling events like these." But the longer I sat with the poem's analogy between the smell of "my own blood" and the smell of a new schoolbook, the more it began to savor of feminist apologetics. In her foreword to *The Fact of a Doorframe* Rich explains that "one task for the nineteen- or twenty-year-old poet who wrote the earliest poems here was to learn that she was . . . a white and also Jewish inheritor of a particular Western consciousness, from the making of which most women have been excluded" (*FD* 1984, xv). Her first day at school would be the day she came into her birthright as an inheritor of that consciousness, a patriarchal inheritance delivered by the "new schoolbook[s]" whose smell she associates with "smelling my own blood." And thus an act of remembering whose ostensible purpose is to summon up her childhood in all of its inconsequent particularity begins to look politically motivated to a degree that undermines that very purpose.

For whom but another radical feminist would getting your first schoolbooks be like getting your forehead cut open?

Rich has written a few poems that are confessional in the fullest sense: their process of autobiographical inquiry is inconclusive, attaching a higher priority to self-knowledge than to self-mastery or self-judgment. "A Woman Dead in her Forties," dated 1974–77, is such a poem. It is also a poem that, in making "you" to find "me," risks harm to the interlocutor it summons back from the dead. She died of breast cancer, and the poem's act of mourning is transgressive on several levels: against canons of female beauty but also of female modesty; against giving love and loyalty to another woman via overtly physical expression; against owning up to grief's unlovely complexity, its component of anger toward the one who has died. The reason the poem's speaker gives for bringing her friend back to speak to is that she can't stop dreaming about her: "Of all my dead," she tells her, "it's you / who come to me unfinished" (FD 2002, 158). The poem makes an effort to bring their relationship to closure by speaking to her friend of things that went unspoken between them while she was alive: "In plain language: I never told you how I loved you / we never talked at your deathbed of your death" (FD 2002, 159). The poem succeeds by failing, since in telling her friend both how much and in what way she loved her, the poet discovers feelings that cannot be summed up in plain language. Their "truth" is complex and many-layered, inextricable from yet irreconcilable with these women's friendship as they actually lived it at a particular moment in the history of same-sex gender relations.

The poem opens with a dream image of "All the women I grew up with" sitting "half-naked on rocks," posed like Sirens with their breasts exposed. Rich "barely glance[s]" at her friend's scarred torso, "as if my look could scald you"; but by averting her eyes she confirms her friend's exclusion from a community of women who "look at each other and / are not ashamed." Her friend then moves to protect her own mutilated body from exposure:

you pull on
your blouse again: stern statement:

There are things I will not share
With everyone (FD 2002, 155)

Her friend's wordless statement "send[s] me back to share / my own scars first of all / with myself." This movement of recoil is emotionally complex, conveying reproach and self-pity along with acceptance of the imagined rebuff. It raises questions that go to the heart of the poem's concern with loyalty and truth-telling: has Rich been loyal or disloyal to her friend in restraining the impulse "to touch my fingers to where your breasts had been"; loyal or disloyal in dreaming this dream about her; loyal or disloyal in publishing it for others to read?

Jahan Ramazani points out, in discussing this poem as "a radical departure in the history of women's elegies for friends," that the mourner's effort to "compensate for loving deeds undone and words unspoken" is at the same time a violation not just of her friend's privacy but of her very selfhood:

> Rich writes poetry for a woman who "never read it much"; she speaks to a woman who preferred "mute loyalty"; she presents her "passion" to a woman with a "calvinist heritage." "I never told you how I loved you," says Rich, but in telling her now, the poet cannot help but betray her friend.[52]

The reason Rich was willing to take such a risk is that in this instance her confession furthers a political project she had already begun to undertake in speeches and essays during this period—that of gaining visibility for "lesbian existence." In the feminist journal *Signs*, in 1980, she would urge feminist scholars to pay more attention to the woman-bonding "that has run like a continuous though stifled theme" through a historical record constructed under the aegis of "compulsory heterosexuality." She wanted the recognition of lesbian existence to become "a politically activating impulse, not simply a validation of personal lives."[53] One contribution she had already made to this project was a 1975 essay that rereads the life as well as the poetry of Emily Dickinson, supplanting the belle of Amherst with a woman who opted out of marriage for the sake of her writing and whose primary emotional allegiances were to other women.[54] In the spirit of this commitment to uncovering "lesbian existence," Rich also undertook to revisit relationships of her own that were implicitly or unconsciously sexual.[55] Under this aegis confession became both an ethically responsible and a politically necessary activity.

Like "Frame," "A Woman Dead in her Forties" is a politically motivated act of witness. It is also a poem that explores "the full range of feelings present in the writing situation." At all times in this poem its speaker seems aware of her own projectionist tendencies, aware that a dialogue with someone who has died cannot but be an exercise in projection. She transcends the solipsism of such an exercise not through self-conscious critique, as in the poems cited earlier, but through the sheer mnemonic power of sensory experience:

> Wartime. We sit on warm
> weathered, softening grey boards
>
> the ladder glimmers where you told me
> the leeches swim
>
> I smell the flame
> of kerosene   the pine
>
> boards where we sleep side by side
> in narrow cots
>
> the night-meadow exhaling
> its darkness   calling
> child into woman
> child into woman
> woman

These memories are sensually vivid and powerfully specific. Perhaps we could read the "narrow cots" allegorically, but there is a richness and thickness to the language of the entire passage—its pacing slowed by enjambment and internal pauses, its sensory power enhanced through subtle sound-music—that discourages allegorical translation. And indeed, the collective tenor of all these details is what is ineffable in relationships between people and unfathomable in the destiny of each of us: the relationship each of us unconsciously carries in her body to the time and manner of her own death. The poem's final stanza completes its confessional project by making a conscious avowal of feelings that were broached in its opening sequence as a dream-wish: "I would have touched my fingers / to where your breasts had been / but we never did such things." Here again, however, the speaker's motive or purpose in wanting to have touched her friend in this way cannot be fully explicated.[56] The best we can do is to recognize a number of tributaries—sexual longing, sheer physical curiosity, protective tenderness, a desire to share in the other woman's bodily knowledge of her own mortality—that are distinct from and even partly at odds with one another.

Rich's most personal poems often end with the rhetorical gesture of deciding or willing the poem to be as it is.[57] She does this, I think, to affirm that the poem's immersion in personal experience and in relationships with significant others has been purposeful. The last line of her "Twenty-One Love Poems" reads, "I choose to walk here. And to draw this circle" (*FD* 2002, 154). "This circle," a space of allegiance to herself as a woman, is at once her own mind, the city of New York in the late twentieth century, and the poem sequence she has just completed. At the end of "Sources" she commits herself to "knowing the world, and my place in it, not in order to stare with bitterness or detachment, but as a powerful and womanly series of choices."[58] This is reminiscent of Lowell's assertion at the end of *The Dolphin* that his "eyes have seen what my hand did," but Rich's formulation entails the inseparability of eye and hand, existential choice and ethical judgment. The last section of "A Woman Dead in her Forties" also has choice for its theme, but in keeping with its more fully confessional stance the poem ends by transgressing against its own expressed commitments to certainty and closure. Recalling a moment of false epiphany in which "I thought: *I understand / life and death now, the choices*," the speaker finds herself forced to acknowledge that she "didn't know your choice / or how by then you had no choice / how the body tells the truth in its rush of cells" (*FD* 2002, 159). Perhaps she was asking the wrong question in wondering, "How am I true to you?" She has discovered that the truth of a life or a relationship cannot be fully captured in conscious gestures and well-chosen words.

In the opening section of "An Atlas of the Difficult World," Rich salutes the poem's readers with a greeting that emphasizes her commitment to a still-ongoing process of "taking in the language of experience different from my own." "This is no place you ever knew me," she explains: she is living and writing from within two miles of the Pacific Ocean. But if, geographically speaking, "these are not the roads you knew me by," still "the woman driving, walking, watching for life and death, is the same" (*FD* 2002, 234–35). Over a long career spent trying out different strategies of "I-you" engagement Rich has remained a poet for whom poetic challenges are also ethical challenges, for whom the best use of the "verbal privilege" that belongs to poets is to engage with others in figuring out what it means to be living in a particular society at a particular time. In that sense she is engaged in a process of "inquiring further" that cannot come to closure—not because it is typically or essentially a confessional process, but because it is a dialogue with others in which it never will be possible to have the last word.

CHAPTER 3

SYLVIA PLATH'S EKPHRASTIC IMPULSE

According to Marjorie Perloff, "Sylvia Plath's 'I,' unlike [Robert] Lowell's, is not subordinated to its attributes or surroundings. Rather, like the 'I' of Rimbaud . . . the self is projected outward; it seems to utter rather than to address anyone."[1] Perloff's description of Plath's poetic stance goes far to explain why even though she was inspired by Lowell and Sexton to write poems that were "Confessional" in their self-exposing candor and in their preoccupation with familial power struggles, the voice that speaks in her poems does not sound like theirs at all. Sexton's and Lowell's speakers have companions and interlocutors; the world they inhabit is realistically peopled. Often we find them reaching out to particular significant others with disconcerting frankness: "Grandpa, hold me, cherish me," they will say, and "Mister, which way is home?" In Plath's poems, on the other hand, figures of address are typically deployed to lift her poems' interlocutors onto a different plane of reality. The speaker of "Daddy" and "The Colossus" and "The Disquieting Muses" does not presuppose or seem to rely on a designated interlocutor's responsiveness; even when she is desperately angry or deeply troubled, she is not asking to be helped, cherished, forgiven, or judged.[2] Unlike the socially embedded and embodied voice that speaks from the pages of Plath's letters and journals, her poetic voice is bodiless and decontextualized, its "kingdom" an ultimate and final space of enunciation.[3]

The key to that kingdom came into her hand in the spring of 1958, when the British journal *Art News* offered to pay her fifty dollars each for one or two ekphrastic poems. Plath was teaching for the year at Smith College, her undergraduate alma mater, and had been doing very little writing, but she had been auditing an art history course and taking out "piles of wonderful books from the Art Library."[4] During an eight-day period over the spring vacation she produced eight poems on paintings, which her journal entry of March 28 proclaims to be "the best poems I have ever done" (*Unabridged Journals*, 356). In these poems it seemed to Plath that she had been able to write from her own experience more deeply than ever before. To her mother she wrote that she was "overflowing with ideas and inspirations, as if I've been bottling up a geyser for a year" (*Letters Home*, 336); her journal entry speaks of "poems breaking open my real experience of life in the last five years: life which has been shut up, untouchable, in a rococo crystal cage. . . ."

Why did Plath need to write about someone else's art to break open her own "real experience of life"? Biographers and commentators, including Ted Hughes, have explained this by singling out the "metaphysical" paintings of Giorgio de Chirico for special emphasis. Judith Kroll explains that de Chirico's paintings—with their deep perspective, their "strong unchanging lights and shadows," and their intimations of supernatural awe and dread—depict a psychic reality Plath knew very well from personal experience.[5] The poem in which she seems to have told us this herself is "The Disquieting Muses," whose speaker confesses that the three weird sisters from de Chirico's painting of the same name have been her secret "travelling companions" since birth:

> Day now, night now, at head, side, feet,
> They stand their vigil in gowns of stone,
> Faces blank as the day I was born,
> Their shadows long in the setting sun
> That never brightens or goes down.
> And this is the kingdom you bore me to,
> Mother, mother. But no frown of mine
> Will betray the company I keep. (*CP*, 76)

This is one of Plath's best-known early poems. Its speaker's feigned allegiance to her mother's resolute optimism, her assiduous concealment of a more fundamental condition of blankness and hopelessness, are so consistent with the troubled adolescence depicted in Plath's autobiographical novel, *The Bell Jar*, that this poem has become a *locus classicus* for her schizophrenic double childhood, the childhood of the Sylvia Plath everybody knows.[6] But as Leonard Scigaj pointed out in 1988, in an article entitled "The Painterly Plath That Nobody Knows," between 1956 and 1959 Plath also did poetic meditations on paintings by Brueghel, Henri Rousseau, and Paul Klee. Scigaj argued that Plath had far more affinity for Klee's comic expressionism than for the eerie fatalism of de Chirico's metaphysical paintings: the Plath Scigaj wanted us to get to know, instead of reading her entire career in the light of its lurid finale, is a poet who shared Klee's "optimism toward human survival powers."[7]

Given the relatively many ekphrastic poems Plath produced over the course of a relatively brief career, along with an even larger number that treat their subject as if it were a painting or a piece of sculpture, Plath's "painterliness" deserves a more extended discussion than it has heretofore received. Indeed I would contend that her affinity for ekphrastic writing, an affinity whose aesthetic, social, and psychic tributaries are complexly interlinked, will take us to the heart of the poetic stance she was beginning to construct for herself as early as 1956, in poems such as the ones Ted Hughes chose to place at the threshold of her *Collected Poems*.[8] As her husband, fellow poet, and poetic mentor, Hughes was deeply implicated in Plath's poetic development; we can therefore learn a good deal from him, as well as from their mutual friend, the poetry critic Alfred Alvarez, about Plath's distinctive process of making "you" to find "me."[9]

This chapter's reconstruction of that process will begin with Hughes's earliest memories of Plath in *Birthday Letters,* a poem sequence he began to work on shortly after her death in 1963 but did not publish until the year of his own death in 1998. These poems are dedicated to his children but addressed to his dead wife, whom he summons back from the dead to listen to his version of the story of their life together. As Diane Middlebrook points out in her book-length study of the Plath–Hughes partnership, the "clever subtext of Hughes's account of their marriage" in these poems is that their speaker is "in dialogue not with an actual woman but with the vivid persona of Plath's well-known texts."[10] An additional subtext of *Birthday Letters*—one that has been hidden in plain sight, like the misogynistic subtext of Lowell's "91 Revere Street"—is a subtext of gender anxiety. Like Sexton and Lowell, both Plath and Hughes had a high-stakes investment in "the gender of things."

In the first of his *Birthday Letters*, Hughes recalls the moment when he may, perhaps, have set eyes on his future wife for the very first time. In downtown London, in the fall of 1955, he was walking past a newsstand when a photograph of "that year's intake of Fulbright scholars" caught his eye. "No doubt," he says,

> . . . I scanned particularly
> The girls. Maybe I noticed you.
> Maybe I weighed you up, feeling unlikely.
> Noted your long hair, loose waves—
> Your Veronica Lake bang. Not what it hid.[11]

What was hidden in the most literal sense by Plath's "Veronica Lake bang" was a scar left over from the suicide attempt that had landed her in a psychiatric hospital in the summer after her sophomore year in college. Plath was self-conscious about the scar and had her hair cut to conceal it. But Hughes is surely also alluding here to the formidable intelligence and ambition of a future poet in embryo, and to the relationship between them whose tragic outcome his visual image foreshadows. The girl Hughes may have sighted among the year's crop of Fulbright scholars did not have the snaky locks of Medusa, but she did have a strategy for encountering the gaze of others—admirers or judges, indifferent strangers or potential suitors like himself. Thus if he had caught sight of her in the photograph, he thinks he must certainly have noticed "your grin. / Your exaggerated American / Grin for the cameras, the judges, the strangers, the frighteners." As he describes it, Plath's trademark "American grin" was at once flirtatious and self-protective, a performance of boldness to mask the anxieties of a frightened girl.[12]

Hughes's depiction of his former wife, and of his erotic susceptibility to her, is double-edged. From the first, he remembers, she aroused his protective instinct—"the mere dog in me, happy to protect you / From your agitation and your stone hours. . . ."[13] At the same time, however, she had a sexy glamour that triggered his vulnerability to a certain kind of erotic performance. Even before he met her, his English girlfriend, who shared a tutorial with Plath at Cambridge, "fed snapshots of you and she did not know what / Inflammable celluloid into my silent / Insatiable future."[14] The memory of their first face-to-face encounter remains with him as a "snapshot . . . stilled in the camera's glare," and that image turns into an extended physical portrait—a blazon, indeed—of the woman whose "monkey-elegant fingers," "loose fall of hair," and eyes like "a crush of diamonds" made her glamorous in a mode his image associates with Hollywood movies, fashion magazines, and pinup bathing beauties:

> Taller
> Than ever you were again. Swaying so slender
> It seemed your long, perfect, American legs
> Simply went on up.[15]

In images such as these it is not just that the memory or the imagination behaves like a camera. The snapshots are seemingly posed for by their subject; Hughes sees, in retrospect, that "You meant to knock me out / With your vivacity."[16]

"Knock me out," a vintage nugget of American slang, is double-edged through being associated with both the hypermasculine boxing ring and the archetypally female glamour of Veronica Lake and her kind. In Plath's "Lady Lazarus," which Hughes may well be citing, this phrase forms part of Lady Lazarus's self-description as the suicide comeback kid:

> It's the theatrical
>
> Comeback in broad day
> To the same place, the same face, the same brute
> Amused shout:
>
> 'A miracle!'
> That knocks me out. (*CP*, 245–46)

In a similar vein, Hughes ascribes a desperate, manic quality to Plath's self-presentation and stresses its theatricality. It seemed she meant to knock *everybody* out with her vivacity; but the social performance she put on like armor for protection from "the frighteners" was one that heightened her exposure and hence increased her vulnerability. Hughes, for his part, took on the role of Perseus without realizing that Plath was both Andromeda and Medusa—both the maiden irresistibly in need of rescue and the Gorgon who "meant to knock me out."

A gender-inflected power struggle was taking shape between them even before they actually met: Hughes knew Plath only by reputation when he helped a friend write a mocking review of a poem of hers that had been published in one of the Cambridge student literary journals.

"We had heard," he explains, "Of the dance of your blond veils, your flaring gestures, / Your misfit self-display"; and so,

> More to reach you
> Than to reproach you, more to spark
> A contact through the see-saw bustling
> Atmospherics of higher learning
> And lower socializing, than to correct you
> With our archaic principles, we concocted
> An attack, a dismemberment, laughing.[17]

It is striking how closely this account of what prompted the *St. Botolph's Review* gang to publish their critical "dismemberment" of a poem corresponds to the double imperative Nancy Vickers uncovers in her now classic essay on the Petrarchan blazon. In the blazon, which became a standard part of the European love poem sequence in the Renaissance and beyond, Vickers finds the poet-lover's desire being sublimated into a ritual of praise that is also an act of "descriptive dismemberment," since it transforms the object of desire into "a collection of exquisitely beautiful disassociated objects."[18] It was a poem of Plath's that Hughes and his friends subjected to dismemberment, but it is clear from his account of the prank that they were mixing up sexual aggression with literary rivalry. It is also clear that they felt themselves licensed to do so by Plath's own behavior—her "flaring gestures," her "misfit self-display."

In *Ways of Seeing* the English art critic John Berger argues that a woman's "presence," which men think of "as an almost physical emanation, a kind of heat or smell or aura," defines for them "what can and cannot be done to her": "every one of her actions—whatever its direct purpose or motivation—is also read as an indication of how she would like to be treated."[19] Berger's thirty-year-old account of the social logic of women's "to-be-looked-at-ness" brings high art and popular culture together in a way that seems particularly apt to gloss Plath's relationship to Hughes at its point of initiation in the 1950s. Their erotic entanglement partook in equal measure of "higher learning" and "lower socializing"; Plath's allure was a function of both her *femme fatale* seductiveness and her flamboyant erudition. In a poem entitled "Chaucer" (*Birthday Letters*, 51), Hughes recalls her stopping a whole herd of Cambridge cows in their tracks with an impromptu recitation, in Middle English, of the General Prologue to *The Canterbury Tales*.

Hughes's portrait of Plath at Cambridge is corroborated in most of its details by Plath's own self-descriptions in her journal for 1956. She had brought with her to England a fantasy nourished by the fiction pages of *The Ladies' Home Journal* and the novels of her mentor, Olive Higgins Prouty, of the magnetic, powerful man who would anchor her to the world in a "smashing act of love." At the *St. Botolph's* party she knew she had met him at last: "He said my name, Sylvia, and banged a black grinning look into my eyes, and I would like to try just this once, my force against his." At first, however, she tells herself she cannot afford to act on this fantasy: "I could never sleep with him," she writes, because all his friends would be "laughing, talking, I should be the world's whore, as well as Roget's strumpet" (*Unabridged Journals*, 212). Plath used Roget's *Thesaurus* to write her poems.[20] The speaker of "Strumpet Song," written right around this time, catches sight of a streetwalker cruising "our street" and wishes for an exceptional man who could "spare breath / To patch with brand of love this rank grimace." "Strumpet Song" is protofeminist in its intimation that to encounter men on a footing of intellectual and social equality women must distort or disavow their emotional, sexual needs. The surprise-twist punch line is that the "grimace" in question is one which "out from black tarn, ditch and cup / Into my most chaste own eyes / Looks up" (*CP*, 34).

That she harbors within herself both the chaste maiden and the strumpet is a theme of Plath's journals even before her first encounter with Hughes. At the beginning of her second term at Cambridge she rededicates herself to a solitary life of reading and writing after a term spent, as she puts it, "going mad night after night being a screaming whore in a yellow dress."[21] Her self-detected propensity to make a spectacle of herself encompasses more than wild party behavior and sexual escapades, however; in an entry dated a few days before the *St. Botolph*'s party, she writes: "I feel like Lazarus . . . and even resort to the mere sensation value of being suicidal, . . . coming out of the grave with . . . the marring mark on my cheek which (is it my imagination?) grows more prominent: paling like a death-spot in the red, windblown skin, browning darkly in photographs against my grave winter-pallor." In the same entry, teetering on the threshold of adulthood, she writes of longing to be protected, like a fatherless child: "I cry so to be held by a man; some man, who is also a father."[22] In these journal entries an explosive mixture of contradictory longings is brought into focus by a self-awareness that is intense, grandiose, and strongly theatrical. If this intellectually and sexually ambitious young woman is prone to making a spectacle of herself for others, she is one to herself as well.

Her journal from this period is full of references not only to the plays she is reading for tutorials, in which she is prone to cast herself in tragic roles ("I *am* Nina in *Strange Interlude*; I *do* want to have husband, lover, father and son, all at once"), but also to painters and paintings. She was an enthusiastic student of art as well as literature at Smith, and her Fulbright postgraduate year gave her the chance to visit not only the paintings she had studied but also the scenes she had encountered first in art books and museums. On a train journey through France, she describes in her journal the stars against the night sky "growing to look like Van Gogh stars. And quarries, steep like a cubist painting in blocks...."[23] Mixed in with these references are painterly images she self-consciously constructs: "the strange black trees ... idiosyncratic pen-sketches against the sky..." (ibid.). Not only the places she visits as a tourist but even her everyday walks through Cambridge are recorded with a self-consciously painterly eye: "Noticed rooks squatting black in snow-white fen, gray skies, black trees, mallard-green water. Impressed."[24]

Hughes recalls in *Birthday Letters* that during their honeymoon trip to the European continent he and his wife were seeing Europe through very different eyes. Paris, for him "the capital / Of the Occupation," was for her a maze of French Impressionist streets and cafés by Toulouse Lautrec; Spain, "where [he] felt at home," was for her a land of nightmare out of Bosch or Goya.[25] In a poem entitled "Your Paris," he addresses her posthumously to speculate, with bitter postmarital hindsight, that her manic and mannered enthusiasms, "the thesaurus of [her] cries" as they roamed the city together, were a way of keeping her real self sealed away from both of them, in an underground chamber "where you still hung waiting / For your torturer / To remember his amusement" (*Birthday Letters*, 37). But in a poem that recalls their time together in Spain he remembers one whole morning spent in mutual "contemplative calm" while Plath sketched the marketplace in the medieval town of Benidorm. Hughes's poem "Drawing" captures both an idyll of simple contentment—"We sat on those steps, in our rope-soles, / And were happy"—and a more sinister intuition of his young wife's psychic economy:

> Drawing calmed you. Your poker infernal pen
> Was like a branding iron. Objects
> Suffered into their new presence, tortured
> Into final position. As you drew
> I felt released, calm. Time opened
> When you drew the market at Benidorm. (*Birthday Letters*, 44)

The "branding iron" metaphor is hyperbolically inflected with hindsight: Hughes deleted some devastating caricatures of their friends and neighbors from Plath's journals the first time they were published.²⁶ But his principal emphasis here is on the calming effect of an activity that allowed her to direct her attention outward while keeping the external world at a safe, objective distance. "Drawing calmed you," he suggests, by letting her keep herself out of the picture, in both a literal and a metaphoric sense. As the marketplace came into focus under the "concentrated quiet" of her gaze, he recalls that she was not distracted either by stall-keepers who came over "to see you had them properly" or by passersby who "crowded round to praise your drawing"; she seemed not to notice that she had an audience:

> You drew doggedly on, arresting details,
> Till you had the whole scene imprisoned.
> Here it is. (Ibid.)

A few of Plath's ink drawings were published in 1970 in *The Art of Sylvia Plath*; this one appeared first in Anne Stevenson's biography, *Bitter Fame*, in 1989. Hughes's poem is thus fully ekphrastic: it treats of a work of visual art that exists and is available for us to compare with the poet's representation.²⁷ John Hollander explains in *The Gazer's Spirit*, his magisterial study of the poetic tradition of ekphrasis, that such poems "range widely in complexity": "they can take a graphic or sculptural representation as a mere particular instance of a conventional sign," but they can also "be acutely responsive to the matter of the medium and its handling."²⁸ Hughes's poem is acutely responsive to the psychological state of the artist, whom he depicts achieving a brief respite from the primal scene of torture she carried inside her by subjecting an external scene to the discipline of her gaze. In this way his poem also contrives to suggest that whereas Plath aroused in him a volatile mixture of predatory and protective impulses, she wielded a powerful gaze of her own that was more than a match for his.

Ekphrasis has been provocatively theorized by W. J. T. Mitchell, James Heffernan, and Paul Fry²⁹ as a practice that enlists and unleashes its practitioner's deepest fears and wishes. Mitchell and Heffernan both cite *The Sister Arts*, by Jean Hagstrum, as a pioneering work in the field, but they stress that in the context of ekphrasis the arts of poetry and painting are not only sisters but rivals.³⁰ According to Mitchell, both artists and critics exaggerate the differences between visual and verbal signification, weaving around them ideologically loaded assumptions about the kinds of meanings and artistic effects that are proper to each. From practical, material differences between text and image we extrapolate "metaphysical oppositions that seem to control our communicative acts."[31] This tendency to fetishize the differences between poetry and visual art renders the ekphrastic project of overcoming those differences attractive yet fearsome, appalling yet seductive. The hope and promise that motivate ekphrasis are of bringing the visual image alive and giving it a voice—or, conversely, of approaching its condition of pregnant stasis. The attendant fear is of falling under the spell of the image's muteness, its Medusan, wordless immediacy. "Yet it is less the horror than the grace / Which turns the gazer's spirit into stone," says Shelley's poem "On the Medusa of Leonardo da Vinci," in the lines from which Hollander's study derives its title.[32] Mitchell and Heffernan both have argued that the relationship presupposed by ekphrastic writing between poetry and painting is often implicitly and sometimes explicitly gender-inflected. "One might argue, in fact," says Mitchell, "that female otherness is an overdetermined feature in a genre that tends to describe an object of visual pleasure and fascination from a masculine perspective." Insofar as a male poet assigns feminine gender to the object of ekphrasis, as Keats does in addressing his Grecian urn as "thou still unravished bride of quietness," the ekphrastic act will have overtones of possessive voyeurism, masturbatory fantasy, even "a kind of mental rape." It will thus be an anxious act, one that is haunted by fear of castration.[33]

An obvious limitation of "castration anxiety" theories, whether in the narrower context of ekphrasis or in the broader context of visual pleasure, is that they presuppose masculine gender for both viewer and creator of the verbal or the painted image. Mitchell ventures to "suspect," in the final paragraph of his widely influential essay on ekphrasis, that "all this would look quite different . . . if my emphasis had been on ekphrastic poetry by women";[34] and indeed this does seem likely, since his account of ekphrasis relies on the fear of *women's* otherness to give "ekphrastic hope," "fear," and "ambivalence" the status of deeply rooted and largely unconscious impulses. James Heffernan seconds Mitchell's observation that the contest ekphrastic poetry stages "is often powerfully gendered" (*Museum of Words*, 1) but argues that a "Medusan" theory of ekphrasis leaves out too much. An important subgenre of the ekphrastic tradition Heffernan constructs in *Museum of Words* falls under the aegis of Philomela, who used visual signs to identify her rapist after he had bereft her of speech. Within this strand of the tradition Heffernan discusses a number of poems that endow a female protagonist with both subjecthood and expressive agency.

And yet only one of the poems he cites in his book-length study is woman-authored, Adrienne Rich's "Mourning Picture," and Heffernan does not use Rich's poem to broach the politics of women's ekphrastic writing.³⁵ In fact, however, Rich's "Mourning Picture" is a pointedly feminist ekphrasis: it lends the daughter of the nineteenth-century American painter Edwin Romanzo Elmer a voice of her own, a century after her death, so that she may belatedly claim the scene depicted in her father's painting for herself and on her own terms.³⁶

Since the European tradition of visual art, especially painting, is one that has authorized and could even be said to have battened on women's objectification, it would not be surprising to find women poets either avoiding ekphrasis altogether—thereby justifying Mitchell's and Heffernan's neglect—or else writing ekphrases that are self-consciously feminist in their choice and treatment of subject matter. Rich's poems about painters and paintings are almost all overtly feminist. Two of the poems in her first published collection celebrate women's tapestry-work;³⁷ during the 1970s and '80s her poems about women artists such as Paula Modersohn-Becker and Emily Carr call attention not so much to their activity of image-making as to their anomalous professional status and the practical difficulties they faced.³⁸ Plath's ekphrastic writing is not self-consciously feminist, but Plath did not opt for the path of avoidance, either. In fact she wrote to her mother in 1958, in connection with the series of poems she had just written for *Art News*, that she had "discovered my deepest source of inspiration, which is art: the art of primitives like Henri Rousseau, Gauguin, Paul Klee, and de Chirico" (*Letters Home*, 336). This intuition about her own aesthetic inclinations is borne out by the relatively many ekphrastic poems she produced as well as by the even larger number that, by treating their subject as if it were a painting or a piece of sculpture, call attention to their creator's "Medusan" proclivities.³⁹

Plath's attraction to ekphrastic writing was overdetermined. She had studied art and liked to draw; she had learned, under the aegis of the New Criticism, to conceive of poetry's formal objectives in a way that made visual art a deeply compatible subject matter. Some of her favorite painters seemed to proffer objective correlatives for her own inner states: Rousseau and de Chirico, in particular, gave her confidence in the art-worthiness of such terrain. But she was also drawn to ekphrastic writing because she was a woman who played to the gaze, self-consciously and with considerable ambivalence. Medusa was her ally and her adversary, inextricably both.

Plath's *Collected Poems* begins with a sonnet that is ekphrastic not in the sense of speaking to or about a painting, but by giving a voice to the human figure at its center. The painting in question, de Chirico's *Conversation Among the Ruins* (figure 1), makes an especially likely candidate for a woman poet's ekphrastic attention because its central female figure has her back to us (art historians call such figures *Rückfiguren*).⁴⁰ Her posture, attitude, and costume furnish a lot of visual information about her ("I sit / Composed in Grecian tunic and psyche knot" is how Plath distills that information into her poem [*CP*, 25]), but instead of offering her up as an object to be contemplated, the painting invites us to look through her eyes at everything else. Costumed *en grecque*, the lady is seated amid the ruin of a nineteenth-century mansion (or more accurately, a stage set to suggest such a ruin); a desolate outdoor landscape is visible beyond her, through the house's broken walls. Facing her across a small table, as if he has just arrived with a message, or perhaps for an interview (the painting's Italian title is *Colloquio*), is a scruffy-looking young man in a twentieth-century three-piece suit. Is the lady meeting his eyes? It's hard to be sure. She may be looking beyond him toward the corner of the room, where a pillarlike fragment of the house wall rises up behind him, displaying a Grecian head that is painted to look like marble and tilted at the same angle as his.⁴¹

The term ekphrasis, Heffernan argues, should be reserved for poems that not only translate visual images into words but also have visual art for their subject.⁴² If so, then "Conversation Among the Ruins" is not ekphrastic in the fullest sense: Plath has turned de Chirico's philosophical and aesthetic allegory into a first-person psychodrama. In her poem there is no Grecian head except the lady's, and her modern suitor is a more commanding presence, a Gothic hero out of a novel by one of the Brontës. And yet Plath has contrived a poetic counterpart for the painting's aesthetic allegory: her poem exhibits the traditional structure of the Petrarchan sonnet (an octave comprising two quatrains, a sestet comprising two tercets), but with off-rhyme throughout and with adjective-noun and noun-verb combinations that alliterate and clash. She has thus "ruined" the sonnet to create for her speaker a predicament that is interchangeably psychological and aesthetic. The lady's interlocutor is responsible for that predicament; he crosses the threshold of her poem as well as her house in the poem's opening line:

> Through portico of my elegant house you stalk
> With your wild furies, disturbing garlands of fruit
> And the fabulous lutes and peacocks, rending the net
> Of all decorum that holds the whirlwind back.

Figure 1 Giorgio De Chirico, *Conversation Among the Ruins,* 1927. Chester Dale Collection. Image courtesy of the Board of Trustees, National Gallery of Art, Washington.

She holds him responsible, if not for the ruin itself of her "bankrupt estate," then for disclosing its true condition to her: "in bleak light / Of your stormy eye, magic takes flight / Like a daunted witch, quitting castle when real days break" (*CP*, 25). Though she keeps up an outward appearance of self-possession—she sits "composed," which both fits the way de Chirico's lady is holding her body and gestures toward the formal dexterity of Plath's poem—she has no idea what lies beyond the fragile boundaries of a poetic form whose "decorum" will now no longer meet her needs. "What ceremony of words can patch the havoc?" she wonders in the poem's final line.

Whether this poem was inspired by Plath's first meeting with Hughes or had been written in wishful anticipation of such an event, we cannot now know for sure: Hughes's note in the *Collected Poems* says only that "a postcard reproduction of [the de Chirico painting] was pinned to the door of the poet's room" in Newnham College.[43] Plath herself did not try to have "Conversation Among the Ruins" published; but as her literary executor, Hughes would have had a number of reasons for choosing to place it at the threshold of her *Collected Poems*. The situation depicted in the original painting is truer than the poem itself to the way he recalls the onset of their professional and marital partnership in *Birthday Letters:* Plath's omission of the Grecian head bears out his conviction that her choice to have him play "the male lead in your drama" was driven by a repressed desire for reunion with the father she'd lost in childhood.[44] Plath's reading of de Chirico's painting also takes the measure of her aesthetic predicament and intentions, marking a boundary between her "Juvenilia" and the poems she herself would later deem publication-worthy.[45] Ambitious of an important career, uncertain whether she has been well or badly served by a demanding apprenticeship in traditional forms, the speaker of this poem is ready to doff her Grecian tunic and make a new beginning. Her attitude of self-conscious composure suggests that she possesses both the intelligence and the courage to find an answer to her own rhetorical question. It suggests, furthermore, that as a woman artist she cannot choose but claim the dual status of a watcher who is being watched, a subject who is also an object of the gaze.

In February of 1958, about five weeks before the spurt of creativity that produced eight new ekphrastic poems in quick succession, Plath set herself a journal exercise she hoped would assist her to live "more deeply and richly" in the here and now. "Now for a picture: . . . I am here: black velvet slacks stuck with lint, worn and threadbare slippers, dun-fuzzed with dark brown leopard spots on a pale tan ground, gilt-bordered, then the polished blond-brown woodwork of the . . . maple coffee table. . . ." Across from her sits her husband, "in the great red chair by the white bookcase of novels, his hair rumpled front, dark brown . . . & his face blue-greening along the jaw. . . . He poises, pen in right hand, propping his chin, elbow on the table and the chartreuse-shaded light behind him." But as she paints this word-picture of two writers at work, an eerie sense of defamiliarization overtakes her; attending so carefully to the surfaces of things brings on a heightened awareness of inner depths less easily fathomed. Her husband works on, oblivious of being watched: "Those faces he makes: owls, monsters: 'The Man Who Made Faces': a symbolic story?" "Who are we, really?" she wonders. Feeling "chilled," she breaks off her description of Ted and goes over to him for a reassuring hug: "HUG his shirts instruct, at the inner neckband, coming back from the Laundry starched and bound."

This journal entry is a window not only on Plath's early married life but also on the mature poet she was in the process of becoming, whose depiction of the external world is often informed by a tension between surface vividness and enigmatic inner depths.[46] The passage highlights what she had to fear from her painterly eye: because it could only deliver surfaces, its promise of enabling her to live more richly in the here and now was finally illusory. By focusing hyperintently on her immediate surroundings she detaches her observing consciousness more and more completely from them—and from her own body also. "Who am I?" she wonders; "how did I get to be this big, complete self, with the long-boned span of arm and leg? The scarred imperfect skin?" By the end of this two-page journal entry she has become a talking head, a consciousness without attributes; her mind's eye has taken her own body hostage.[47]

Ten days later Plath wrote exultantly in her journal of having had a visionary experience of a different order while attending a slide lecture on African masks: "I had a vision in the dark art lecture room today of *the* title of my book of poems. . . . It came to me suddenly with great clarity that *The Earthenware Head* is the right title, the only title."[48] A year earlier she had written "The Lady and the Earthenware Head" about a terra-cotta model of her own head that an art-student friend had given her. The lady in the poem wants to be rid of the head, but as she considers various expedients she finds herself superstitiously "loath to junk it" (*CP*, 69).[49] In her journal entry Plath transforms it from an evil-omened "basilisk" into a "sacred object, a terrible and holy token of identity." Before long she would reject this prospective title for a first book of poems and begin to dislike the poem itself, "with its ten elaborate epithets for head in five verses";[50] but for now, both the poem and its title symbolize "release" from the "crystal-brittle and sugar-faceted voice" of her apprenticeship phase. The earthenware head helps her claim for herself a creative genius that is far-seeing, prophetic, yet rooted in the earth: "I see it . . . stamped with jagged black and white designs, signifying earth, and the words which shape it." In "The Lady and the Earthenware Head" the head had seemed to be all eye; it threatened to paralyze the lady with its "basilisk-look of love." As she now re-envisions it, what strikes Plath instead is the "dusky orange-red terra-cotta color" of its "flesh." Whereas the head in the poem had mocked the lady with a "spite-set / Ape of her look," its potential now is to figure forth a self that is recognizably her own, yet magnificently other: "rough, crude, powerful and radiant . . . flushed with vigor . . . its hair heavy, electric" (*Unabridged Journals*, 332).

Its "heavy, electric" hair gives the earthenware head of Plath's journal entry an unmistakable resemblance to the head of Medusa, but in other important respects it is less Medusan than it was in her poem a year earlier. The head in her poem leers and glowers and steadfastly ogles her; in her journal entry she dwells instead on its faculty of speech, its power of "world-making" through "word-making": "I feel great works which may begin to speak from me. . . . I feel beginning cadences and rhythms of speech to set world-fabrics in motion." As emblems of visionary power, the earthenware head and the head of Medusa are both sublimely totalizing, but the earthenware head is patient of time, of change, of organic process: "as the earth-flesh wears in time, the head swells ponderous with gathered wisdoms." Under its aegis Plath conceives of working in three dimensions rather than two, not reproducing what she sees but drawing on a deep reservoir of past and future experience. But like Medusa's head, and also like the African masks she was looking at "on Mrs. Van der Poel's screen," Plath's "holy token of identity" is bodiless, decontextualized. And the poetic voice it assists her to aspire to is unlike the voice she is actually using in her diary—as different as prophecy is from quotidian, social speech. As a poetic mask or persona, the head affords access to a kind of ultimate utterance that transcends any and every particular context of speech—"sucking into itself magnetwise the farflung words which link and fuse to make up my own queer and grotesque world. . ." (*Unabridged Journals*, 332). This is the voice Marjorie Perloff hears in Plath's late poems, a disembodied voice that speaks from the page.

Through writing about acknowledged masterpieces in another artistic medium, Plath could lay claim to a different kind of authority than she needed for writing directly from her own life experience. The ekphrastic poems she wrote for *Art News* in the spring of 1958 fairly bristle with erudition, flaunting their author's intimacy with both classical and contemporary art and literature. Ekphrasis also freed her from the necessity of working up an event or scene or image from scratch; the shapeliness, vividness, and complexity of the painting's images were given to her, instead of being enjoined upon her as part of her creative task. But even more important than these reasons for gravitating toward ekphrastic writing was the way in which it enabled Plath to harvest her own experience while at the same time securing a necessary measure of detachment from it. She could project herself into the painting as its protagonist, as she does both in "Conversation Among the Ruins" and, with less encouragement from the painting itself, in "The Disquieting Muses"; but the "world" this protagonist inhabits is in no way contiguous or continuous with the world of the poet's everyday existence. And thus even while reading herself into it she can remain outside the painting—reading about herself, as it were, from a safe distance.

Of the eight ekphrastic poems Plath brought to completion in the spring of 1958, the one that has the most to tell us about what she hoped to achieve as a poet and what she saw herself having to struggle against is "Perseus: The Triumph of Wit Over Suffering." This is an ungainly poem that doesn't quite come off, either poetically or rhetorically, but the aesthetic issues it raises are directly relevant to the direction Plath's poetry took in the last few months before her death. "Perseus" is uncannily prefigurative of poems such as "Daddy" and "Lady Lazarus," poems Plath acutely predicted would "make my name,"[51] but which have done so misleadingly under the banner of Confessionalism.

The subtitle of Klee's *Perseus* is *Der Witz hat über das Leid gesiegt;* the etching depicts a struggle whose locus is mental and emotional, transforming the classical hero's warrior-prowess into a feat of psychic or spiritual resiliency. In a diary entry Plath translated into her course notebook, reproduced by Scigaj in his article on these poems, Klee explains that "this new Perseus has done away with the lugubrious monster, suffering, by beheading it"; but the etching does not depict a beheading, nor does it rehearse any part of the mythical story of Perseus's triumph over Medusa. Instead, as Klee's diary entry goes on to explain, "the action is depicted physiognomically in the features of Perseus whose face enacts the deed."[52] Klee's new Perseus (figure 2) is a massive head and shoulders in three-quarters profile that fills the space of representation from top to bottom, thrusting out of the picture plane toward us. In presenting him thus, Klee has actively resisted the Medusan tendency of his own visual medium—its tendency to still the life it captures on a two-dimensional surface. "Added at the side," Medusa's head seems not to belong to the same three-dimensional space as Perseus: her head is in two-dimensional profile, with a small pouting mouth, grotesquely flattened nose, and one eye staring open. Medusa's head is "without nobility—the skull shorn of its serpentine adornment except for one ludicrous remnant," a single snake-braid that hisses impotently downward into the empty space beneath. Perseus, in contrast, appears robust and fleshy; he has a strong, sinewy neck and shoulders and a virile stubble of whiskers. On his face, according to Klee's own ekphrastic description, "a laugh is mingled with the deep lines of pain & finally gains the upper hand." In this way the latter-day hero resists any inclination we might have to resolve his expression into a mask of either comedy or tragedy: Klee intended, as he explains in the diary entry Plath translated, for Perseus's facial expression to "[reduce] to absurdity the unmixed suffering of the Gorgon's head." This is a feat that depends on the viewer for its realization: we have to read Perseus's facial expression and make eye contact with him in order for his face to "enact" its "deed."

Plath begins her poem with a witty salute to Perseus and by implication to Klee, whose tragicomic vision she seeks to approximate with her poem's mannered rhetoric, heavy jocularity, and ponderous cadences. Scigaj faults her for an opening catalogue of pain and suffering that "taxes the poem's tone with flaccid, pedantic rhetoric" (Scigaj, 244); clearly, however, she took this risk in order to have her poem enact a process of "digestion" equivalent to the one it salutes and celebrates:

> Head alone shows you in the prodigious act
> Of digesting what centuries alone digest:
> The mammoth, lumbering statuary of sorrow,
> Indissoluble enough to riddle the guts
> Of a whale with holes and holes, and bleed him white
> Into salt seas. Hercules had a simple time,
> Rinsing those stables: a baby's tears would do it.
> But who'd volunteer to gulp the Laocoön,
> The Dying Gaul and those innumerable pietàs
> Festering on the dim walls of Europe's chapels,
> Museums and sepulchers? You. (*CP*, 82)

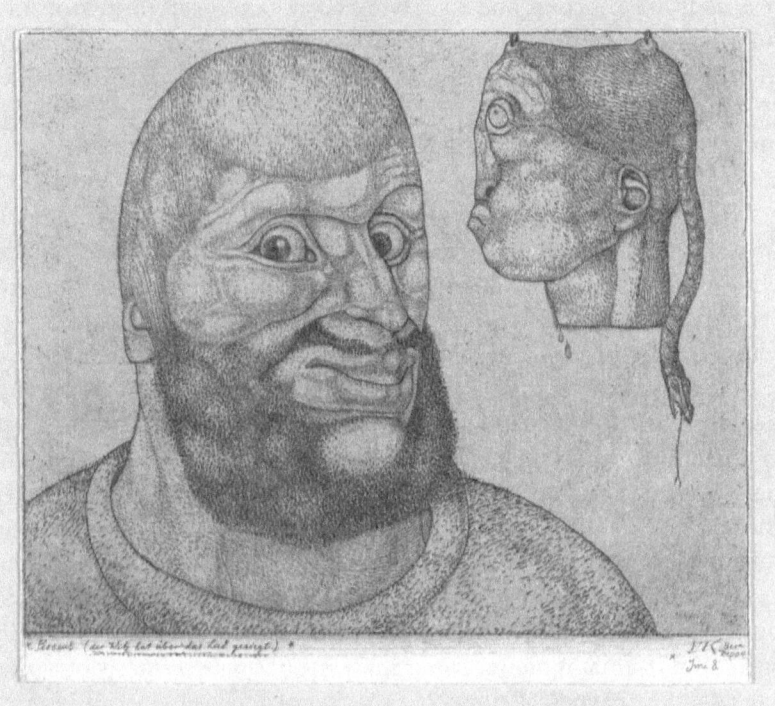

Figure 2 Paul Klee, *Perseus. (Der Witz hat über das Leid gesiegt.)* 1904, 12; *Perseus (wit has triumphed over grief)*: etching, 12.6 x 14 cm. Zentrum Paul Klee, Bern.

The poem's ekphrastic conceit is that Klee's Perseus has just dined, quite literally, on a load of old rocks: all the statues and monuments to grief on the face of the earth, along with the "accumulated last grunts, groans, / Cries and heroic couplets" of all the tragedies that have been staged since Aeschylus, in the theater and on the more encompassing stage of western history.

>   Grit in the eye or a sore
> Thumb can make anyone wince, but the whole globe
> Expressive of grief turns gods, like kings, to rocks.
> Those rocks, cleft and worn, themselves then grow
> Ponderous and extend despair on earth's
> Dark face.
>   So might rigor mortis come to stiffen
> All creation, were it not for a bigger belly
> Still than swallows joy. (*CP*, 83)

It is as if the Laocoön and the Dying Gaul, Sophocles' Antigone and the Duchess of Malfi, had been arrested forever by a Medusan muse of tragedy in a posture of suffering that amounts to a kind of death-in-life. Perseus's feat, and also Klee's, has been to reassimilate these monuments to sorrow and suffering into an ongoing life process, one that is earthy rather than stony.

Plath's tribute to Perseus's feat of digestion is very much in keeping with the aesthetic intuitions of her journal entry on the earthenware head. It is also a thinly veiled tribute to her husband and fellow poet, "the man who made faces." Ted's physiognomic likeness to Klee's Perseus—the big jaw with its shadow of beard, the closed-mouth grin—must have struck her as an uncanny physical token of spiritual kinship between them (cf. figure 3). She liked to cook for Ted; his bear hugs and healthy appetites bespoke a level of comfort in the world that she herself aspired to, and that comforted her. He kept encouraging her to write poems that tapped more directly into her own deepest layers of experience and feeling. As a tribute to Ted, "Perseus" picks up the conversation she had begun with him among the ruins of the European poetic tradition, at the threshold of her *Collected Poems*. "With such blight wrought on our bankrupt estate, / What ceremony of words can patch the havoc?," that poem's speaker had melodramatically wondered, even while bringing her "ruined" sonnet successfully to closure. The witty poet-speaker of "Perseus" has seen beyond that young woman's and that fledgling poet's courage, as well as her propensity for melodrama. Even though she hasn't yet written "The Eye-mote" or "Cut," she is irreverent and playful at the expense of "anyone's" tendency to let a sore thumb or a piece of grit in the eye get blown up into a catastrophe of life-mangling proportions.[53]

Plath deploys two different metaphors in her poem for the triumph of wit over suffering, neither of which is directly suggested either by the etching itself or by Klee's verbal gloss. Her digestion metaphor involves a witty pun on two different senses of "digestion": the physical processing of food for bodily nourishment, and an intellectual process that works analogously to condense and organize a set of texts. In the opening lines of the poem, she calls attention to Klee's having given us Perseus's "head alone," but in such a way that a body is strongly entailed. The digestion metaphor may have been suggested to her by the expression on his face—the "cosmic / Laugh" she sees imminent there (*CP*, 83) could also be described as a belly laugh. Her second metaphor is taken from the myth: the apotropaic mirror-shield Perseus borrowed from Athena becomes "a fun-house mirror that turns the tragic muse / To the beheaded head of a sullen doll."

Figure 3 Sylvia Plath and Ted Hughes in Paris, August 1956. Mortimer Rare Book Room, Smith College, © Warren J. Plath.

These metaphors point in different directions: the fun-house mirror and the digestive process are both transformative, but differently so. Digestion enlists the body's own wisdom—or at any rate its survival capacities, including the capacity to assimilate and work through suffering instead of flinching away from it. Plath's journal entry on the earthenware head affirms both the difficulty and the desirability of such an approach. But her fun-house mirror metaphor suggests a different approach to suffering, an apotropaic use of wit and of art that fends off suffering by refusing to take it in. By insisting that comedy have the last word, a fun-house mirror approach transforms the muse of tragedy into "the beheaded head of a sullen doll"—impotent, absurd, no longer attached to a body or nourished by the heart's blood. Klee's image of Medusa takes this approach, disarming her gaze and divesting her of her snaky locks. But in his verbal account of the etching he stresses that Medusa appears thus impotent by contrast with Perseus; it is his laugh, which mingles and copes with pain, that reduces her "unmixed suffering" to absurdity. Perseus shares that laugh with us by making eye contact, and Scigaj finds Plath accepting the etching's invitation to intimacy with Perseus by addressing him in a tone of "warmth and sincerity" (Scigaj, 244). But in restoring Perseus's mythological bag of tricks, Plath has given him the means of going beyond his own humanity, whereas the earthy humanity of Klee's "new Perseus" is inconsistent with, and indeed refuses, that kind of transcendence.

Plath mixes the digestion metaphor and the fun-house mirror metaphor in her tribute to Perseus without seeming to notice that they point in different directions. In the long run she herself would opt for an apotropaic, "fun-house mirror" approach to suffering. At the same time, however, in poems such as "Medusa," "Lady Lazarus," and "Daddy" she would contrive to transform the conflict between Perseus and Medusa into a paradoxical, unholy alliance. After decapitating Medusa, Perseus carried her head around with him for a time; as long as he did not look at the head himself, it was a potentially deadly weapon against his own enemies. In poems such as "Daddy" and "Medusa" Plath has taken this approach to her own suffering: "the gorgon-grimace / Of human agony" belongs to Plath herself in these poems. They triumph over suffering by enlarging and intensifying the sufferer's agony in speech that seems to belong nowhere else but in a poem, yet explodes the "well wrought urn" of New Critical poetics.

Paul Klee's real importance to Plath, Scigaj argues, is that he helped her "conflate what she learned about modern art from Van der Poel with the content of one of her bibles . . . Cleanth Brooks' *Well Wrought Urn*" (Scigaj, 227). Plath's "New Critical art," Scigaj suggests, "is in some respects the exact equivalent of Klee's formalism," since the "essence" of both artists' work resides in its "power to harmonize and synthesize contradictions . . . in mobile, open gestalts that readjust and grow with every artistic venture" (241). To explain how a poem can be formally equivalent to a painting, Scigaj cites an analogy Plath herself coined to frame some of her early poems for a 1961 BBC broadcast: "A poem can't take the place of a plum or an apple. But just as a painting can recreate, by illusion, the dimension it loses by being confined to canvas, so a poem, by its own system of illusions, can set up a rich and apparently living world within its particular limits." The way a poet creates the illusion of a third dimension, Plath goes on to explain, is through fidelity to the emotions and a persuasive dramatization of human experience.[54]

How is this actually managed; what does a poem's "system of illusions" consist of? According to the New Critics, a lyric poem's three-dimensionality, its inner drama, consists in being able to hold conflicting or contradictory feelings and attitudes together by means of irony and paradox. In a passage Plath underlined in her copy of *The Well Wrought Urn*, Cleanth Brooks explains that "the essential structure of a poem (as distinguished from the rational or logical structure of the 'statement' which we extract from it) resembles that of architecture or painting: it is a pattern of resolved stresses."[55] "Limits" are crucial to the achievement of a pattern of resolved stresses, as Plath points out in her BBC commentary. The limits, the boundedness, of a painting are given to the beholder as an inescapable dimension of the aesthetic experience. This is also true of a poem, in the sense that it sits on a page in a book with white space around it; but because a poem's medium is language, the medium we also use to extrapolate its meaning, its boundaries are more permeable and precarious. What Brooks called "the heresy of paraphrase," a naïve interpretive procedure that looks for a poem's meaning in the statements its speaker explicitly makes, is a procedure that neglects to find the poem's boundedness meaningful; so too is the intentional fallacy, the mistake we make if we assume that the speaker of a poem by Wordsworth is just Wordsworth thinking aloud.[56] Even after Plath stopped writing sonnets and villanelles and began working in looser meters, with sound-patterns subtler than rhyme, she continued to give her poems strong, definite boundaries. The poems of her final period, which we know she wrote quickly, are no less bounded and internally cohesive than her early, thesaurus-driven villanelles and sestinas; arguably they are more so, but in a different way.

Plath received Brooks and Warren's *Understanding Poetry* as a book prize for academic achievement in the ninth grade, and bought her own copy of *The Well Wrought Urn* during her junior year at Smith; Scigaj says its underlinings indicate that she "read the book cover to cover."[57] That she took its lessons to heart can be inferred not only from the kinds of poems she wrote, poems that are highly patterned and "wrought," but also from her working habits. Hughes recalls, in his introduction to *The Collected Poems*, that Plath's "attitude to verse was artisan-like" (*CP*, 13), and he explains in "Notes on the Chronological Order of Sylvia Plath's Poems" that "every poem grew complete from its own root . . . as if she were working out a mathematical problem" (188). In a poem in *Birthday Letters* entitled "Portraits," he recalls watching her write her poem "Medallion":

> Entranced, gnawing your lips, your fingers counting
> The touches of your thumb, delicately
> Untangling on your fingers a music
> That only you could hear. . . . (*Birthday Letters*, 105)

Interestingly enough, the poem Hughes depicts Plath writing in this vignette is a still life of sorts, a poem that gazes unflinchingly at a dead snake she had come across in the grounds at Yaddo while they were in residence there in the fall of 1959.[58]

In Hughes's poem the snake's deadness is eerily prophetic: his wife is pregnant, and whereas a small bronze snake that is "glistening life" has just appeared in the room where he watches her portrait being painted, he is reminded of how she appeared to him a week earlier, "Bowed as over a baby, / Conjuring into its shrine, onto your page, / This thing's dead immortal doppelganger." The "doppelganger" conceit intimates what earlier poems in Hughes's sequence have already suggested—that Plath's artistic creativity concealed a death sentence within its promise of immortality. But in suggesting that it was no accident she had chosen to write about a dead snake rather than a live one, Hughes may also be passing an aesthetic judgment on Plath's "New Critical art."[59] His poem highlights a difference in orientation between Plath and himself as poets that persisted in spite of his strong influence on her aesthetic commitments. Her poem uses metaphor to hold and fix and "icon"-ize a sharply focused image. "The yardman's flung brick perfected his laugh" (*CP*, 125)—but it is really the poem that has "perfected" an ordinary garden snake, by turning it into a "Medallion." The poem's metaphoric blazon intensifies the snake's deadness, thereby lending it a kind of eerie posthumous afterlife.

Hughes thought Plath worked over her poems too assiduously, that their formal intricacy inhibited her mature poetic voice from asserting itself.[60] They both suspected her of using formalism apotropaically, to ward off psychic truths she could not yet bear to acknowledge. While they were at Yaddo she worked at allowing her poems to draw upon her own experience more directly than before. It seemed to Hughes that Theodore Roethke, an American contemporary whose poetry she discovered that year, was the poet who helped her the most to move in this direction;[61] but by the time she wrote the Roethke-esque "Poem for a Birthday," Plath had also made the acquaintance of Anne Sexton and W. D. Snodgrass, through Robert Lowell's Harvard poetry workshop. Like Hughes, however, the Confessional poets had a strong penchant for narrative, whereas Plath would remain a poet of the image. Scigaj thinks her early poetry "offers us as lucid a retrospect of the end of American New Critical poetry as Marvell did of the end of English metaphysical poetry" (249). I would argue that the analogy with Marvell is even more appropriate for late poems such as "Lesbos," "Medusa," "Daddy," and "Lady Lazarus," poems that remain caught within a New Critical aesthetic while dealing with subject matter the Confessional poets opened up to Plath. Such poems' power is a function of their boundedness, their refusal of narration, their achievement of a pattern of *un*resolved stresses.

Plath's poems have become inseparable for us as readers from the story of her troubled life and early death, even though—or perhaps because—her stance as a poet was strongly antinarrative. In an annotated bibliography of early reviews and responses to Plath's poetry, Mary Kinzie points out that not until a biographical story began to be told to contextualize her poems did they begin to receive the kind of deep reading that would in due course garner her the stature of a major "Confessional" poet. Early reviews of both *The Colossus* and *The Bell Jar* were "brief, reserved, entirely conventional," and Kinzie wonders whether the meanings M. L. Rosenthal found "to call out from nearly every poem" when he revisited *The Colossus* in 1967 "would even have been divined, had people not been motivated by her death to go back and re-read."[62]

Margaret Dickie argues in an article on "Sylvia Plath's Narrative Strategies" that Plath was a storyteller whose "social" lyrics, along with Robert Lowell's more "documentary" confessional poems, "recouped the ground lost to poetry when Poe insisted on the brevity and Mallarmé on the autonomy of the poem."[63] But as Dickie takes apart several of Plath's late poems to show us how she worked with narrative materials, it becomes apparent that these poems incorporate such materials without giving up the compression and "autonomy" that were the hallmarks of Symboliste and Imagist poetics. Dickie's analysis of poems such as "Lesbos," "The Tour," and "Eavesdropper" shows the social situation or story that seems to have generated the poem in the first place becoming distorted and fractured almost beyond recuperation by temporal compressions and distortions, rapid shifts in perspective, and metaphoric patterns that "erupt from narrative details" to take on a life of their own.

Plath attributes an antinarrative bias to her own imagination in a BBC broadcast excerpted by Hughes in his Notes to her *Collected Poems*, where she explains the genesis of a poem whose subject Hughes suggested to her: "The Moon and the Yew Tree."[64] With deadpan playfulness, she accuses the yew tree of having taken the poem out of her hands quite early in the composition process and begun, "with astounding egotism, to manage and order the whole affair."

> It was not a yew tree by a church on a road past a house in a town where a certain woman lived . . . and so on, as it might have been in a novel. Oh no. It stood squarely in the middle of my poem, manipulating its dark shades, the voices in the churchyard, the clouds, the birds, the tender melancholy with which I contemplated it—everything! I couldn't subdue it. And, in the end, my poem was a poem about a yew tree. (*CP*, 292)

Plath's claim that this piece of her surroundings had a mind and will of its own is often implicit in her poems also, as Marjorie Perloff has pointed out.[65] In "The Moon and the Yew Tree" we are told that "the grasses unload their griefs on my feet" and the moon is "terribly upset," but the poem's speaker neither shares in these feelings nor takes responsibility for them. Only four of the poem's sentences are predicated of her, two dispassionate status reports ("I live here" and "I have fallen a long way"), and two that call attention to her profound alienation from ordinary human feelings and purposes: "I simply cannot see where there is to get to," and "How I would like to believe in tenderness." The last of these "I"-predicates is especially interesting in view of Plath's BBC reference to "the tender melancholy with which I contemplated [the scene]." To her poem's speaker emotions such as tenderness and melancholy seem utterly alien, transfixed as she is by the yew tree's message of "blackness and silence."

In many of Plath's poems from this time onward the speaker is merely a vantage point, a seeing "I." The speaker of "Tulips," who is in the hospital recovering from an operation, has "given my name and my day-clothes up to the nurses / And my history to the anesthetist and my body to surgeons" (*CP*, 160). What she has been given in return is a temporary respite from being the focus of anyone's need or desire or special attention. But this status is crucially endangered by a bouquet of hospital flowers. "Nobody watched me before," she says crossly, "now I am watched" (*CP*, 161); somebody out there is asking her to take all that unwanted baggage back on board.[66] In "Tulips," as in "The Moon and the Yew Tree," agency and emotion seem to originate in the world around a preternaturally passive speaker, whose own capacities for emotion and action have been attenuated or lost.[67] This is the same poetic strategy Hughes found Plath using to "rhyme [her]self into safety" in "The Lady and the Earthenware Head," in which an inanimate object becomes a "terrible and holy token of identity." The logic of this strategy is that of the fetish, whose psychic cathexis accrues from the psychic energy that is invested in disowning it. "Tulips" is a better poem than "The Lady and the Earthenware Head" because its self-defensive logic is better orchestrated and more wittily self-detected: the poem mocks its own apotropaic strategy by building an escalating series of increasingly outlandish metaphoric claims. "The tulips should be behind bars like dangerous animals; / They are opening like the mouth of some great African cat" is the climax of this series, followed by a metaphor that begins to acknowledge the speaker's susceptibility to ordinary human attachments and purposes: "And I am aware of my heart: it opens and closes / Its bowl of red blooms out of sheer love of me" (*CP*, 162).

An alternative strategy for achieving the triumph of wit over suffering is deployed in poems whose speakers own up to an enormous capacity for pain and rage, but are themselves "behind bars"—transfixed by the boundedness of their own utterance, its linguistic inventiveness, its incantatory rhythms and phantasmagoric images. "Daddy, I have had to kill you"; "A squeal of brakes. Or is it a birth-cry"; "Viciousness in the kitchen! / The potatoes hiss": the transitive force of these poem-initiating exclamations, questions, and statements of intention is considerable, but has been surreally decontextualized.[68] "Medusa" may well be the most bizarre and unreadable of these poems, despite Sister Bernetta Quinn's having untangled its riddling apostrophes in a definitive reading that owes as much to the OED as to biographical backlighting.[69] The poem consists of a series of apotropaic epithets that fend off their common referent both by overt imprecation ("Off, off, eely tentacle!") and by plays on words that force very disparate linguistic registers—vernacular and scientific, literal and figurative, religious and secular—to interact and fuse with each other.

> Off that landspit of stony mouth-plugs,
> Eyes rolled by white sticks,
> Ears cupping the sea's incoherences,
> You house your unnerving head—God-ball,
> Lens of mercies. . . . (*CP*, 224)

Plath's mother, Aurelia, unnerved her daughter by paying her a transatlantic visit while her marriage was falling apart; the jellyfish *aurelia medusa* "unnerves" its victims with a poisonous secretion. What unnerves "Sylvia," more abstractly, is Aurelia's motherhood: the daughter must resort to a kind of blasphemy to shore up her own inadequate sense of self. "Who do you think you are," she asks her mother truculently in stanza seven: "A Communion wafer? Blubbery Mary?" and then fiercely but farcically declares that "I shall take no bite of your body, / Bottle in which I live, // Ghastly Vatican" (*CP*, 225). Her enormous rage is both dramatized and disabled by a seeming inability to contain the metaphoric fertility of her own language. The poem's funhouse mirror is thus doubly apotropaic: the apparent magnitude of its speaker's need to fend off her mother's concern and worry is itself "unnerving," and renders her grotesque.

A poem like this is very far from being a cry for help: the condition of its possibility is the determination to achieve a triumph of wit over suffering. When Plath read "Daddy" and "Lady Lazarus" aloud to her friend Alfred Alvarez, he remembers her calling them "light verse."[70] Although "there was no avoiding how much she was part of the action" of such poems, he recalls that she gave him no encouragement to notice or comment on this: "if only by her blank refusal to discuss them otherwise, she insisted that her poems were purely poems, autonomous."[71] Plath's relationship to the speaker of such poems was essentially Perseus's relation to the head of Medusa; a secondary, derived meaning for "gorgon," as she was presumably well aware, is "a woman regarded as ugly or terrifying."[72] To achieve the triumph of wit over suffering, she had knowingly be-monstered herself.

I have been suggesting that Plath's penchant for ekphrastic writing was overdetermined by the desire to take control of her own "to-be-looked-atness." The poem in which she came closest to realizing that ambition is one of the last she completed before she took her own life; Hughes placed it last in her *Collected Poems,* and his choice is eerily suggestive. "What ceremony of words can patch the havoc?" This poem answers that poem's rhetorical question, and thereby gives us a measure of the distance Plath had traveled as a poet since "Conversation Among the Ruins." "Edge" is a "notional ekphrasis," John Hollander's term for the description of a "purely fictional painting or sculpture that is indeed brought into being by the poetic language itself" (*The Gazer's Spirit,* 4). But to classify this poem as ekphrastic, even as notional ekphrasis, we must allow Plath to have stretched the limits of what the term has traditionally encompassed:

> The woman is perfected.
> Her dead
>
> Body wears the smile of accomplishment,
> the illusion of a Greek necessity
>
> Flows in the scrolls of her toga,
> Her bare
>
> Feet seem to be saying:
> We have come so far, it is over. (*CP,* 272)

The poem's first four stanzas could be describing the effigy of a woman on the lid of an ancient sarcophagus; but in the next four stanzas, with their description of her dead children "coiled" beside her and the metaphor of her having "folded them back into her body as petals / Of a rose close when the garden // Stiffens," we are looking not at an image in *bas relief* but at an actual dead body—the body of a woman whose self-composure is so "perfect" that she has become her own effigy in death.

Plath's poem also wears the smile of accomplishment, and the secret of its uncanny poise lies in the rigor and diffidence of its ekphrastic posture. The poem will only tell us how this woman *appears,* what her posture and expression "*seem* to be saying" (emphasis mine). Plath has thus declined to exercise the power that has given ekphrasis its traditional mandate and *raison d'être*—the power of a verbal description to make a silent image "speak." The passive construction in the poem's opening line is both confident and inscrutable: "The woman is perfected"—but is it death that has perfected her, or is that her own "accomplishment"? "The illusion of a Greek necessity flows in the scrolls of her toga": her pose is seemingly transparent to the shape and meaning of her life's completed journey, but this could well be an illusion we have practiced on ourselves by assuming that how a woman looks will tell us all we need to know of her inner self. The poem eschews "I"-reference entirely, and yet in reading it we experience a strong sense of being spoken to—not from within the visual image, as in "Conversation Among the Ruins," but from above and behind, by a voice that directs our gaze with an objectivity as rigorous as it is discreet.

The poem's ekphrastic description is patient of diametrically opposite readings.[73] The woman's smile could be a triumphant affirmation of female self-sufficiency: the rose-garden metaphor for her relationship to her two dead children is one that renders a husband and father superfluous. But if we take our cue from "the illusion of a Greek necessity," her pose might instead be taken to epitomize women's predicament under patriarchy: perhaps its "necessity" is only illusory, but like the protagonist of "The Disquieting Muses," she will not be the one to say so. Are the dead children "coiled" beside her, "One at each little // Pitcher of milk, now empty," said to be white serpents to suggest that their mother is "perfected" by a biological destiny that has also proved deadly to her? Or is the image intended to remind us of Shakespeare's Cleopatra, whose final words as she put asps to her breasts were "Dost thou not see the baby at my breast / That sucks the nurse asleep?" If so, this woman's "perfection" is more sexual than maternal, and the deepest meaning of her "presence" (John Berger's term) lies in the seductiveness of its inscrutability.

Having awakened our desire to penetrate its perfect surface and pluck out the heart of its mystery, the poem's last four lines bring its ekphrastic project to closure by invoking a celestial onlooker whose spectatorial presence trumps our own. For us the image may be tragic, but "the moon has nothing to be sad about" (*CP*, 273); for us it may be enigmatic and mysterious, but she does not find it so. She is "used to this sort of thing" (ibid.): she has seen it all, thus rendering our gaze redundant and superfluous. In a cryptic but suggestive discussion of "the pacifying, Apollonian effect of painting," Jacques Lacan argues that the function of a picture, "in relation to the person to whom the painter, literally, offers [it] to be seen . . . is not, as it might at first seem, that of being a trap for the gaze." The painter "invites the person to whom this picture is presented to lay down his gaze there as one lays down one's weapons."[74] Implicitly, thus, Lacan is suggesting that a painting allows the viewer not to take responsibility for what he sees: you can relax, the painter seems to be telling its viewer, I've done the gazing for you. In this poem's notional ekphrasis, the artist seems instead to be saying, "Whether you lay down your gaze or not is of supreme indifference to me. Having already filled both positions in the structure of the gaze, I have rendered you superfluous to its exercise." This is the aesthetic counterpart of the statement the woman's suicide makes: "By killing myself I have occupied both positions in the structure that would otherwise have given others the power to hurt me; no one can hurt me now." I do not mean to suggest that we read this poem as a suicide note, even though Hughes has encouraged us to do so by placing it last in the *Collected Poems;* my analogy is intended instead to call attention to the redoubled triumph of its aesthetic self-sufficiency.[75]

In one of his *Birthday Letters,* in lines that could serve as an epigraph for the entire sequence of poems, Hughes depicts himself "stilled / Permanently now, permanently / Bending so briefly at your open coffin."[76] His inability to close his wife's coffin—to stop writing poems to and about her—was owing, at least in part, to the way in which her late poems, such as this one, gesture toward a story they refuse to tell. In his "Notes on the Chronological Order of Sylvia Plath's Poems," Hughes insists that the order of their composition harbors a tragic story line Plath herself was not in a position to narrate; he speculates that this may be "one of the privileges or prices of being a woman and at the same time an initiate into the poetic order of events" (187). On this reading of her poetic corpus, Plath becomes a latter-day sibyl who was gifted with prophecy but could not make sense of her own experience in narrative terms. "A woman like that is not a woman, quite," was Anne Sexton's wry comment on the status that kind of prophetic stance confers; but for Hughes it was quintessentially a woman's prerogative. Meanwhile, however, with his reordering of the *Ariel* poems and his suppression of the last two volumes of Plath's journals, he laid himself open to the charge that the plot he claimed to find in Plath's life and writings was the one he had imposed. By rearranging the *Ariel* volume, as Marjorie Perloff has shown, he turned a sequence of poems Plath would have arranged to end in rebirth into one that confirmed the inevitability of her self-inflicted death.[77] His choice of beginning and ending poems has produced a similar trajectory in her *Collected Poems,* one that is consistent with the story he tells in *Birthday Letters.* That choice confirms Hughes's need to give Plath's career a tragic story line that is inextricably personal and aesthetic; other versions of that story have proliferated since her death.

In an important essay on the *Ariel* poems, the poet and critic Alicia Ostriker recalls that for countless women her age and older, those poems had a kind of prophetic authority for at least two decades after Plath's death. When Ostriker first read the *Ariel* poems they seemed to mirror her own loves and hatreds, her own domestic predicament, her own secret sense of helplessness and self-loathing. She accounts for this by suggesting that Plath's addiction to loneliness was a peculiarly American predicament.[78] Be that as it may, the Medusan quality of Plath's late poems is a rhetorical and aesthetic achievement, as I have tried to show. It is a function of the way in which, like the act of suicide that both completed her life and cut it short, these poems uncannily gesture toward, and thus involve us as readers in constructing, a story they refuse to tell. Their prophetic authority is all the greater if we are inveigled by them into telling Plath's story for her, a story which thereby indeed becomes our own.

Plath used ekphrasis to achieve "the triumph of wit over suffering" at moments of personal existential crisis. Many of her ekphrases are apotropaic; like fun-house mirrors, they afford a bounded space, a screen or scrim on which extreme states of rage, of hatred, or of apathy can be projected. Gwendolyn Brooks, as we shall see in chapter 4, has used ekphrastic writing in an entirely different way. In Brooks's quasi-ekphrastic poems it is never her own private identity or personal future that is at stake. What is at stake is "Blackness" as a problem, a conundrum, and a resource for African Americans.

CHAPTER 4

RACE AND RHETORIC IN THE POETRY OF GWENDOLYN BROOKS

One wants a Teller in a time like this.
—Gwendolyn Brooks, c. 1949 (Poem XI from
Annie Allen: "The Womanhood")

Many things can be meant by the word that is capitalized in my epigraph to this chapter, the first line from a poem in Gwendolyn Brooks's Pulitzer Prize–winning volume, *Annie Allen*. In common parlance a "teller" might be one who narrates a story, counts out your money, or gives evidence against you; a "Teller" with a capital "T" is more likely to be someone who speaks the truth or explains what's what. In this particular poem "one wants a Teller" to furnish guidance and reassurance, as if "one" were still a child or the world were a safe and predictable place in which to live out one's adult life:

> Put on your rubbers and you won't catch cold.
> Here's hell, there's heaven. Go to Sunday School.
> Be patient, time brings all good things—(and cool
> Strong balm to calm the burning at the brain?)—Behold,
> Love's true, and triumphs; and God's actual.[1]

Prudence, patience, faith in a beneficent God and trust in the ultimate triumph of goodness—these virtues are invoked in a spirit of irony, to highlight their inadequacy to the times in which the poet and her readers are living:

> One cannot walk this winding street with pride,
> Straight-shouldered, tranquil-eyed,
> Knowing one knows for sure the way back home.
> One wonders if one has a home.
> One is not certain if or why or how.
> One wants a Teller now:— (*BLACKS*, 132)

Brooks spent her whole career as a poet trying to be the Teller her readers "wanted" by keeping a certain ironic distance from the certainty, clarity, and authority such a role would seem to entail. One "wants" a Teller both in the sense that such a one is desired and in the sense that she or he is missing—but "in a time like this," perhaps necessarily so.

"What shall I give my children? who are poor, / Who are adjudged the leastwise of the land," asks the second poem in her sonnet sequence, "the children of the poor" (*BLACKS*, 116). That poem's Teller is a mother, but it could also be a preacher or prophet whose children "have begged me for a brisk contour," an image of who they are and could be. Both mother and prophet/preacher are roles that have authority and resonance within the black community—more so, indeed, than the role of poet—and they are roles whose authority white people acknowledge. Black women have historically been the caretakers of white as well as black children; black preachers have wielded the power of words, and of the Word, to promote racial justice without recourse to violence.[2] These are roles that Brooks would intermittently invoke and inhabit throughout her career as a poet but always aslant, or with a difference. Another way to be a Teller that she was drawn to was the role of reporter or journalist: *The Chicago Defender* published poems of hers from the time she was seventeen, and she had interviewed for a job with the *Defender* after graduating from Wilson Junior College in 1937.[3] With its forceful reporting of racial atrocities, its successful campaign in support of the Great Migration, its protest against the treatment of black soldiers in World War I, and its coverage of the race riots of 1919, the *Defender* had been a catalyst of solidarity for the African American community not only in Chicago, but nationally as well.[4]

Mother, preacher, prophet, and journalist were all ways of specifying the role of Teller that Brooks found attractive, yet problematic. A mother's pride and compassion may inhibit her from telling her children the whole truth of their condition; a preacher may encourage them to turn their problems over to God instead of taking responsibility for their own lives. A prophet may allow his vision of the collective good to distance him from the lives and struggles of actual people, so that he becomes willing to have that vision realized by any means necessary; a journalist may feed her neighbors' tabloid cravings with reportage that is devoid of any larger vision of the community's needs and purposes. The teeming urban microcosm of "In the Mecca," Brooks's most ambitious single poem, is full of false prophets and preachers, inadequate mothers, and reportage that is irrelevant or exploitive. And yet toward the end of that poem one of the Mecca building's residents, the failed poet Alfred, has the intuition of "an essential sanity, black and electric, / [that] builds to a reportage and redemption" (*BLACKS*, 433). Alfred is the Mecca resident who comes closest to envisioning a possible future for the black community: what he glimpses is the paradoxical possibility of redemption without a savior and of "reportage" as a self-actualizing vision his community might come to have of itself.

What the roles of mother, reporter, and prophet/preacher have in common is other-directedness: they are more closely akin to the balladeer or the bard of epic than to the lyric poet, whose favorite pronoun is "I." For Suzanne Juhasz, endeavoring in 1976 to construct a "new tradition" of American poetry that "speaks in the voice of women," the other-directedness of Brooks's poetry indicated two things about her: first, that although she "developed a black consciousness . . . she [did not develop] at the same time a feminist consciousness"; and second, that "she does not speak in the lyric voice, since the lyric is preeminently the poem of the self." Those two characteristics of Brooks's writing were interconnected for Juhasz: Brooks was not a feminist poet because, even though "women have always been prominent as subject matter in her poems," Brooks wrote about women "as subject, never as self."[5] As an exponent of "feminist consciousness" Juhasz believed it was crucial, both psychologically and politically, for women poets to begin to give the pronoun "I" its fullest possible weight and scope: "It takes a strong ego," she insisted, "to send out one's work, be rejected, send it out again. But even more profoundly, it takes an enormous ego to say: My experience of the world, my vision of the world, are worth—*I* am worth—your attention. What I say is important!" (Juhasz, 2). But as Barbara Jean Bolden points out in response to Juhasz, you need not make your own experience the subject of a poem to assert that your vision of the world is worth your readers' attention.[6] And Juhasz's assertion that Brooks never put her own subjective experience and "sense of self" at the center of a poem is mistaken.[7] What she was unwilling to do, and in this refusal she is akin to Adrienne Rich, was to write of her own experience in the confessional mode.

From her first published volume on forward, Brooks found herself writing simultaneously for black and white readers, "Negroes" and "Gentiles." What kind of political work was she in a position to do with each of these constituencies? Could she deliver home truths to both groups of readers in the same poem? Over more than five decades, beginning with the publication of *A Street in Bronzeville* in 1945, Brooks's conception of how this might be managed, of whether it should even be attempted, and of what her own evolving "sense of self" had to do with these questions has shifted several times. This chapter will track those shifts by looking closely at poems of hers that have especially "telling" strategies of address.[8]

PART I
THE POET OF BRONZEVILLE

A good place to begin looking at complexities of address in Brooks's first published volume, *A Street in Bronzeville*, is "the mother," a woman-centered poem whose subject, abortion, was an intimate and risky one.[9] Richard Wright suggested leaving this poem out of the series that became "A Street in Bronzeville" when he read it for Harper & Row in 1943: "Wright did not feel," according to Brooks's biographer George Kent, "that the poet had yet appeared who could 'lift abortions to the poetic plane'" (Kent, 63). Brooks persuaded her editor at Harper to let the poem stand, and she continued to include it in her poetry readings up until her death in 2000. Unlike Rich's poem "Rape," "the mother" has thus survived important changes in Brooks's intentions with respect to her audience. The embeddedness of its rhetorical structure is what has enabled it to survive these changes both in the poet's political outlook and in the political leanings of successive generations of readers.

The first stanza of "the mother" is in second-person voice, but the second stanza shifts to first person, and this shift has prompted several commentators to give the poem as a whole a confessional trajectory. According to Barbara Jean Bolden the first stanza's "inchoate second-person voice" signifies its speaker's unwillingness to "take ownership of her own deed and pain" (Bolden, 27). In the second stanza, suggests D. H. Melhem in a congruent reading, the mother's "defenses fall away" as she responds to her children's ghostly voices with an attempt to explain and take responsibility for her "crime" against them.[10] Brooks herself, commenting on this poem in *Report from Part One*, observes that the mother's decision not to bring these children into the world is "not nice, not simple, and the emotional consequences are neither nice nor simple."¹¹ But whatever emotional consequences we may suppose the poem to be staging, confessional readings underplay its ethical and political agenda. The decision to have an abortion is one that many women must consider, especially in economically disadvantaged communities; it is a decision in which the society as a whole may be presumed to have something at stake. The poem's first stanza uses second-person voice not to shirk responsibility, but to secure a vantage point for reflection: "Abortions will not let you forget" (*BLACKS*, 21).

I have already argued, in taking issue with Cary Nelson's reading of "Rape" in chapter 2, that second-person voice promotes empathy while securing detachment, in poems as well as in everyday conversational exchanges. In second-person voice we can generalize about situations and events that are highly subjective and must be experienced individually, but with respect to which many individuals may be supposed to have had similar thoughts and feelings. In this instance, the mother uses "you"-statements to reach out to any woman who has been a mother—and indeed to anyone, female or male, who is willing to imagine what it would be like to have "(be)got" children you "did not get."¹² Second-person voice leaves her free to conjure up a range of hypothetical acts of mothering ("You will never neglect or beat / Them, or silence or buy with a sweet. / You will never wind up the sucking-thumb / Or scuttle off ghosts that come"): not least among the poem's many ironies is that by frustrating the body's procreative mandate, abortions provoke the imagination to an exercise of compensatory procreativity.

The poem's second stanza, even as it shifts to first-person voice, provides for its mother-speaker to continue to be detached from her own confessional impulse. She has used apostrophe, she tells us—and in this way her poem challenges comparison with Sexton's "The Double Image"—to stage a dialogue she could not have had with her children in real life, in which she has confessed to having failed them in crucial ways:

> I have heard in the voices of the wind the voices of my dim killed children.
> I have contracted. I have eased
> My dim dears at the breasts they could never suck.
> I have said, Sweets, if I sinned, if I seized
> Your luck . . . (*BLACKS*, 21)

But this strategy of self-quotation sets up an abyssal structure that enables the mother in Brooks's poem to hear her own confession. The poem's abyssal structure might be unpacked as follows: the poet both is and is not the poem's speaker;[13] its speaker both is and is not a mother; the mother both is and is not the person she was when she said to her "dim killed children," "Sweets . . . / Believe that even in my deliberateness I was not deliberate"; the one who said that to her children both is and is not the one who decided not to let them be born. The poem's temporal and rhetorical distancing of its confessional apostrophe makes room for all kinds of ironies to blossom, and allows the mother herself to share in the poet's claim to having intended them—a claim the poet stakes in the inescapably ironic relation between her poem's title and its opening line. Thus when its speaker assures her aborted children in the poem's closing lines that—

> Believe me, I loved you all.
> Believe me, I knew you, though faintly, and I loved, I
>   loved you
> All. (*BLACKS*, 22)

—this assurance is believable: she is in a position to subsume all of the poem's ironies into a loving benediction, a "true" mother's hail and farewell.

In 1975, outlining a new aesthetic for aspiring poets from the vantage point of the Black Arts movement in *A Capsule Course in Black Poetry Writing*, Brooks was ready to assign much of her earlier work to a category she called "condition literature." Recalling that Walt Whitman, in "Song of Myself," "loves animals because they do not tirelessly 'whine about their condition,'" she acknowledges that "a good many of us who preceded the pioneering influence of Baraka did a lot of poetic, dramatic, and fictional whining. . . . One of my own twenty year old poems semi-begs: 'Grant me that I am human, that I hurt, that I can cry.'"[14] "The mother," by then thirty years old, is not the poem she had in mind, but this poem's mother-speaker does accuse herself of whining. Having begged her "dim killed children" to "Believe that even in my deliberateness I was not deliberate," she pulls back to comment on the futility, if not cowardice, of this claim: "Though why should I whine, / Whine that the crime was other than mine?— / Since anyhow you are dead." By the early 1970s black activists had an answer to this rhetorical question; they could unpack the conundrum of a "deliberateness [that] was not deliberate." And thus when Brooks read "the mother" in the 1970s, her audiences could begin to hear, not an apologia for black people's humanity, but a provocation to wonder: if not this mother herself, who *is* it who does not want black children to be born? In 1970 Brooks wrote of a young artist-activist she admired that he "teaches dolls and dynamite. / Because he knows / there is a scientific thinning of our ranks. / Not merely Medgar Malcolm Martin and Black Panthers, / but Susie. Cecil Williams. Azzie Jane."[15] The earlier poem's speaker doesn't "know" this, but by 1970, in virtue of its embedded structure of address, the poem would seem to know it on her behalf.

Had Brooks herself had one or more abortions by the time she wrote "the mother"? The poem's rhetorical structure discourages us from asking such a question, and so does its placement in the larger context of *A Street in Bronzeville*, where it is preceded by a poem that begins "But in the crowding darkness not a word did *they* say," and another whose first line is "*We* are things of dry hours and the involuntary plan" (my emphasis). Arriving thence at a poem that begins "Abortions will not let *you* forget," we are bound to notice that the poet of Bronzeville has a range of options available to her for speaking of and from the lives of its residents: third-person omniscience for "the old marrieds" who share a bed and a silence that comments enigmatically on their life together; "first-person communal voice"[16] for the family that shares a too-small apartment in a "kitchenette building"; second-person voice for the Bronzeville mother's dialogic monologue. How to sequence and voice the poems in this volume are choices that have clearly been made with care. Brooks needed to be careful: the success or failure of *A Street in Bronzeville* with readers and reviewers largely depended on how she positioned both herself and her potential audience in relation to these poems.

In a 1967 interview with Paul Angle, citing Whitman's injunction to "vivify the contemporary fact," Brooks explained that for her part, she liked "to vivify the *universal* fact, when it occurs to me."[17] "Once," she told Angle, "I considered burying my precious manuscripts in the back yard so that in the future—at some time in the hundreds of years to come—they would be discovered and loved."[18] But she would learn first from whites, in trying to get her first volume published, and then from blacks after her second, *Annie Allen*, won the Pulitzer Prize, that this was an exceedingly naïve conception of her predestined poethood. In this same interview, when asked if "the fact that you are a Negro" had placed her "under any handicap in a writing career," she replied that "if it has, I don't know about it," and insisted that whenever she submitted poems for publication, if they were any good they were published (*RPO*, 136, 140). But elsewhere in *Report from Part One* she tells a more nuanced, ironical story of how being a Negro came into play as she was trying to pull together a first book of poems.

In a vignette that is sharply drawn even though the exchange it recalls is almost thirty years in the past, she recalls being approached by Emily Morison, an editor at Knopf, at a conference where she was being honored with an award for one of her poems. When Morison asked her if she "had enough poems 'for a book,'" Brooks recalls that she "rushed home in high hysteria" to pull together for Morison's perusal some forty of the "love poems, war poems, nature poems, patriotism poems, 'prejudice' poems" that she had been writing since her early teens (*RPO*, 71). Morison wrote back to say that she "liked the 'Negro poems'" and "hoped that, when I had a full collection of these, I would try Knopf again." Brooks was in no position to disregard Morison's advice. "Always ready to make lemonade out of lemons," she remarks mock-modestly, "I availed myself of Emily Morison's wisdom. I culled nineteen 'Negro poems' from the medley before me, and I sent them, not to Knopf, for I was too shy to approach that door again, but to Harper and Brothers..." (ibid.). Harper and Brothers sent them to Richard Wright, who pronounced them "hard and real, right out of the central core of Black Belt Negro life in urban areas" (quoted in Kent, *A Life*, 62).

In the original "Street in Bronzeville" series, Brooks establishes her authority as a chronicler of urban life through the range of voices and perspectives she captures and the ironies she builds into these poems by various means. Each poem is differently voiced from the one that immediately precedes it: some go inside a particular neighborhood resident's house and head, while others have the impersonal stance of a ballad or an epigram. Whether the vantage point of any one poem is internal or external to the lived experience of its central figure, whether the poet comes across as clairvoyant or merely nosey, she is speaking from within her own community. In so doing, however, she is putting that community "on the map"—the social and political map of the United States of America, whose citizens officially share a common set of civic and social values. She seems, in other words, to have achieved what James Weldon Johnson was calling for in an essay he wrote for the *American Mercury* in 1928 concerning "The Dilemma of the Negro Author": a "fusion" of black and white America into "one interested and approving audience."[19]

Johnson argued in 1928 that the "Aframerican" writer is in the position of having "to solve, consciously or unconsciously, [the] problem of the double audience." It is "axiomatic that [he] achieves his best when working at his best with the materials he knows best," but black and white audiences will each insist that he abide by certain limiting conventions in his depiction of Negro life. "White America has a strong feeling that Negro artists should refrain from making use of white subject matter"; black America will attempt to "hold [his] work down to literature of the defensive, exculpatory sort."[20] Johnson insists that a fusion of the two audiences is possible even if neither is ready to let go of its demeaning or defensive stereotypes, but he offers no specific advice as to how this can be achieved, saying only that "standing on his racial foundation, [the Negro author] must fashion something that rises above race and reaches out to the universal in truth and beauty."[21]

In 1970, in a disparaging response to that injunction from the vantage point of the Black Arts movement, A. D. Miller argued that in citing Keats's "Ode on a Grecian Urn" Johnson betrays his own allegiance to "the specious universality of a European aesthetic."[22] And yet Miller's "Observations on a Black Aesthetic" also imply the desirability of bringing to bear on "black life" a perspective that is humanly inclusive. "When we write about ourselves," he suggests, "from a point of view that takes black life seriously, that *views it in scale, with human dimensions*, then we are creating a black aesthetic."[23] Perhaps, then, Johnson's effort to think through the possibility of addressing both audiences in terms of what they have in common is not so easily dismissed. If not a common hunger for truth and beauty, white and black readers might nevertheless be supposed to share a common set of ethical norms, a common sense of what is absurd or poignant or simply noteworthy in human experience, a capacity to respond intelligently to irony and understatement, and a preference for the story that seems to tell itself over the one that carries a burden of explicit didacticism. Richard Wright's reaction to the nineteen poems Brooks originally submitted to Harper and Brothers suggests that a fusion of horizons was, on something like these terms, both possible and desirable. The poet of Bronzeville "takes hold of reality as it is and renders it faithfully," Wright wrote to Edward Aswell, his own editor at Harper. "There is not so much an exhibiting of Negro life to whites in these poems as there is an honest human reaction to the pain that lurks so colorfully in the Black Belt." And he adds, approvingly, that "a quiet but hidden malice runs through most of them."[24]

Wright suggested that to have enough poems for a book Brooks would need to add one longer, more ambitious poem that "strikes a personal note and carries a good burden of personal feeling."[25] In making this suggestion he may have been thinking of T. S. Eliot's début volume, *Prufrock and Other Observations,* and it is tempting to think that Brooks wrote the *Bronzeville* volume's longest poem, "The Sundays of Satin-Legs Smith," with "The Love Song of J. Alfred Prufrock" in mind. George Kent lists "Prufrock" among the poems Brooks particularly admired, along with "Portrait of a Lady" and "The Waste Land."[26] But

"The Sundays" invites its readers to "go and make our visit" to a physical and psychic destination that is as different as may be from that of Eliot's sexually and sartorially timid protagonist. And a "personal note" is struck not by displacing the poet's anxieties onto a fictive persona, but by giving the poem's third-person speaker a higher profile than in the original "Street in Bronzeville" series.

The poem's weighty cadences and florid diction set it apart from the other poems in the *Bronzeville* volume, and so does its labored construction of an audience whose vision of the world is blinkered by race and class privilege. "The speaker's vocabulary and attitudes," says George Kent, "create sardonic tones of cool condescension and contempt . . ." (Kent, *A Life*, 70). "The Sundays" thereby shows that Emily Morison's reaction to her Bronzeville poems had made Brooks newly aware of white readers as a distinct group, an audience that was eager to extend its patronage to a new Negro poet as long as she was offering to take them into her neighborhood and not endeavoring to "set the world a-boil" by taking up residence in theirs:[27]

> You might as well—
> Unless you care to set the world a-boil
> And do a lot of equalizing things,
> Remove a little ermine, say, from kings,
> Shake hands with paupers and appoint them men,
> For instance—certainly you might as well
> Leave [Satin-Legs] his lotion, lavender and oil. (*BLACKS*, 43)

In this poem Brooks is self-consciously (and even maliciously) exhibiting Negro life to whites, anticipating readers who cannot be trusted to accord her poem's protagonist a full measure of humanity. We are encumbered, she assumes, with a frame of reference so different from his that a good deal of corrective mediation will be required to open up his outlook and values—his hedonism, his capacity for living in the present, his appetite for fancy women—to a sympathetic reading. As the chronicler of one of Satin-Legs' typical Sundays, the position she reserves to herself is that of a Janus-faced intermediary between mutually exclusive frames of reference:

> Down these sore avenues
> Comes no Saint-Saëns, no piquant elusive Grieg,
> And not Tschaikovsky's wayward eloquence
> And not the shapely tender drift of Brahms.
> But could he love them? (*BLACKS*, 43–44)

Have readers who are themselves from Bronzeville been anticipated or made room for by this poem's strategy of address?[28] No such question arises in relation to the original "Bronzeville" series, whose vignettes of daily urban life are equally accessible for insiders and outsiders, blacks and whites. Many of those poems have an epigrammatic pointedness that implies a judgment passed on behalf of the neighborhood concerning the person whose achievement or dilemma or failure the poem epitomizes; their ironies are for every reader to be moved by or to relish. In "The Sundays of Satin-Legs Smith" the narratorial voice is passing judgment *on* the neighborhood, instead of on its behalf. If, as Kent has suggested, "the drama of the poem arises" from this omniscient speaker's condescension to a not-from-Bronzeville interlocutor (Kent, *A Life*, 68), a black reader might enjoy watching that other reader taken down and set straight; but she or he must also reckon with the omniscient speaker's evident distaste for Satin-Legs' "heritage of cabbage and pigtails," and with the pity and shame in which her depiction of his Bronzeville neighborhood is drenched. Her protagonist both "hears and does not hear" the sounds that signify his neighbors' physical and spiritual victimization by the machinery of modern urban life:

The alarm clock meddling in somebody's sleep;
Children's governed Sunday happiness;
The dry tone of a plane; a woman's oath;
Consumption's spiritless expectoration . . . (*BLACKS*, 45)

These sights and sounds speak volumes, but in a language of generalizing abstraction and tendentious metonymy that is as estranged from the people and the behaviors it catalogues as they are said to be "from music and from wonder and from joy." "Would a greater involvement in the reaches of black traditions have helped?," Kent wonders (*A Life*, 70). It's a fair question, in view of how the residents of Bronzeville have been stranded in this poem between "Tschaikovsky's wayward eloquence" and "I Want a Big Fat Mama," the song that is pouring out of the jukeboxes in the restaurants Satin-Legs passes as he "loiters" along the street—between, that is, an effete high culture that will not or cannot speak to their experience and an urban popular culture that infantilizes and degrades them.

"Negro Hero," the poem that comes next in the *Bronzeville* volume, was clearly also written for a divided audience. But whereas "The Sundays of Satin-Legs Smith" brings white visitors into an urban black neighborhood, both "Negro Hero" and the off-rhyme sonnet sequence "Gay Chaps at the Bar" follow Negroes out of Bronzeville to serve their country in the South Pacific. "Gay Chaps" was inspired by letters Brooks received from friends who served overseas and is dedicated to her brother, "Staff Sergeant Raymond Brooks." The speaker of "Negro Hero" is a man she did not know personally; he is "to suggest dorie miller," a naval mess attendant who received the Navy Cross for bravery in combat when, in violation of a military regulation against black soldiers serving in combat positions, he shot down several enemy aircraft and carried his wounded captain to safety. In these poems Brooks took on a contemporary topic that would indeed seem bound to divide blacks from whites: the second-class status of blacks in the military. But unlike "The Sundays of Satin-Legs Smith," they are poems that actively seek to achieve a fusion of black and white horizons, even while reminding both groups of readers that we live in a racially divided nation whose institutional practices are at odds with its creed of equality.

Dorie Miller's status as a war hero, and even the particulars of what he did to deserve that status, could well have been familiar to both white and black readers of *A Street in Bronzeville:* as the poem reminds us, his picture had appeared "in the Caucasian dailies / As well as the Negro weeklies."[29] But wherever we may have read about him, the poem's first-person speaker quickly puts himself on easy, confidential terms with us. Having acted quickly, with the instinct of a hero, he invites us to reflect with him on the complex interweaving of motives that go to inform an act of this kind. Brooks has used a standard American vernacular "to suggest dorie miller"; if you are white, he comes across as "your" equal. He also comes across as a pungent talker or "teller" who expects you to share his sense of irony:

> I had to kick their law into their teeth in order to save them.
> However I have heard that sometimes you have to deal
> Devilishly with drowning men in order to swim them to shore.
> Or they will haul themselves and you to the trash and the fish beneath.
> (*BLACKS*, 48)

Delivered with an easy, colloquial wryness, the drowning-man analogy is race-neutral: your drowning man will cause you, his rescuer, to "have to deal devilishly" with him no matter what color the two of you happen to be. This analogy continues to resonate throughout the poem with a message for black and white Americans that each group will find hard to live with for different reasons—that "we" are in the same boat, and will sink together if it sinks.

As the poem unfolds, the footing of easy give-and-take on which its opening stanza has placed the speaker and his audience continues to be subtly reinforced by the rhetorical armature of his discourse: "Of course," he says, "I was rolled on wheels of my boy itch to get at the gun."[30] A number of his sentences begin: "Of course . . ." or, "Naturally . . ."—but readers are not paying enough attention if they fail to notice, behind the veneer of geniality, a shrewd appraisal of the motives *everyone* has for keeping it simple:

> It is good I gave glory, it is good I put gold on their name.
> Or there would have been spikes in the afterward hands.
> But let us speak only of my success and the pictures in the Caucasian dailies
> As well as the Negro weeklies. For I am a gem. (*BLACKS*, 48)

With everyone in sight colluding to call him a hero, why bother with troublesome complexities: "let us speak only of my success." But *of course* his agenda, which is also the poem's agenda, is ethically and politically more ambitious. The poem's fifth stanza uses indirect discourse to recall a conversation that was going on inside his head the whole time with a second interlocutor who continues to be referred to as "they": his white fellow servicemen, the ones he could save only by "[kicking] their law into their teeth." His recourse to self-quotation is reminiscent of "the mother's" past-tense apostrophe to her unborn children, but here the nesting of interlocutors is potentially more unsettling. Until the stanza's second line resituates his questions as indirect speech in past tense, they appear to be directed at us:

> Still—am I good enough to die for them, is my blood bright enough to be spilled,
> Was my constant back-question—are they clear
> On this? Or do I intrude even now?
> Am I clean enough to kill for them, do they wish me to kill
> For them or is my place while death licks his lips and strides to them
> In the galley still? (*BLACKS*, 49)

If this stanza's questions had been openly addressed to the reader (". . . are *you* clear on this?"), the poem's easy dialogue would have turned confrontational; as it is, white readers can continue right to the end of the poem to play the racially unmarked role of conversation partner and confidante. The final stanza begins with another of those rhetorical gestures that gather "us," and even potentially "them," into the same human family: "*Naturally, the important thing is,* I helped to save them, them and a part of their democracy" (emphasis mine).

In between the poem's fifth and its final stanza falls a stanza in parentheses that is conspicuously *not* in "dorie miller's" voice:

(In a southern city a white man said
Indeed, I'd rather be dead;
Indeed, I'd rather be shot in the head
Or ridden to waste on the back of a flood
Than saved by the drop of a black man's blood.) (*BLACKS*, 49)

As Ann Folwell Stanford points out, the white man's words have been cast into a singsong tetrameter that invokes "childish playfulness" while articulating "malicious hatred." The appalling little jingle is cited as if in response to the previous stanza's rhetorical questions, and yet the genial, thoughtful voice of the Negro Hero resumes speaking in the poem's final stanza as if he were merely continuing his own train of thought. In this way, Stanford explains, his monologue "shifts the balance of power" by surrounding the southern white man's words with "a more mature, more searching, more logical, and certainly more heroic discourse."[31] The poem's final stanza completes the self-appointed work of that discourse, balancing Miller's conviction that he has done "a good job" against the possibility that "their" preference for a segregated military is widely enough shared to render the ship of state unseaworthy (*BLACKS*, 50). In this way the poem contrives to suggest that the presence of black enlisted men at Pearl Harbor has opened up a dialogue about the meaning of American citizenship that is cognizant of, but need no longer engage directly with, the backwater racism they left stateside.

In the same way, the sonnet sequence "Gay Chaps at the Bar" gives expression to a set of attitudes and concerns that are both generic and particular: the sequence is proffered as a "souvenir for Staff Sergeant Raymond Brooks *and every other soldier*" (*BLACKS*, 64; emphasis mine). The paramount concern of this sequence of twelve sonnets is not race prejudice, but how the experience of facing death in combat changes every soldier, those who "come out standing up" as well those who do not. The only sonnet in the sequence that makes an issue of race is the seventh, entitled "the white troops had their orders but the Negroes looked like men," where the point is made that despite an official policy of second-class status for black soldiers, their common humanity ultimately trumped their racial status:

Such [among the white troops] as boxed
Their feelings properly, complete to tags—

> A box for dark men and a box for Other—
> Would often find the contents had been scrambled,
> Or even switched . . . (*BLACKS*, 70)

And yet the poem goes on to suggest that instead of learning from this experience that all men are created equal, what it teaches them is that death renders everyone's life equally meaningless: ". . . Who really gave two figs? / Neither the earth or heaven ever trembled. / And there was nothing startling in the weather." The rest of the sequence continues to pursue the implications of this experience of ultimate disillusionment: the final sonnet, speaking for the veterans of a war that has ended in victory, discloses their "inward" awareness of incapacity to resume civilian life on the old, prewar terms.

> For even if we come out standing up
> How shall we smile, congratulate: and how
> Settle in chairs? Listen, listen. The step
> Of iron feet again. And again   wild. (*BLACKS*, 75:11. 11–14)

Is the returned soldier expecting to relive his worst memory of entrapment and loss of control for the rest of his life, or is he listening forward, into the future? If the latter, is it the inevitability of a fascist resurgence that he senses, or the struggle for full civil rights that lies ahead for black Americans now that so many of them have proved good enough to die for their country? However we may choose to fill this in, the poem's injunction to "Listen" is urging its readers to realize that neither these soldiers nor the country whose freedoms they fought for will ever be the same again.

If we read both "The Sundays of Satin-Legs Smith" and "Gay Chaps at the Bar" as having been conceived and written in response to Emily Morison's directive to produce additional "Negro poems," then the long poem and the sonnet sequence represent two different ways of "making lemonade out of lemons." Brooks's interlocutory strategy in the former poem smokes out the hypocrisy of white readers for whom Negro poetry represents an opportunity to go slumming in Bronzeville. Following as it does upon the "Street in Bronzeville" sequence, "The Sundays of Satin-Legs Smith" puts white readers on notice that if Negro poetry has its limitations, so too does the high-art tradition on which they preen themselves. "Gay Chaps," on the other hand, deploys a poetic form whose association with the European high-art tradition is unmistakable and uses it to produce a fusion of horizons, but without ignoring or "transcending" racial difference.[32] In the sonnet sequence, as in "Negro Hero," white readers are brought not only to assign normative, generic humanity to blacks, but to acknowledge that they have done so. They are also brought to recognize that a Negro poet is the equal of any white sonneteer in America, Brooks having produced a sonnet sequence whose off-rhyme pentameter is the distinctive music of a distinctively American situation—the "off-rhyme situation"[33] of a U.S. soldier hailing from Bronzeville.

PART II
RACE AND RHETORIC IN
"THE ANNIAD" AND "IN THE MECCA"

With *Annie Allen*, published in 1950, Brooks became the first African American writer to win the Pulitzer Prize. This achievement was cited by African American critics both to affirm her stature as a major American poet and to infer that she had turned her back on her own community. Her second volume differs from the first in two key ways: most of the poems are more "difficult," and they are woman-centered to a greater degree. Annie is the protagonist of the entire volume: after an opening series entitled "Notes from the Childhood and the Girlhood," "The Anniad" gives (mock-) epic treatment to her passage from girlhood into womanhood, and in a third section entitled "The Womanhood" her first-person voice becomes indistinguishable from the poet's own. The first line of the volume's opening poem, "Weeps out of western country something new," is a portentous announcement that contrives to refer both to Annie's birth and to the advent of "something new" in the history of western poetry. The volume's new stylistic orientation is thereby associated from the outset with a female protagonist who is "sweet and chocolate" and thus in several respects an unlikely candidate for this kind of poetic attention.

Contrasting "the birth in a narrow room" with "the old marrieds," the poem that opens *A Street in Bronzeville*, George Kent points out that because of the elliptical syntax and mythically resonant images that typify the Modernist allegiance of Brooks's second volume, "careful and repeated readings [are needed] to grasp the theme."[34] But what is new here is a function not only of difficulty, and not only of the "Modernist convention" Bolden identifies of "thrusting newness on old forms" (*Urban Rage*, 93–94), but of a poetic stance that is loftier, less dialogic, and more self-concealing than before. In *A Street in Bronzeville* most of the poems reach out in various ways to a hypothetical interlocutor: they gossip, pray, or "ruminate";[35] they apostrophize other denizens of

Bronzeville from the vantage point of a mother, neighbor, or wife. The sonnets and ode-like poems that invoke a European high-art tradition are outnumbered by poetic genres associated with oral storytelling and the common reader: epigrams, ballads, blues, and poems in dialect. Even the rhetorically more ambitious poems, the ones addressed to a reader who is not from Bronzeville, make an active show of taking that reader into their confidence. The poems in the first two sections of *Annie Allen* are not discursive and conversational; they are voiced, for the most part, by an omniscient speaker who is in dialogue neither with the people she is writing about nor with an actively constructed reader-interlocutor. "The Anniad" frequently enjoins its reader to "think of" Annie under a series of adjectival rubrics ("Think of sweet and chocolate," "Think of ripe and rompabout," "Think of tweaked and twenty-four"), but these injunctions are formulaic and declamatory: they are stylized deictic flourishes rather than openings toward dialogue or invitations to acknowledge common ground.

What readers of "The Anniad" are presupposed to have in common is not a black neighborhood in a major American city or a common destiny as American citizens, but a cultural heritage that includes *The Iliad*, "The Rape of the Lock," and the poetry of Tennyson and Swinburne. This, presumably, is what Don Lee had in mind when he suggested in 1972 that *Annie Allen* "seems to have been written for whites" and that in having chosen to "[use] their ground rules . . . [Brooks] suffers by not communicating with the masses of black people."[36] In 1950, however, in a special issue of *Phylon* devoted to the "New Negro Poetry," Margaret Walker speaks instead of "a growing global perspective which has become a key note of current poetry" in the Cold War period. For Walker, Brooks's contemporary and a poet herself, the most pressing issue of the moment is the question of the survival of western civilization: "Is the Negro as a poet doomed to annihilation because he is part of a doomed Western world," she asks, "or is that Western culture really doomed?"[37] In the shadow of the arms race and the hydrogen bomb, Walker congratulates Brooks for having given "Western culture" a new lease on life with poems that have "universal appeal."[38]

And yet in *Annie Allen* Brooks paid a high price for "universality," adopting a stance that keeps both her readers and her protagonist at arm's length and thereby makes her rhetorical intentions difficult to fathom. In "the birth in a narrow room," just as in "The Anniad," there is an ironic disproportion between the poem's discourse and its protagonist's life circumstances. Having opened with an epic claim for this birth's importance, the poem then lards its account of an ordinary Bronzeville childhood with flagrant poeticisms:

> Now, weeks and years will go before she thinks
> "How pinchy is my room! How can I breathe!
> I am not anything and I have got
> Not anything, or anything to do!"—
> But prances nevertheless with gods and fairies
> Blithely about the pump and then beneath
> The elms and grapevines, then in darling endeavor
> By privy foyer, where the screenings stand
> And where the bugs buzz by in private cars
> Across old peach cans and old jelly jars. (*BLACKS*, 83)

The poem's discourse is mock-heroic, but who or what is being mocked: the naïveté of a young girl who will be led into an unhappy marriage by a head full of romantic (and Romantic) notions? Those "western" notions themselves? Or is the poem mocking, instead, a hypothetical reader's readiness to assume that Annie's girlhood couldn't possibly be important in this way? Annie is not Aeneas, nor was meant to be, but why would it be foolish for her to dream of having an important, interesting life? Who decides how much the life of a young Negro girl ought to matter, or is really worth?

"Well, the girl's name was Annie, and it was my little pompous pleasure to raise her to a height that she probably did not have," said Brooks to George Stavros in 1969 (*RPO*, 158). Whenever she was asked about "The Anniad," she would speak impenitently of how pleasurable the poem had been to write. Poets and critics whose judgment she respected had pronounced it overwritten, mannered, obscure to no good purpose.[39] Yet when Stavros quotes verbatim a stanza he has clearly found obscure to the point of indecipherability, Brooks responds as if freshly struck with admiration for her own use of language: "What a pleasure it was to write that poem!" Stavros asks her why, and she responds that she was "just very conscious of every word," and that every stanza was "worked on and revised, tenderly cared for" (*RPO*, 159). Even conceding that "some of it just doesn't come off" (ibid.), she does so with an air of finding it easy to rise above that kind of negative judgment; if her interlocutor cannot see his way to joining her, so much the worse for him!

Well, *Annie Allen* did, after all, win a Pulitzer Prize. But "my little pompous pleasure" also bespeaks the degree to which Brooks's own girlhood and young womanhood are retrospectively enshrined in "The Girlhood" and "The Anniad." From the age of eleven, when she first began to save her poems in notebooks, Brooks had been as full of dreams as her protagonist, "fancying on the featherbed / What was never and is not." "I think my dreams were based on the fairy tales I was reading," she told Ida Lewis in a 1971 interview for *Essence* magazine: "The future was very vague, but it was very beautiful; it had a fascinating sort of glamour. So that's what those poems were made of."[40] In *Report from Part One* she recalls that she "was always mooning over some little boy or other" (*RPO*, 57), and would "go to bed and dream of embracing and marrying Him." In spite of having had to reckon early in life with His preference for lighter-skinned girls she remained, by her own account, a "very sweet" and dreamy girl well into her twenties.[41] Annie dreams of a "paladin . . . With a dimple in his chin" and marries a "man of tan"; at twenty-one Brooks met her own "man of tan," dimpled chin and all, in the person of Henry Blakely, whom she remembers deciding she would marry the moment she first laid eyes on him (*RPO*, 58).

Unlike her poem's protagonist, Brooks had a mostly successful married life;[42] unlike Annie, Brooks made poems out of her dreams. And unlike many of her critics, she found the disillusionment of a naïve, imaginative young black girl to be as important as any other "western" Bildungs-narrative. In "The Anniad" she constructed an enduring monument both to her earliest experiences of romantic yearning and disillusionment and to the "lofty meditations" of the poet she had dreamed of becoming (*RPO*, 55) before she had to settle for the narrower niche of Negro poet in order to get her first volume published. "The Anniad" is loyal to its "thaumaturgic" protagonist for some of the same reasons that "The Sundays of Satin-Legs Smith" is loyal to a Bronzeville dandy whose hunger for the good life is stubborn and strong. In "The Sundays" that loyalty is explicit: in pointed asides, the poem's narrator anticipates white readers' contempt for her protagonist, challenging them to recognize that he is the pawn of larger social forces and is making the best of the life he has been dealt. Brooks's defense of Annie's need to dream is subtler and more indirect: it is embodied in lavishly poetic language that mocks but at the same time upholds the naïve lyricism of her own earliest poems.[43]

Black women critics such as Barbara Jean Bolden, Claudia Tate, and Hortense Spillers have found encrypted in the "extreme artifice" of "The Anniad" (the phrase is Claudia Tate's) not only pleasure—a poet's pleasure in giving free rein to her own powers of language—but anger. It is anger, suggests Spillers, that fuels and motivates the virtuoso display of poetic craftsmanship: the poem's highly wrought metaphoric language is a weapon "mobilized against" what is, for any woman, the "most dangerous life-encounter—the sexual/emotional entanglement." "Thus women don't cry in Brooks's poetry nor does she cry over them," remarks Spillers: "Hers is a tough choice of weapons. . . ."[44] Spillers's intuition that this is a deeply angry poem helps to account both for the political readings it has garnered from white feminist critics[45] and for its having been singled out by Nikki Giovanni and Sonia Sanchez, two of the most outspokenly angry poets who came of age during the Black Arts movement of the 1960s, as having given them permission to speak from the vantage point of their own racially and sexually inflected experience.[46] I would build on Tate's and Spillers's intuition by suggesting that the poem's "extreme artifice" has been mobilized not only against "the sexual/emotional entanglement" but also against a hypothetical reader's indifference to the fate of people like Annie and her "man of tan." The loftiness of the poet's stance, the elusiveness of her intentions, and the difficult complexity of her highly wrought conceits have armed and armored "The Anniad" not only on Annie's behalf, but on behalf of the poet's conviction of her story's importance.

"The Anniad's" most cryptic passages are those that translate inner states and interpersonal encounters into vividly expressionistic metaphors:

> What a hot theopathy
> Roisters through her, gnaws the walls,
> And consumes her where she falls
> In her gilt humility. (*BLACKS*, 100)

> Cries "I am bedecked with love!"
> Cries "I am philanthropist!
> Take such rubies as ye list.
> Suit to any bonny ends.
> Sheathe, expose: but never shove.
> Prune, curb, mute: but put above." (*BLACKS*, 106)

> In the indignant dark there ride
> Roughnesses and spiny things
> On infallible hundred heels.
> And a bodiless bee stings.
> Cyclone concentration reels.
> Harried sods dilate, divide,
> Suck her sorrowfully inside. (*BLACKS*, 109)

The first of these three passages depicts Annie's erotic thralldom to "Tan Man"; the second, her attempt to recover from his infidelity by reaching out to other friends; the third, her sense of inner desolation over his death and that of her own youth. Anger is encrypted in all three passages: in the coinage of "hot theopathy" to designate the whole-souled devotion to Tan Man that will be her undoing; in the posture of abjection she adopts in the second passage to resuscitate her own capacity for feeling; in the phrase "indignant dark," which turns the indignation she suppressed while he was alive into the medium of her torment after his death; in the image of a grave whose hunger has not been slaked by his body, but yawns to claim her soul as well. The harrowing strangeness of what is envisioned in the extended metaphor of the third passage—darkness that is "indignant," a "bodiless bee"—burns away any residual parodic inflection, investing the poem's protagonist with capacities for feeling and for suffering that do indeed seem "stupendous."

Whereas the poet of "The Anniad" opted for virtuosity and loftiness—poethood with a vengeance—the stance Brooks crafted for her second epic poem is one that returned her to the Bronzeville community as the teller, or Teller, of its residents' struggles to envision a better life for themselves. "I was to be a Watchful Eye; a Tuned Ear; a Super-Reporter": the book jacket of *In the Mecca* invoked the stance of a journalist while expressing a prophet's sense of having been called to speak to and for this community. A "Watchful Eye" is detached, but pays close attention: in the prospectus Brooks produced for her publisher she explained that she was "interested in a certain detachment, but only as a means of reaching substance with some incisiveness." Her detachment would not be that of "a statistical report"; like a journalist, she would "present a large variety of personalities against a mosaic of daily affairs" (*RPO*, 189). Her "Tuned Ear" would be that of a bard or singer: in her prospectus Brooks notes that "*to touch every note* in the life of this block-long block-wide building would be to capsulize the gist of black humanity in general" (*RPO*, 189; my emphasis).

In describing herself as a "Super-Reporter," Brooks later emphasized that she was thinking of "one who is 'just supremely *accurate*'";[47] implicitly, however, she was also claiming access to truths and realities that lie beyond a journalist's grasp. The dust-jacket statement, says D. H. Melhem, "confirms Brooks's own view of her work as quasi-divine reportage";[48] and indeed, the stance she adopts in this poem is almost that of an Old Testament prophet. "*Now the way of the Mecca was on this wise*": sitting by itself on the verso page across from the poem's opening stanzas, this sentence sets the stage for a work that, according to Brooks's prospectus, "[was] to be Leisurely and massive" (*RPO*, 190) in keeping with the massive size and ruined grandeur of the Mecca building itself.[49] By the time Brooks's poem was published in 1968 the Mecca building had long since ceased to exist: it was razed in 1952, to make room for a new urban campus for the Illinois Institute of Technology. Two of the poem's epigraphs are drawn from a powerful journalistic piece written for *Harper's* by John Bartlow Martin in 1950, after the demolition plan had been unveiled: Martin's interviews with individual Mecca residents, including a mother whose nine children shared a single bed in a one-room apartment, showed Brooks how a complex social microcosm might be constructed one vignette at a time.[50]

The poem's language is both "leisurely" and "massive," full of archaisms, portentous polysyllables, cryptic epithets, and many-layered, sylleptic formulations. Its complexity and density are as great, at times, as in "The Anniad," but Brooks's second epic poem is different from the first in two key ways that give readers more incentive to grapple with its challenges. Whereas the poetic register of "The Anniad" is relentlessly "monologic," the flexible free verse of "In the Mecca" is hospitable to an interweaving of many different poetic registers. Mecca residents' own voices can be quoted; ponderous pentameters can give way to the rhyming tetramers of the folk ballad at a moment's notice. The voice of the poet is also more directly and variously engaged with her characters—and with the poem's readers, for whom she serves as a much-needed guide to the labyrinthine complexities of the building's human microcosm.[51]

Before introducing us to the particular Mecca resident whose search for her lost child will drive its unfolding panorama of black urban life, the poem's opening lines establish, for the poet and her readers, "a certain detachment" from the attitudes and preoccupations of Mrs. Sallie Smith and the building's other residents: "Sit where the light corrupts your face. / Miës Van der Rohe retires from grace. / And the fair fables fall" (*BLACKS*, 407). We are told in due course that Mrs. Sallie's children hate the "sewn suburbs" whose children have all the things she can't afford to give them: "Lace handkerchief owners are enemies of Smithkind" (*BLACKS*, 412). But German-born architect Miës Van der Rohe is the enemy of Smithkind in a more important sense, did they but know it, since it was his vision of an enlarged urban campus for the Illinois Institute of Technology that was immediately responsible for the building's demise.[52] In retiring him from grace the poet announces her intention to rescue "the way of the Mecca" from oblivion by telling a single story that branches into countless others: the story of the Smith family's search for their youngest member, who is eventually found to have been raped and murdered by another Mecca resident. The death of Pepita, whose name means "golden seed" or "grain of gold," signifies that indeed the Mecca building does not have a viable future, not only in the sense that it will be (has been) physically destroyed but insofar as it has become a site of social fragmentation, political impotence, and spiritual bankruptcy.[53] Its lost souls can be redeemed only to the extent that their successors come to know themselves as having a common stake, not in Miës Van der Rohe's vision of a Modernist oasis in high relief against a chaotic surrounding slum,[54] but in their own blackness, and hence in coming together as a community. By getting her readers to care about the disappearance and destruction of "a little woman" who "never learned that black is not beloved," Brooks places at the heart of her poem an absence that paradoxically has the potential to become "their joining thing."[55]

In helping to place the poem's readers at a certain critical distance from "Smithkind," Miës Van der Rohe's proper name does the same kind of work in this poem as the names of European composers in "The Sundays of Satin-Legs Smith." But whereas "The Sundays" constructed a not-from-Bronzeville reader whose intimacy with European classical music was the marker of reluctance to grant the poem's protagonist a full measure of humanity, both the audience to whom "In the Mecca" is addressed and Brooks's intentions with respect to that audience have significantly changed. "The Sundays" presupposed a dichotomy between "your" world and "Negro life" that only the poet could bridge; "In the Mecca" orchestrates a more fluid interpenetration between "their" world and "ours." The poem's representative sample of Mecca residents is drawn from many different educational levels and walks of life, and as Pepita's family members go through the building knocking on doors to search for their sister, individual Meccans speak for themselves in many different registers. Great-great Gram, who grew up in a slave cabin in the Old South, recalls how "something creebled in that dirt"; Hyena, an urban girl who bleaches her hair and puts on airs, pronounces Pepita "a puny and a putrid little child." Mrs. Sallie's repeated questions, "where Pepita?" and "Where Pepita be?," carry standard markers of Black English, the lingua franca of Smithkind; elsewhere in the building Loam Norton, who is presumably white and Jewish, uses Standard American English to insist that he is "not remote, / not unconcerned." Boontsie De Broe, whose "clear mind is the extract / of massive literatures," has a "clear voice [that] tells you life may be controlled"; Alfred is a poet manqué who reads "Bob Browning." Brooks's poem is thus a site of what Bakhtin called "heteroglossia": it encompasses a great variety of speech patterns that coexist without blending, inflected by differing levels of education, different regional and class backgrounds, differences in age and station in life.[56] Whereas "The Sundays of Satin-Legs Smith" was intent on claiming full humanity for blacks vis-à-vis whites, this poem is more interested in taking stock of a broad gamut of subcultural formations and deformations that coexist within an urban black community. By anachronistically including the perspectives of Way-Out Morgan, Amos the revolutionary, and Black Arts movement activist Don Lee, Brooks has also constructed a dialogue within the poem itself about the community's future—a dialogue that includes the voices of Mrs. Sallie Smith and even, finally, of Pepita herself.[57]

"WHERE PEPITA BE?" None of the neighbors knows—except the one who has raped and killed her, and he too "denies ... a dealing / of any dimension with Mrs. Sallie's daughter." And so each Mecca resident responds to the question of Pepita's whereabouts by giving an account of him- or herself. Like the denizens of Dante's *Inferno*—or of Eliot's "Waste Land," "Each in his prison, thinking of the key"—they live unknown to one another, each preoccupied with his or her own particular fantasy of escape from their common condition of poverty and helplessness. "One wants a Teller" to put that condition into perspective for them, but within the social microcosm Brooks has constructed, both reportage and prophecy have been debased. Meccans have newspapers and magazines to connect them with current events in a wider world, but these media have not helped them form a usable image of how they fit into that world. "One reason cats are happier than people," thinks Pepita's brother, Tennessee, "is that they have no newspapers...." "Delicate Melodie Mary" finds it "interesting" that in China children are suffering, but "where," she wonders, "are the frantic bulletins" on behalf of a rat caught in a trap or a roach "smashed in the grind of a rapid heel?" Marian, another Mecca resident, "craves crime": she longs to be murdered herself, so that "her community, / her Mecca," will finally "stop / and See her." Prophet Williams advertises his Love Balls, Pay-check Fluid, and Voodoo Potions "in every Colored journal in the world"; ironically, however, the "Prophet" has no premonition of a future conflagration that will consume him too when the frustration he feeds on reaches a boiling point: we are told that his lawyer, the fat and prosperous Enrico Jason, "soon will lie beside his Prophet in bright blood."

Many of the building's residents are Christian, but they have no sense of being called to a common destiny—except, perhaps, Way-Out Morgan, prophet of "Death-to-the-Hordes-of-the-White-Men," and Amos the revolutionary, who "prays, for America, prays: 'Bathe her in her beautiful blood.'" For most Meccans, "America" is a meaningless abstraction: the ubiquity of religious language to express their needs and longings is a symptom of the absence from their lives of any viable language of secular citizenship. "The Lord was their shepherd. Yet did they want," muses Loam Norton. The history of his own, Jewish people is on his mind, and he reflects that African Americans have comparably good historical reasons to despair of the future:

> They were comforted by no Rod,
> No Staff, but flayed by, O besieged by, shot a-plenty.
> The prepared table was the rot or curd of the day.
> Anointings were of lice. Blood was the spillage of cups.
> (*BLACKS*, 418)

This is the most arresting biblical parody in the poem, but its entire fabric is steeped in the language of biblical prophecy and organized religion, ironically inflected to call attention to Meccans' incapacity to meet one another's most basic needs. Old Saint Julia Jones also parodies the Twenty-Third Psalm when she affirms that her Lord lets her sleep late and "hunts me up the coffee for my cup"; Aunt Dill is "a Christ-like creature, Doing Good" when she comes over to tell the Smiths in ghoulish detail about another little girl who was recently molested and killed nearby. Mrs. Sallie spends her days tending to a white child whose "pink-lit image" she loves and loathes, since she cannot hope to give her own children adequate sustenance on any level: "What shall their redeemer be? / Greens and hock of ham," says the poet sarcastically of their all-too-meager evening meal (*BLACKS*, 414).

Jamaican Edward "denies *and thrice denies* a dealing / of any dimension with Mrs. Sallie's daughter" (*BLACKS*, 433; emphasis mine): like the disciple Peter he is lying under duress, but Pepita herself is no Christ figure. She is a powerless though feisty little girl, and the poem ends with a haunting depiction of her death throes from the uncomprehending perspective of the man who is hiding her murdered body.[58] And yet the poem's final stanzas intimate an alliance between Pepita, who like Alfred and Satin-Legs Smith is a poet manqué ("'I touch'—she said once—'petals of a rose. / A silky feeling through me goes!'"), and the poet who has constructed a resonating chamber for the "chopped chirpings" that signify the extinction of her voice (ibid.). Such an alliance is also suggested by the climactic, twice-repeated question, "How many care, Pepita?"—which could only be asked by a poet, since it is an apostrophe in the fullest sense.[59] "Turning aside" to address "an imaginary person," this question goes to the heart of what ails the Mecca building and its inhabitants; ironically, the innocence of a child who "never went to kindergarten" has made her its only conceivable interlocutor. Pepita died believing she was worth caring for and assuming that other people thought so as well. "She never learned that black is not beloved" (ibid.); in death she becomes the Mecca building's *genius loci*.

The paratactic structure of "In the Mecca" has made it easy to suggest, by citing the poem selectively, that it underwrites the revolutionary stance of the most extreme wing of the Black Power movement. "Amos from *In the Mecca* has transcended Dorie Miller," writes Addison Gayle, Jr.; Don Lee, who is himself in the poem calling for "a new music screaming in the sun," cites the profile of Way-Out Morgan as an instance of the "new music" that Brooks herself "becomes" by "re-directing . . . her voice to her own people—*first and foremost*."[60] Whereas *A Street in Bronzeville*'s "Negro Hero" risked his life for his country because "Their white-gowned democracy was my fair lady," Way-Out Morgan, whose fair lady is "Blackness stern and blunt and beautiful," "smacks sweet his lips" as he thinks of the rapes and beatings and murders white people will have to answer for on "the day of Debt-pay," with "flesh-rip in the Forum of Justice at last!" (*BLACKS*, 431). But to assume that by the time Brooks wrote "In the Mecca" she was ready to endorse a revolutionary commitment of this kind is to answer the poem's central question, "How many care, Pepita?" by brushing it aside or indefinitely postponing its claims.[61] "*Ain seen er I ain seen er I ain seen* er": the Smith children's defensive response to their mother's discovery that Pepita is missing is re-echoed throughout the Mecca building by neighbor after neighbor who "ain seen no Pepita" or has "never known Pepita S." or "has not seen Pepita anywhere." By placing Amos and Way-Out Morgan alongside all the others who have neglected her welfare in favor of "other importances,"[62] Brooks implicitly holds them accountable for her disappearance along with the rest. At the same time, however, by including their perspectives she puts the poem's readers on notice that a powerful rage is building within the black community. It is an open question whether that rage, and the political abstractions it fosters, will prove less or more hospitable to the survival of "Smithkind" than the "fair fables" of Miës Van der Rohe.

As the poem unfolds, the poet is continually posing hard questions, sometimes in an extradiegetic voice, sometimes in the voice of the Mecca building, and sometimes on behalf of individual Mecca residents. These questions go a long way toward establishing her authority and presence as "Super-Reporter," one who is both detached and concerned, in a position to know the Mecca building's inhabitants better than they know themselves but with a vested interest in helping them come to know themselves better. In her presence, even practical questions resonate beyond their immediate context. From the moment that

Mrs. Sallie asks "WHERE PEPITA BE?" and none of her other children can answer, it begins to seem that any question, however straightforward and practical, could without warning take on a portentous unanswerability. And yet it is chiefly by means of questions, many of them rhetorical questions to which no answer is expected or seems possible, that the Mecca building's residents become, paradoxically, answerable to one another.

The poet comes close to saying this in so many words when Mrs. Sallie asks a rhetorical question that epitomizes her frustration over the impossibility of turning her run-down, roach-infested apartment into a home she could be proud of. "What can I do?" She intends that question as an admission of defeat, an expression of helplessness, but the poet intervenes in second-person voice to "call" her to answerability:

> "What can I do?"
> But World (a sheep)
> wants to be Told.
> If you ask a question, you
> can't stop there.
> You must keep going. (*BLACKS*, 410–11)

The "you" pronoun is used to upbraid and correct, but also to empathize, and while ostensibly addressed to Mrs. Sallie, its force is generic and generalizing. Whether we like it or not, our lives are in conversation with our world. A question is itself an action: to ask a question is to issue a challenge, but if your interlocutor is God or "World" you will find that the only one who is available to take up the challenge is you yourself. Mrs. Sallie wants a Teller, but "World (a sheep) wants to be Told": the world throws her question back in her face.

And indeed, her daughter's disappearance does constrain Mrs. Sallie to "keep on going," as she and her other children fan out through the building to search for Pepita—

> Knock-knocking down the martyred halls
> at doors behind whose yelling oak or pine
>   many flowers start, choke, reach up,
>   want help, get it, do not get it,
>   rally, bloom, or die on the wasting vine.
>
> "One of my children is missing. One of my children is gone."
> (*BLACKS*, 416–17)

The metaphor of "yelling oak or pine" transfers the agency and urgency of their knocking to the physical fabric of the building; in this way, the lament that "one of my children is missing" seems to come from the Mecca building itself, summoning its inhabitants to give an account of themselves. The "Super-Reporter" becomes their Teller, not in the sense that she can tell them how to rally or get help, but in the sense that she gathers and weaves into a single complex fabric what all of them individually have to say for themselves.

"How many care, Pepita?" The only living Mecca resident who comes close to sharing the poet's sense of that question's urgency is Alfred, who is introduced near the beginning of the poem and reappears thereafter several times. A high school English teacher, Alfred "'fails' no one" by forming no serious attachments and by not attempting to do very much with his life *(BLACKS,* 409). He reads widely in the European classics and is very much taken with Leopold Senghor, the contemporary African philosopher-king who theorized "negritude" and became President of Senegal. We are told that Alfred "might have been a poet-king" himself, and "might have been an architect" (ibid., 421–22)—like the rest of his neighbors, but with greater self-awareness, he has missed his calling in life. Importantly, however, the callings Alfred has missed are ones that would have put him in a position to create new conditions of existence for his African American neighbors. And while it seems at first that his reading and his philosophical inclinations are just one more way of taking evasive action, like Mrs. Sallie's dream of changing places with her white employer or her son Thomas Earl's of becoming Johnny Appleseed, Alfred is the only Meccan whose outlook changes over the course of the poem and the only one who begins to grasp the big picture—what Brooks referred to in her prospectus as "the gist of black humanity in general."[63] Thus Alfred "has not seen Pepita Smith," but near the end of the poem he comes close to being able to hear what the Mecca building itself is saying:

> I hate it.
> Yet, murmurs Alfred—
> Who is leaning at the balcony, leaning—
> something, something in Mecca
> continues to call! Substanceless; yet like mountains,
> like rivers and oceans too; and like trees
> with wind whistling through them. And steadily
> an essential sanity, black and electric,
> builds to a reportage and redemption.
>   A hot estrangement.

A material collapse
that is Construction. (*BLACKS*, 432–33)

At this moment Alfred seems to cross over from the world of the poem into the World of its readers—or perhaps he has had one foot there all along, since at times throughout the poem his voice is difficult to distinguish from the poet's extradiegetic commentary. Seeming to foresee the "material collapse" of the building itself, he begins to have faith in the possibility of life after Mecca for a community that is being forced to confront itself and take stock of its own resources. In tuning his ear to "something in Mecca," Alfred is listening both *to* his neighbors and *beyond* them.

PART III
RACE AND RHETORIC AFTER MECCA

In 1950, a year after *Annie Allen* won the Pulitzer Prize, Brooks contributed a one-page essay entitled "Poets Who Are Negroes" to a special issue of the journal *Phylon* whose topic was the status of Negro literature at mid-century.[64] In that essay she asserted that "at present" the Negro poet's "most urgent duty" is "to polish his technique." Simply being a Negro gives him "impressive advantages"; "many a Gentile poet, longing for a moving, authoritative and humane subject," is inclined to envy him the "major indignities" he has suffered, since these are such as to "make the pen run wild." But he cannot afford to let his pen run wild; he must polish his technique so that "his truths and his beauties ... may be more insinuating, and, therefore, more overwhelming."

> Every Negro poet has "something to say." Simply because he is a Negro; he cannot escape having important things to say. His mere body, for that matter, is an eloquence. His quiet walk down the street is a speech to the people. Is a rebuke, is a plea, is a school.

That said, "no real artist is going to be content with offering raw materials" as if they "required no embellishment, no interpretation, no subtlety." What you must do, instead of "throwing dough to the not-so-hungry mob," is "to cook that dough, alter it, until it is unrecognizable."

Implicit in Brooks's emphasis on technique is a goal to which she and other writers attached a high priority at mid-century: that of building a canon of Negro poetry whose technical proficiency would speak for itself.⁶⁵ She is suggesting, however, that for poets who are Negroes, "craft" in the usual sense is not all that will be needed; they will also need to be *crafty*—subtle, devious. Her own rhetoric not only recommends but models *craft* in this additional sense—with the ironical suggestion that poets who are Negroes are advantaged by their disadvantages, with the insinuation that when you are a Negro there is no such thing as minding your own business. Interestingly enough, however, even as she advises would-be poets to "insinuate" their truths rather than speak them openly, Brooks adumbrates an interlocutory relationship between "the people" and the Negro *qua Negro* that is open, direct, and unmediated. As poet he should not speak plainly; as Negro he cannot choose not to do so.

Fifty years after it was first published, the metaphor of a "mere body" that is an eloquence, a "quiet walk down the street" that is "a speech to the people," is the *Phylon* essay's most vivid conceit. It is the only place in the essay where the general public is referred to not as "the mob" but as "the people," in keeping with the depiction of encounters at street level and of speech genres that promote education through dialogue. In this image of a body that is eloquent without speaking, whose behavior and "body language" are themselves a medium of speech, we can already find the kernel of the task Brooks would set for herself as a poet "After Mecca," from the 1970s until her death in 2000—that of envoicing and personifying "Blackness."

In 1972 Brooks announced that her aim, "in my next future, is to write poems that will somehow successfully 'call' (see Imamu Baraka's 'SOS') all black people: black people in taverns, black people in alleys, black people in gutters, schools, offices, factories, prisons, the consulate . . . black people in pulpits, black people in mines, on farms, on thrones . . ." (*RPO*, 183). Phillip Brian Harper cites this announcement as an index of the enormous influence of Amiri Baraka's "Black Aesthetic" even amongst "black writers from different generations and disparate backgrounds";⁶⁶ but for Harper, Baraka's "SOS" is problematic because "the objective for which it assembles the black populace is not specified in the piece itself."⁶⁷ What Brooks felt called to do by Baraka's poem was not, however, to specify objectives; she saw something else that needed doing first, which if done successfully would enable the populace to come up with its own, as yet unforeseeable, goals and purposes. The most effective way to be "calling all black people" was to arrange for their Blackness *itself* to call them together, in the name of "black identity, black solidarity, black self-possession and self-address" (*RPO*, 183).

"SOS" is a poem you cannot read to yourself without having it become mentally audible, so tellingly does Baraka's poem capture the rhythms of oral speech. Through flamboyant mimicry of the way an urban policeman might use his two-way radio to summon reinforcements, Baraka hijacks the vocative force of a distress signal that is conspicuously unpoetic, oral, of the street. But then, abruptly yet seamlessly, by means of a strategic enjambment, he converts an SOS into a different kind of summons altogether:

> Calling black people
> Calling all black people, man woman child
> Wherever you are, calling you, urgent, come in
> Black People, come in, wherever you are, urgent, calling
> you, calling all black people
> calling all black people, come in, black people, come
> on in.[68]

The edge of the poem's climactic gesture of welcome has been sharpened for its collective addressee by a history of having been made *unwelcome* in public venues of all kinds. Poetry is one such venue, but that, says Baraka's poem, is about to change! This *is* a poem, after all, by virtue of its use of apostrophe, its stylized repetitions, its rhythmic tensions, brevity, and pointedness. Indeed, an entire poem has been made out of the figure traditionally associated with the summoning of poetic inspiration and thus with poetry's transcendent status. Baraka has renovated this quintessentially poetic figure and carried it into the street. The poem's implied message for other Black artists is that it's time for bringing the community together to acknowledge its own existence and begin to shape a collective identity.

Brooks had arguably been engaged in such a project since the 1940s, but "until 1967," as she explains in *Report from Part One*, "my own blackness did not confront me with a shrill spelling of itself" (*RPO*, 83). The metaphor at the heart of this arrestingly worded formulation sounds a theme that was present in her poetry as early as the "ballad of chocolate mabbie," in *A Street in Bronzeville*, but its 1967 context is a Black Arts conference at Fisk University at which Brooks found herself upstaged by a group of younger artists who had already begun to heed Baraka's "call." At Fisk, Brooks found the "Websterian" definition of blackness,[69] the definition chocolate mabbie learns to "spell" at the age of seven, being annulled and set aside by these younger artists' determination to reclaim both the word and the concept from within the black community. To her own delight, Brooks felt very much at home with this new collective sense of purpose: "I had never been before," she says, "in the general presence of . . . such determination to mold or carve something DEFINITE" (*RPO*, 85). A new sense of what she needed to be doing as a poet took shape accordingly. The task she set herself was epideictic, in the fullest sense: it was a question of reaching out to black people in the name and in the spirit of their blackness so that, metaphorically speaking, their ears could become attuned to its frequency.

Classical and Renaissance rhetoricians speak of epideictic rhetoric as a discourse of praise and blame, but contemporary scholars of classical rhetoric have begun to articulate a broader understanding of its traditional mandate: "the establishment, reconfirmation, or revision of general values and beliefs."[70] Epideictic lyric, according to Lawrence Rosenfield, is poetry that "calls upon us to join with our community in giving thought to what we witness."[71] It presupposes, according to Jeffrey Walker, an occasion that must be seized, "about which something can or must be said."[72] The epideictic occasion Brooks understood herself to be seizing was the emergence from within the black community of a "new black ideal"—one that, as she explained in 1975 in *A Capsule Course in Black Poetry Writing*, "italicizes black identity, black solidarity, black self-possession and self-address." In "subscrib[ing] to these," the new black literature no longer addresses itself to whites with the cry, "We are equal!" Instead, the "prevailing understanding" is that "black literature is literature BY blacks, ABOUT blacks, directed TO blacks" (3).[73]

Brooks would later come to stress, as Zofia Burr reminds us, that writing "to" blacks was not at all the same as writing exclusively "for" them.[74] She continued to accept invitations to read for mixed or predominantly white audiences all through the 1980s and '90s, and on such occasions she would choose poems to read aloud that strongly thematized poetry's "flexible addressivity" (Burr, 145).[75] If the gestures of address her poems were making began to look simpler, to the point where they strike us when we read them as "too 'direct' for writerly conceptions of the poetic," Burr suggests we heed Toni Cade Bambara's suggestion that by the early 1970s Brooks had already begun to move "'more toward gesture, sound, intonation, attitude, and other characteristics that depend on oral presentation rather than private eyeballing'" (Burr, 142).

Although I would heartily endorse Burr's emphasis on the complex "addressivity" of Brooks's poems both before and after Fisk, I think Bambara has overstated Brooks's inclination to break with "writerly conceptions of the poetic." She greatly admired the work of poets such as Sonia Sanchez and Ntozake Shange, which is scripted for oral performance,[76] but her own intention to write "for blacks" did not commit her to turning away from on-the-page literariness. This is confirmed in the very passage from the 1988 poem "Winnie" that Burr says she would often use "to orient her audience to her stance as a poet" at the beginning of a reading:

> I pass you my Poem.
>
> A poem doesn't do everything for you.
> You are supposed to go *on* with your thinking.
> You are supposed to enrich
> the other person's poem with your extensions,
> your uniquely personal understandings,
> thus making the poem serve *you*.[77]

As Burr points out, these lines challenge their audience in no uncertain terms to "engage with poetry as purposeful speech" (Burr, 144). At the same time, however, "I pass you my Poem" is a gesture of address that models the poet's transaction with her audience as implicitly textual and writerly. In its original context, it is a boldly direct gesture that nonetheless retains a crucial *in*directness. When "Winnie" says "I pass you my Poem," she is using "my Poem" to refer to *herself*: she means something like "I give you my life to reckon with for your own purposes as black Americans." When she read the poem at Ithaca College, Burr recalls Brooks having "specified that the lines are spoken by Winnie Mandela *to* black Americans." What that specification highlights, with Burr's italics to record Brooks's emphasis, is that it is really the poet, or more precisely the poem, that is speaking to black Americans on Winnie's behalf. The fiction of Winnie speaking is just that—a strategic fiction whose purpose is to give black Americans a Winnie they can use, a figure of heroic proportions who "speaks" to them of their African origins and of their own (potential) Blackness.

Such poems have a quasi-ekphrastic function: they undertake to envoice behavior that is not already speech, arranging in this way for "Blackness" itself to speak to the black community. Such a poem is calling on its audience to engage with an action or a set of behaviors or a way of life that "speaks out" or has a message for them.[78] At the same time, however, the poem's very existence presupposes that the message's legibility—that is to say, its intelligibility, its timeliness, its relevance to the community's problems and aspirations—is to some degree a problem and a challenge. "Winnie" may well be the least successful of these poems, insofar as its speaker is induced to say too much, belying her own insistence that "a poem doesn't do everything for you." The most successful of Brooks's poems in this mode construct a provocatively bounded image that speaks without foregoing its status as action, and hence without converting its eloquence entirely into speech.

The work the poem is doing to capture such an image and make its eloquence legible is especially obvious in poems whose speakers lack the verbal resources to explain themselves, or do not feel inclined to do so. In what may well be Brooks's single best-known poem, "we real cool," the poem's ostensible speakers ("The pool players / seven at the golden shovel") are far too "cool" to pronounce *themselves* cool, too intent on the activity that defines them and gives them a public identity to notice that they have an audience.[79] What is speaking in "we real cool" is their style, their behavior, their way of life—or rather, what is speaking is a poem that deciphers, disseminates, and commemorates the message of this mute speech, this behavior-that-is-speech. Just as in Baraka's "SOS," the rhythms of oral speech have been tellingly captured: Brooks would later explain, for example, that she had placed the recurring pronoun "we" at the ends rather than the beginnings of lines to convey that the pool players are "a little uncertain of the strength of their identity."[80] But the poem's lightly submerged couplet rhyme scheme is also crucial to the message it leaves us with, and that message is the poem's, not the pool players'. Its final words are not asserting their conscious intention or foreknowledge but projecting an outcome that is implicit in their way of life—an early death that will come upon them as surely as "Jazz June" rhymes with "die soon."

In chapter 3 we found Sylvia Plath turning to an ekphrastic mode of writing to achieve "the triumph of wit over suffering" at moments of personal crisis. Plath found that ekphrastic images, someone else's or ones that she herself had killed into art,[81] could furnish a fun-house mirror on which to project inner states of personal foreboding, murderous hatred, or suicidal apathy. The triumph of wit over suffering counted for Plath as art rather than therapy (her acknowledged mentors in this mode were the classical tragedians and the Gorgon-slayer Perseus), but such poems were almost always triggered by events in her own life and by her own "suffering," in the broadest sense. In Brooks's quasi-ekphrastic poems it is almost never her own private life that is at issue or at stake. Instead what is at stake is "Blackness," which her poems depict as both a conundrum and a resource for African Americans.

Blackness is not a chosen identity in the first instance, and choosing not to have your blackness be meaningful is not an option, as

Brooks had emphasized in "Poets Who Are Negroes." Most black children learn this early: "The Life of Lincoln West"[82] is the story of a little boy who learns what it means to look African from a conversation between two white strangers in a movie theater. As they pronounce his physical "ugliness" to be "the real thing," these men's intention is by no means to give him a way of thinking of himself that will "[comfort] him." But the poem contrives to leave its readers with the thought that whereas black identity is foisted upon Americans of African descent by a history not of their making, they nonetheless have a choice with respect to that identity. They can fend it off or try to outrun it, like the little girl who runs away from Lincoln West in the schoolyard, or they can opt instead, as he does, for "black self-possession" and "self-address."[83]

In *Report from Part Two*, Lincoln West is cited along with Satin-Legs Smith in a section Brooks calls "my gallery," in which she also lists actual friends and acquaintances who have figured in her poems. "All the aforementioned," she explains, "are among my Family Pictures. ... 'Family' therein referred to is Blackness" (*RPT*, 127). Brooks's poetic mandate as it took shape post-Fisk was to give Blackness many names and faces, many arresting and intelligible ways of living in the world. Whereas the would-be poet Alfred in "In the Mecca" has a prophetic intuition of Blackness that is powerfully abstract—"an essential sanity, black and electric"—these "pictures" depict specific ways of being Black, some of which are more fully chosen than others. "After Mecca" has elegies for Medgar Evers and Malcolm X, along with "Boy Breaking Glass"; a volume of poems entitled *Family Pictures*, published with Broadside Press in 1970, includes "The Life of Lincoln West," "Paul Robeson," and a three-part "YOUNG HEROES" series. The larger purpose of these poems, as the title of the 1970 volume suggests, is to forge a sense of "family" or of "nation" for African Americans—which is not only a matter of identifying leaders and qualities of leadership, but also of discerning grounds for solidarity among "black brothers and sisters."[84]

Underlying all of Brooks's poems in this mode is the principle adumbrated in the *Phylon* essay, that a person's "mere body" is "an eloquence" that speaks "to the people." In "The Wall" she depicts Val Gray Ward, the leader of the Chicago dance troupe Kuumba, as "a little black stampede / in African / images of brass and flowerswirl" who "leans back on mothercountry and is tract, / is treatise through her perfect and straight teeth."[85] Medgar Evers and Malcolm X were orators, but Brooks's commemorative poems for them do not quote their words; instead they conjure up contrasting bodily stances whose eloquence is undeniable. In the presence of Malcolm X, her poem tells us, "We gasped. We saw the maleness. / The maleness raking out and making guttural the air / and pushing us to walls" (*BLACKS*, 441). Medgar Evers, by contrast, is depicted "lean[ing] across tomorrow. People said that / he was holding clean globes in his hands" (*BLACKS*, 440). In both poems heroism is not only the ascribed status of an individual, but an index and expression of the community's ability to create its own values and envision its own collective destiny: "He [Malcolm] opened us— / who was a key, // who was a man."[86]

What speaks to "us" of who we are and could be is not always a message of uplift in the person of an acknowledged hero. The protagonist of "Boy Breaking Glass" is a nameless young boy from the projects, whose "broken window is a cry of art." Brooks's poem has set itself the task of translating that "cry" into articulate speech in order to disclose the latent eloquence of behavior that is, on the face of it, pointlessly destructive:

> "I shall create! If not a note, a hole.
> If not an overture, a desecration."
> . . .
> "Nobody knew where I was and now I am no longer there."

To the poet's "Tuned Ear," the boy's vandalism has an urgent message for his neighbors and for the larger society that refuses to acknowledge his existence:

> "It was you, it was you who threw away my name!
> And this is everything I have for me." (*BLACKS*, 438–39)

He is sending out an "SOS." And indeed, all of Brooks's hero poems insist on the vocative force of the hero's behavior or stance. There are, as it turns out, many degrees of urgency, many ways of reaching out, many tones of voice in which black people can be called to engage with what a body or its actions have to "say."

The "YOUNG HEROES" series juxtaposes three styles of heroism that are strikingly different from one another, personified respectively in South African artist-activist Keorapetse Kgositsile, teacher-publisher-poet Don Lee,[87] and youth organizer Walter Bradford.[88] In the first of these tributes Kgositsile's "message" for black Americans is epitomized by the title of a book of his poems, *My Name is Afrika*, whose symbolic act of self-naming the poem commends to its African American readers in a more colloquial register:

"MY NAME IS AFRIKA!"
>Well, every fella's a Foreign Country.
>This Foreign Country speaks to You. (*BLACKS*, 491)

"You" is the poem's final word in order to maximize its deictic force, so that it can reach out beyond the poem to provoke recognition and response. In "To Don at Salaam" a more traditional use of apostrophe calls attention to its subject's everyday, private individuality through a quasi-ekphrastic reading of his body language:

> I like to see you lean back in your chair
> so far you have to fall but do not—
> your arms back, your fine hands
> in your print pockets.
>
> Beautiful. Impudent.
> Ready for life.
> A tied storm. (*BLACKS*, 492)

The poem's mode of address is intimate and playful, performing an act of friendship which the reader is permitted to overhear notwithstanding its intimacy. "Walter Bradford" honors another good friend of Brooks's by using alliterative kennings to depict him in a Herculean mode of response to crisis.[89] "It's Walter-work, Walter," the poet affirms—

> Not overmuch for
> brick-fitter, brick-MAKER, and wave-
> outwitter;
> whip-stopper.
> Not overmuch for a
> Tree-planting Man.
>
> Stay. (*BLACKS*, 493)

Both "To Don at Salaam" and "Walter Bradford" conclude with a vocative gesture that is directed not toward the poem's readers, as in "To Keorapetse Kgositsile," but toward its eponymous protagonist on the reader's behalf. The last line of "To Don" is "I like to see you living in the world"; in "Walter Bradford" the single word "Stay" brings a sterner voice to a more conventionally heroic tribute. Both are vocative gestures whose indirect message is: black people need you to be this, to model this way of living in the world.

In each poem Brooks has made a conspicuous and telling use of apostrophe—in "To Keorapetse Kgositsile" to provoke a response from the reader, in "To Don at Salaam" to perform friendship and conjure intimacy,[90] in "Walter Bradford" to confer heroic status. All three poems have made "you" to find "us"; at the same time, however, all three contrive to suggest that their eponymous heroes are self-made. Each man's existential stance is already "an eloquence"; what the poet has done is put *her* capacity for eloquence at the service of *his*.

In the *Phylon* essay Brooks makes the point that a Negro "speaks" without having chosen or even wished to do so: perfect strangers feel themselves to be addressed, apostrophized, put on the spot by his very existence in their city or neighborhood. If the logic of that metaphor is pushed to the limit, it points toward Martin Luther King, Jr.'s definition of a riot as "the language of the unheard": a riot is what will happen if the Negro's "quiet walk down the street" goes unheard for too long. Brooks uses this definition as the epigraph for her three-part poem "RIOT," in which the vocative force of action-that-is-speech is brought to crisis, along with the vocative force of reportage, prayer and pulpit oratory, songs, legends, expletives, and distress signals of all kinds. In "RIOT" Brooks's epideictic agenda and the strategies of address that subtend it disclose a contradiction that is implicit in its metaphoric premise, which is that ordinary everyday Blackness, not the Blackness of heroes but of "people in taverns . . . in alleys . . . in gutters, schools, offices, factories, prisons," has "something to say" that is eloquent, but at the same time inscrutable.[91]

The first section of this three-part poem was commissioned by Don Lee for the Chicago magazine *Black Expression* in April of 1968, when widespread rioting occurred in the wake of King's assassination: its entire focus is the death of a rich white Chicagoan who finds himself in the wrong part of town when the riot breaks out and is trampled to death. The second section, entitled "The Third Sermon on the Warpland," consists of a series of disjunct vignettes and comments that capture the chaotic fluidity of the riot as it unfolds. This ironically labeled "sermon" consists largely of announcements, rhetorical questions, exclamations, and cries of varying degrees of urgency, but the prevailing voice is that of the riot itself: "Crazy flowers / cry up across the sky, spreading / and hissing **This is / it**" (*BLACKS*, 473). The poem's third section, entitled "An Aspect of Love, Alive in the Ice and Fire," is a love poem from a black woman to a black man whose placement prompts the inference that their relationship may be the harbinger of a phoenix-like rebirth for the black community.[92]

At the end of this third section the lovers go off "in different directions / down the imperturbable street" (*BLACKS*, 480). Ironically, however, in the first section of the poem it is a rich white man whose walk down the street is an eloquence: not only "John Cabot's" name but his clothing and grooming and physical carriage bespeak "the nourished white / that told his story of glory to the World" (*BLACKS*, 471).[93] His verbal speech, however, is conspicuously futile. "Don't let It touch me! The blackness! Lord!' he whisper[s]"; "But in a thrilling announcement, on It drove / and breathed on him: and touched him." "'*Que tu es grossier!*'" he hisses toward "the 'Negroes'" coming toward him "in rough ranks"; but "They were black and loud. / And not detainable. And not discreet" (*BLACKS*, 471–72). Repeatedly the poem depicts the rioters' mere movement as speech: the unwilling ambassador of white America, much as he would wish to have nothing to do with their poverty, their loudness, their blackness, cannot now fail to hear what "It" has to say. At the same time, however, he and the rioters are talking past each other. His inability to make any sense of their "thrilling announcement," his instinctive shrinking away from its "terrific touch," stand in metonymically for white America's refusal to take responsibility—or even cognizance—of the volatile condition of black urban ghettos throughout the United States in the 1960s.

In counterpoint to John Cabot's horror of being "touched" by "the blackness," "An Aspect of Love" introduces a black man and woman who "laugh," "smile," and "touch each other" in a perfectly reciprocal yet wordless dialogue. The poem's speaker is watching her lover ready himself for the new day's business after the night of love they have spent together:

> You rise. Although
> genial, you are in yourself again.
> I observe
> your direct and respectable stride.
> You are direct and self-accepting as a lion
> in African velvet. You are level, lean,
> remote. (*BLACKS*, 479)

Here again we have a man whose "mere body" is "an eloquence," but unlike the "Negro" invoked by the *Phylon* essay a half-century earlier, whose "walk down the street" is emphatically legible even though it may well be "saying" different things to different people, he projects a powerful yet enigmatic remoteness. In *Report from Part One* Brooks offers a prose description of this figure, whom she claims to have first encountered and recognized at the Fisk Conference about a year before this section of the poem was written:[94]

> There is indeed a new black today. He is different from any the world has known. He's a tall-walker. Almost firm. By many of his own *brothers* he is not understood. And he is understood by *no* white. Not the wise white; not the Schooled white; not the Kind white. (*RPO*, 85)

A big part of what makes him seem remote and mysterious is that he does not seek to be understood: respectable in the eyes of others he may be, but the completeness of his self-acceptance makes that kind of respectability superfluous.

The poem's speaker, identified as "LaBohem Brown," is a "bohemian" successor to Maud Martha Brown, the Bronzeville protagonist of Brooks's novel *Maud Martha* who came of age in the early 1950s.[95] The man she apostrophizes is her lover, but also her comrade in struggle.[96] In choosing the most intimate of love poems, the aubade, as the genre in which to recognize and acknowledge him, Brooks has flown in the face of the European tradition of using the aubade to lament a merely private relationship's vulnerability to encroachment from the public world of business and politics. D. H. Melhem helpfully plays Brooks's aubade off against Donne's "The Sun Rising";[97] as she points out, to the extent that we are familiar with what this lyric genre has been used to do in the past, that history underscores the newness of the relationship Brooks's poem celebrates. Instead of insisting, like "The Sun Rising," that the public world does not exist for the lovers, and instead of casting the female partner as the one who will be left behind when her lover does accede to the call of that world, the last stanza of Brooks's poem sends the lovers out into the world together, to be about their daily business:

> On the street we smile.
> We go
> In different directions
> Down the imperturbable street. (*BLACKS*, 480)

This is predominantly a "we" poem, but the "I"-perspective is also kept alive so that both the one who is speaking and the one who is being addressed will retain their distinctness and independent agency. In the lines that celebrate their partnership—"There is a moment in Camaraderie / when interruption is not to be understood. / I cannot bear an interruption."—Brooks told Melhem she had considered and rejected "*We* cannot bear an interruption." Her reason for going with "I" in this context may have been to suggest that "she" is more romantic than "he" is, but it may also have been to strike a careful balance between independence and mutuality. Brooks's female speaker is speaking "to" the man she loves but not "for" him; their partnership is reciprocal, but she is her own woman just as much as he is his own man. At the same time, however, she is using the traditional resources of love poetry: the apostrophe that "turns away" from the poem's readers to construct a world that is for two people only, the invocation of a time-transcending fullness in the lovers' presence to each other ("This is the shining joy; / the time of not-to-end").[98]

The poem's celebration of an intimate relationship, its invocation of "lyric time," its use of apostrophe to "turn away" both from readers and from the riot itself, might suggest that poetry has been enlisted here as a refuge from "the gut issue, the blood fact" of the riot.[99] Perhaps, however, just as she did with the off-rhyme sonnets of "gay chaps at the bar" in *A Street in Bronzeville*, Brooks was bringing the aubade into hitherto uncharted territory. Perhaps she intended, in so doing, to pass her readers a poem whose relationship to its own literariness, as well as to the mute eloquence of the riot itself, is unstable and even a little troubling, thereby provoking us to "go on with [our] thinking" about poetry's institutional viability. If so, then its speaker's act of making "you" to find "me" is one that, by troubling its own reception, heightens the political stakes of poetic address.

CODA

PRESENCE AND ABSENCE

I have been arguing throughout this book that in lyric poetry figures of address are crucial to the construction of a viable poetic persona, an "I" to take ownership of the voice that speaks from the page. When Louise Glück explains, in "The Education of the Poet," that her preference as both reader and writer has always been for "poetry that requests or craves a listener," she is suggesting that not all poems express that craving or make that request; but while we need to allow for varying degrees of explicitness and urgency, I would argue that "addressivity" is a key constituent of lyric utterance.[1] Poems are written for the ear not only in the sense that their sound shape is meaningful, but also in the sense that they are getting a "hearing" for what their speakers have to say.[2]

Who "I" can be in a poem depends on whom I have chosen to address and what is at stake between us. Is my supposed interlocutor an intimate or a stranger? Does "she" share my values and allegiances, or are "his" fundamental assumptions unjust to me and my kind? Am I addressing the poem's readers directly, or constraining them to witness a summons or disclosure I have "turned aside" to address to someone else? In *Invisible Listeners: Lyric Intimacy in Herbert, Whitman, and*

Ashbery, Helen Vendler has recently called attention to certain poets' preference for conjuring up "nonexistent" listeners: a deity who is an intimate friend, a reader who has not yet been born, a long-dead artist from the past.[3] The four poets this book has brought together were speaking instead from within existing social relations: those of parenthood; of a patient and her therapist; of lovers, friends, or spouses; of neighbors or of citizenship more broadly conceived. Their choice to inhabit and work from within existing social relations arose in part from the realization that who they were as social beings could not easily be bracketed or kept out of play. Each of them sought to claim the status of poet for herself in the teeth of a prevailing assumption that poetic authority and masculine gender were indissolubly connected. If you were a woman poet, coming of age at the middle of the twentieth century, could you afford to "sound like" a woman in your poems? Could you manage *not* to?

In attending closely to how four poets faced these interrelated questions, I have not been trying to sketch the contours of a poetic movement or a shared aesthetic. Far from it: I decided to write this book when I noticed how differently each of them came to grips with "the gender of things," even though they began to have their poems published within a few years of each other. Anne Sexton learned from Robert Lowell's poetry class to mistrust her propensity for writing "as a woman writes," and yet it was by speaking as a woman in her poems that she found her poetic voice in the first place.[4] Sexton's interlocutory strategy typically calls attention to the power dynamics of socially constructed relationships in order to leverage those relationships to a female speaker's advantage. Sylvia Plath, encouraged by Sexton's example, openly aspired to become "The Poetess of America": Plath's speakers inhabit the gendered roles of daughter and wife, *femme fatale* and high priestess, with a hyperbolic intensity that has proved even more "unnerving"[5] than Sexton's high-profile performances. But whereas Sexton's poems are aggressively sociable, Plath's figures of address are stylized and poetic; they assist her female speaker to withdraw from the terrain of ordinary social life into a "kingdom" apart, a realm of mythic permanence and inevitability.[6]

In contrast with Plath and Sexton, Adrienne Rich tried for a poetic stance in her first two published volumes that would be gender-neutral and hence generically human. Rich embarked on her poetic career with the goal of making "you" to find "we"; like Gwendolyn Brooks, she had an affinity for what Brooks called "the universal fact." Rich came to want to position herself as a woman in her poems only gradually, as she became an activist on behalf of radical feminism during the 1970s.

Her ongoing involvement in the women's movement brought home to her, however, that speaking as a woman entailed speaking as a white woman, an American woman, a woman of comparative privilege who has received a good education. The "difficulty of saying 'we,'"[7] a difficulty she had hugely underestimated at the outset, was a function of race and class as well as being a function of her gender.

Gwendolyn Brooks had no choice but to speak as a woman who was black rather than white, but she did not wish to disown or bracket either her gender or her racial status. When she first began to have her poems published by a mainstream publishing house, Brooks's goal was to bring the lives of urban blacks into focus for the society at large. The question, however, of whether she could address her poems to "American" readers without compromising her allegiance to "blackness" is one that she had to revisit at intervals throughout her career, as the racial climate changed around her both in the city of Chicago and in the country at large. At mid-career, in the context of the Black Arts movement, Brooks explicitly redefined her poetic mission by turning away from white readers in order to concentrate on "calling all black people," in the name of "black self-possession" and "self-address."[8]

Brooks is the outlier in this foursome; whereas Rich, Plath, and Sexton were very much aware of each other's careers as they went along, her sphere of activity and of influence scarcely overlapped with theirs.[9] But just as Rich's attempt to keep her gender out of play in her first two published volumes renders Sexton's choice to speak as a woman all the more interesting, and just as Plath's use of apostrophe to "borrow the stilts of an old tragedy"[10] makes Rich's and Sexton's allegiance to the realm of ordinary social life appear that much more chosen and hence meaningful, so Brooks's bardic stance is all the more striking in its difference from the more self-involved, "I"-focused stances of Sexton and Plath, and her strategies for reaching out to potential readers come more sharply into focus when they are juxtaposed with Rich's. As I have worked with Brooks's poems alongside Rich's, Plath's, and Sexton's, I have come to understand more fully how a poet's political goals might come to inform her poetic practice; I hope that has been the experience of this book's readers as well.

Two of these poets cut their own lives short; the other two finished out the century. One of them, Adrienne Rich, is still calling attention to the importance of the "I-you" relation in her poems, and she is still experimenting with that relation in ways that are both familiar and surprising. Her latest volume, suggestively titled *Telephone Ringing in the Labyrinth,* has for one of its epigraphs a categorical assertion by the African American poet Sterling A. Brown that *"Poetry is not self-expres-*

sion, the I is a dramatic I." "To which I would add," says Rich over her own initials, *"and so, unless otherwise indicated, is the You."*[11] Together, these epigraphs put us on notice that an "I-you" relation is crucial to each of the poems in the volume, but that the "I" is never simply Adrienne Rich. Is she reminding us of what we should have known all along about even the most apparently "confessional" poems, or calling attention to what is especially true of the poems in this volume? Perhaps the latter, since although Rich's hunger for dialogue is everywhere apparent in these poems, collectively they seem bent on persuading us of the insuperable difficulty, notwithstanding the crucial importance, of constructing a viable "I-you" relation.[12]

Never has the possibility of dialogue been in so many ways attenuated, the prospect of it so often rendered moot. A poem entitled "Even Then Maybe" gives a startlingly kinesthetic account of how it feels in your mouth and throat to be the bearer of speech that is withheld, swallowed, begrudged, or "taken back half-spoken":

> *I told her a mouthful*
> *I shut my mouth against him*
> Throat thick with tears
> how words sound when you swallow
> —and under the roof
> of the mouth long stroke
> reaching from the tongue's root (*Telephone*, 58)

The volume's third section consists of a single poem entitled "Letters Censored, Shredded, Returned to Sender, or Judged Unfit to Send." In "Hubble Photographs: After Sappho," the poem's speaker maintains that "the most desired sight of all" is not the person you love beyond all others, "turning to look at you," but the "impersonae" we encounter in the photographs of "galaxies / so out from us there's no vocabulary // but mathematics and optics": "we look at them or don't from within the milky gauze // of our tilted gazing / but they don't look back and we cannot hurt them" (*Telephone*, 50–51). The pathos of this poem's longing for an encounter with beings who are not in any danger from the possessiveness, the self-interest, or the messy human inadequacy of our desire for contact with them is enormous as it resonates against the fifty-year career of a poet who has used both poems and essays to call for the kinds of human encounters that might address the difficulties of a "difficult world" with clarity and compassion.

If a telephone is ringing in the labyrinth, then who is the intended recipient of its peremptory summons? If she decides it's for her, will she be able to find her way to the phone before it stops ringing? Even if she gets there in time, a telephone conversation is a machine-mediated exchange that will distort her caller's voice and emphasize their physical separation. We have to use the telephone because we are in different locations—on different sides of the country perhaps, or even the world. The title poem begins by addressing, it seems, some particular person of the poet's acquaintance—"You who can be silent in twelve languages"—but then its surreal opening section unfolds an "I-you" relation that is complexly mediated, wordless, and at best hypothetical. "You" are depicted walking along the shoulder of a highway at sunset, "after the car broke down"—somewhere in the United States presumably, but the location is not specified—while "I" am accidentally breaking a bowl "by midsummer nightsun in, say, Reykjavík" (*Telephone*, 99).[13] Perhaps you have "sighted" me in your rearview mirror; perhaps the "convex reflection" in one of the shards of the bowl that has just been broken has "caught you walking / the slurried highway shoulder . . ." (ibid.). Who are these people, and what is their relationship to each other? Is the geographic distance between them symbolic of other kinds of distance; is it deliberately chosen or merely circumstantial? In subsequent sections of the poem there is just as little information as to who is speaking and who is being addressed. In section iv, in the context of what appears to be an erotic encounter in a hotel room, the telephone rings and one of "us" says, or thinks, "(Don't stop! . . . they'll call again . . .)" (*Telephone*, 102). Is it the telephone in the poem's title that is ringing? If so, are the poem's "dialogic urgencies" being impeded or furthered by the decision to ignore its summons?[14]

In most of the poems in this volume so little is done to identify or "locate" the one who is speaking that the onus is on us to give his or her predicament a context: such poems are reading *us*, in effect, by testing our capacity to do so.[15] Their purpose seems to be to distill the essential dynamics of situations that are symptomatic of the trouble we are in, both as Americans and as citizens of a wider world: the disorientation of immigrants who have "seen [their] world wiped clean" (in "Behind the Motel"); the impact of economic globalization (in "Voyage to the Denouement") and of natural disasters inadequately foreseen and addressed ("The University Reopens as the Floods Recede"); the legacy of a war that sends its veterans home with their spirits shattered and parts of their bodies gone (in "Calibrations"). The speaker of a balladlike poem entitled "Rhyme" has returned to find nothing left of the place she or he called home (the refrain changes each time it is used, beginning with "O tell me this is home" and ending with "So tell me where is my home"). Instead of telling us what happened to bring this about, the poem ends with the question "so what happened here so what / are the facts . . ." (*Telephone*, 44–45). That its questions go unpunctuated enhances the impression of a speaker who is not fully present and a "rhyme" that has not been fully voiced.

Throughout the volume even poems that carry dedications to indicate that the "you" being addressed is someone in particular stage acts of communication that are attenuated and ghostly. In "Via Insomnia," a poem addressed to the poet Tory Dent within a few weeks or months after her death,[16] it is impossible to distinguish cleanly between an "I" (presumably Rich) who is speaking and the "you" (presumably Dent) who was a friend of hers. It is "you" whose voice gets the poem going in the first place—"Called up in sleep: your voice: / *I don't know where I am* . . . ." But the speaker's encounter with that voice on the "via insomnia" gives her a premonition of what her own death might be like, in the context of which their voices become eerily interchangeable as the deictic force of "you" is broadened to encompass them both: *"you don't know where you are // Is this how it is to be newly dead?"* (*Telephone,* 81).

As of the summer of 2008, Anne Sexton has been dead for thirty-four years and Sylvia Plath for forty-five. Yet in contrast with the abstracted, ghostly voice that speaks from many of the poems in Rich's latest volume, Sexton and Plath are even more distinctly audible now than when they were alive to read their poems aloud. If, as Christopher MacGowan has suggested in a recently published guide to *Twentieth-Century American Poetry*, the "neo-confessional" lyric was predominant throughout the second half of the twentieth century in mainstream poetry journals and creative writing programs, then these two poets, along with W. D. Snodgrass and Robert Lowell, have left a powerful legacy.[17] It is a legacy that has been taken up by both male and female poets; the domestic arena has proven to be a goldmine of exemplary stories whose tellers are men *and* women, fathers *and* mothers, daughters *and* sons. Meanwhile, however, Plath's and Sexton's voices are themselves still with us; the passage of time has confirmed and even strengthened their power to speak from the page.

In Plath's case this is partly owing to the publication of her *Unabridged Journals* in 2000 and Ted Hughes's *Birthday Letters* in 1998; it is also a function of the aura of celebrity that attached itself to such poems as "Daddy" and "Lady Lazarus" as soon as they first appeared in print. But the continued "presence" of Plath's poetic voice is also an achievement of the poems themselves—of their intensely stylized interpersonal gestures and kinesthetically powerful patterns of sound and rhyme. In my upper-level "Women Poets" seminar this past spring my students asked me as we came to the end of a month-long unit on Plath to read her poem "Daddy" aloud. "We want you to sound like Plath," one of them said, to gloss their collective request. I can do a passable imitation of Plath's recorded voice, but I think what they were really asking for was a live performance of our collective readerly intimacy with the poem: *"You do not **do**, you **do** not **do** / Any more, **black shoe** . . . ."* Plath's late poems have flourished posthumously in a state of undeadness that continues to claim successive generations of woman readers; we keep them alive by lending them our own life's blood.

Sexton's voice is still vividly audible for different reasons. Her poems' performance of mid-century suburban American femininity stays in the past, but it belongs to a historical moment we are very much inclined just now to revisit, on television and in the movies. If that performance seems "dated," so much the more successfully does it recall a particular moment in the twentieth-century history of American gender relations. In one of her elegies for Sexton, Maxine Kumin says to the friend she has missed so much, "You haven't changed. / I, on the other hand, am forced to grow older."[18] Like Kumin, Brooks and Rich were "forced to grow older," but Sexton is still the desperate housewife whose problem can be known but not yet named; her poems still speak to us from within a way of being female whose historical moment has passed, but is currently enjoying a kind of "retro" stylishness.

Both here and throughout this book as a whole, I confess to having overemphasized the extent to which lyric poetry sponsors the illusion of a speaking voice; I have said comparatively little about the capacity poems also have to withhold "voice," and with it the illusion of a self or soul made present in the act of reading. As the L=A=N=G=U=A=G=E poets, among others, have emphasized, a poem can also make us aware of the ownerlessness of written or printed speech and the extent to which we are always being spoken by prefabricated discourses, "found" phrases, clichés of all kinds. Rich's latest volume calls attention not only to the fragility of the "I-you" relationship, but also to its fictive, hypothetical status and to a variety of ways in which that relationship can be hollowed out or attenuated. And yet the withholding of voice would not be a powerful gesture if we did not "crave" what is being withheld. When all is said and done, "you" and "I" are the words that most enable poems to matter to us.

NOTES

INTRODUCTION

1. *The Poet Speaks: Interviews with Contemporary Poets,* ed. Peter Orr (London: Routledge, 1966), 168. The interview took place on October 30, 1962, a few months before Plath ended her life. She had written almost a poem a day during that October, including "Daddy," "Lady Lazarus," and "Ariel."

2. I am indebted to Barbara Johnson for this piece of ephemera, which she cites in *The Feminist Difference: Literature, Psychoanalysis, Race, and Gender* (Cambridge, Mass.: Harvard University Press, 1998), 102, in a chapter on the French poet Marceline Desbordes-Valmore.

3. Alicia Ostriker also discusses the problematic status of the "poetess" in her introduction to *Stealing the Language: The Emergence of Women's Poetry in America* (Boston: Beacon Press, 1986), a pioneering study that takes a broad thematic approach to the emergence of women's poetry in America post-1960.

4. *The Unabridged Journals of Sylvia Plath, 1950–1962,* ed. Karen V. Kukil (New York: Anchor Books, 2000), 360. The mixture of admiration and jealousy in this passage is vintage Plath, yet not unusual among the women poets of this and earlier generations. As Betsy Erkkila points out in *The Wicked Sisters: Women Poets, Literary History and Discord* (New York and Oxford: Oxford University Press, 1992), claiming a female lineage by no means precludes thinking of female mentors and sister poets as rivals.

5. The first poem in the volume is an elegy for a friend and fellow poet who was killed in Germany in 1945, but "the birth in a narrow room" is the poem that opens "The Childhood and the Girlhood" by getting the volume's protagonist born.

6. In chapter 4, my account of Brooks's poetic formation will stress the interweaving of compliance and resistance in her response to mentors and editors.

7. My project differs from those of both James Breslin, in *From Modern to Contemporary: American Poetry, 1945–1965* (Chicago: University of Chicago Press, 1984), and Thomas Travisano, in *Midcentury Quartet: Bishop, Lowell, Jarrell, Berryman, and the Making of a Postmodern Aesthetic* (Charlottesville: University Press of Virginia, 1999). Although my four poets do belong to roughly the same midcentury generation, my reason for bringing them together is not that they shared a particular set of aesthetic objectives, as Travisano argues for his quartet, nor that each of them represents a "major innovating movement of the late fifties," as in Breslin's study, but that they all came of age as poets at a moment of significant intersection between the history of American poetry and the history of gender relations.

8. Adrienne Rich, *The Fact of a Doorframe: Poems Selected and New 1950–1984* (New York: W. W. Norton, 1984), xv.

9. My first chapter will look more closely at Rich's attempt to construct a gender-neutral stance in her first two published volumes, *A Change of World* (New Haven, Conn.: Yale University Press, 1951) and *The Diamond Cutters* (New York: Harper, 1955).

10. Feminist critics who have done important work with this topic already include Jan Clausen, Joanne Feit Diehl, Elizabeth Dodd, Betsy Erkkila, Karen Ford, Sandra Gilbert and Susan Gubar, Cynthia Hogue, Margaret Homans, Suzanne Juhasz, Linda Kinnahan, Helena Michie, Jan Montefiore, Cheryl Walker, Lesley Wheeler, Kim Whitehead, and Liz Yorke. I will be citing their work where it bears directly on the poems and poets my study is concerned with, but must acknowledge a more diffuse and pervasive debt to their engagement with the institutional politics of poetic authority and poetic stance.

11. Cited in Richard Gray, *American Poetry of the Twentieth Century* (New York: Longman, 1990), 223.

12. In *Poetry's Touch: On Lyric Address* (Ithaca, N.Y.: Cornell University Press, 2003), William Waters points out that "poetry is, of all the ways we use language, the one with the most tenuous relation to a context of use" (10). The term "self-focused" is from "Linguistics and Poetics," Roman Jakobson's classic account of "the poetic function of language": *Selected Writings* (The Hague: Mouton, 1981), 18–51.

13. Susan Stewart arrestingly glosses this complexity in suggesting that "when speakers speak from the position of listeners, when thought is unattributable and intention wayward, the situation of poetry is evoked" ("Lyric Possession," *Critical Inquiry*, 22 [Autumn 1995]: 34).

14. John Stuart Mill, "What Is Poetry?" in *Essays on Poetry*, ed. F. Parvin Sharpless (Columbia: University of South Carolina Press, 1976), 12. Herbert Tucker points out that Mill was giving "a memorable but by no means unique voice" to a "subjectivist" approach that "governed the reading of English poetry circa 1830" and has persisted into the present. Cf. "Dramatic Monologue and the Overhearing of Lyric," in *Lyric Poetry: Beyond New Criticism*, ed. Chaviva Hosek and Patricia Parker (Ithaca, N.Y.: Cornell University Press, 1985), 226–27.

15. T. S. Eliot, *The Three Voices of Poetry* (New York: Cambridge University Press, 1954), 27, 33 (Eliot's emphasis).

16. Northrop Frye, *Anatomy of Criticism* (Princeton, N.J.: Princeton University Press, 1957), 271, 249.

17. Jonathan Culler, "Apostrophe," in *The Pursuit of Signs* (Ithaca, N.Y.: Cornell University Press, 1981), 142.

18. Charles Altieri, *Canons and Consequences: Reflections on the Ethical Force of Imaginative Ideals* (Evanston, Ill.: Northwestern University Press, 1990), 133–34.

19. Ann Keniston, "'The Fluidity of Damaged Form': Apostrophe and Desire in Nineties Lyric," *Contemporary Literature* 42, no. 2 (Summer 2001): 307.

20. Virginia Jackson, "Dickinson's Figure of Address," in *Dickinson and Audience*, ed. Martin Orzeck and Robert Weisbuch (Ann Arbor: University of Michigan Press, 1996), 79; cf. *Dickinson's Misery* (Princeton, N.J.: Princeton University Press, 2005), 128.

21. Helen Vendler, *Poems, Poets, Poetry: An Introduction and Anthology* (Boston: St. Martin's Press, 1997), x–xi.

22. Cf. Vendler, *The Art of Shakespeare's Sonnets* (Cambridge, Mass.: Harvard University Press, 1997), 18: "The words of a poem are not 'overheard' (as in the formulations of J. S. Mill and T. S. Eliot); this would make the reader an eavesdropping voyeur of the writer's sensations." But Vendler has arguably misconstrued what Mill and Eliot have in mind; according to Jackson's, Altieri's, and Keniston's construal of the reader's relationship to the poem that is overheard, the reader is *drawn into* the poem by its speaker's supposed unconsciousness of having an audience.

23. In *The Three Genres and the Interpretation of Lyric* (Princeton, N.J.: Princeton University Press, 1983), William Elford Rogers elaborates Vendler's claim that the lyric "I" is an alter ego for the reader by citing Hans-Georg Gadamer's conception of a fusion of horizons and George Poulet's phenomenological account of the experience of reading, in which "I mentally pronounce an *I*, and yet the *I* which I pronounce is not myself" (cited in Rogers, 53, from Poulet, "Criticism and the Experience of Interiority," in *The Structuralist Controversy* [1972]).

24. In *Lyric Poetry: The Pain and the Pleasure of Words* (Princeton, N.J.: Princeton University Press, 2007), Mutlu Konuk Blasing uses this definition of lyric poetry's generic distinctiveness to argue that "the lyric presents us with poetic language per se," and thus with "the otherness of the material medium of language to all that humans do with it—refer, represent, express, narrate, imitate, communicate, think, reason, theorize, philosophize" (2). Blasing argues that the "I"-position "is occupied by anyone reading or speaking a poem" (29), but for Blasing the poem's "I" is standing in not for a person whose purpose is to communicate but for the very possibility that language can have such a purpose. Blasing's approach to lyric "subjectivity" is thus very much at odds not only with Vendler's but also with my own. The only twentieth-century poet her study and mine have in common is Anne Sexton, whose "hysterical" relationship to language is the subject of Blasing's chapter 8.

25. W. R. Johnson, *The Idea of Lyric: Lyric Modes in Ancient and Modern Poetry* (Berkeley: University of California Press, 1982), 3 ff.

26. In the poetry of Mallarmé's epigones, among whom Johnson numbers Gottfried Benn, "it is very seldom that we meet with a You of any kind, nor are we likely ever to encounter an authentic I" (Johnson, *The Idea of Lyric*, 12).

27. Ibid., 19–21.

28. Cf. Barbara Johnson, "Apostrophe, Animation, and Abortion," in *A World of Difference* (Baltimore, Md.: Johns Hopkins University Press, 1987), 184–99.

29. Louise Glück, *Ararat* (Hopewell, N.J.: Ecco Press, 1990), 15.

30. *Poems, Poets, Poetry*, 179. Vendler is alluding to W. B. Yeats's memorable dictum that we make rhetoric out of the quarrel with others, poetry out of the quarrel with ourselves.

31. Glück is on record as having "a conscious preference for a poetry of intimate and urgent address," as Bruce Bond notes in his review essay in the *New England Review* 14, no. 1 (Fall 1991): 219. "My preference from the beginning," she explains in "Education of the Poet," "has been the poetry that requests or craves a listener" (*Proofs and Theories: Essays on Poetry* [Hopewell, N.J.: Ecco Press, 1994], 4).

32. Jonathan Holden, *The Rhetoric of the Contemporary Lyric* (Bloomington: Indiana University Press, 1980), 55.

33. Glück, *Ararat*, 34–35; Keniston, "Apostrophe and Desire in Nineties Lyric," 307.

34. *Dark Fields of the Republic: Poems 1991–1995* (New York: W. W. Norton, 1995), 4; repr. in *The Fact of a Doorframe: Selected Poems 1950–2001* (New York: W. W. Norton, 2002), 253. Readers will find it worthwhile to consult the entire poem in the opening section of the former volume, where it appears among poems that share its formal strategies and thematic emphasis.

35. Will "people" then be in a stronger position than we are now relative to "the great dark birds of history"? Perhaps this is what history becomes if we cease to be capable of grasping the historical import of our personal lives. Ann Keniston finds an allusion to Walter Benjamin's "angel of history," who is "condemned helplessly to witness a past he cannot repair"; but if so, the pathos of the angel's helplessness has not found its way into the poem. Keniston, "'To feel with a human stranger': Adrienne Rich's Post-Holocaust Confession and the Limits of Identification," in *Modern Confessional Writing: New Critical Essays*, ed. Jo Gill (London and New York: Routledge, 2006), 59.

36. *An Atlas of the Difficult World: Poems 1988–1991* (New York: W. W. Norton, 1991), 25; repr. in *The Fact of a Doorframe: Selected Poems 1950–2001*, 235. The poem is dated 1990–91.

37. *What Is Found There: Notebooks on Poetry and Politics* (New York: W. W. Norton, 1993), xiv.

38. Other critics who have discussed these "Dedications" include Joshua S. Jacobs, who suggests in "'An Atlas of the Difficult World': Adrienne Rich's Countermonument," *Contemporary Literature* 42, no. 4 (Winter 2001) that they are a monument to the capacity for "powerfully self-defining acts of reading" even among "people who might seem unconnected to a broader community" (745). Cf. also Alice Templeton, *The Dream and the Dialogue: Adrienne Rich's Feminist Poetics* (Knoxville: University of Tennessee Press, 1994), 163, and Cynthia Hogue, *Scheming Women: Poetry, Privilege, and the Politics of Subjectivity* (Albany, N.Y.: SUNY Press, 1995), 196–200.

39. Robert Pinsky takes a more conventional approach to conjuring up an interlocutor for "An Explanation of America," a poem that, like "An Atlas of the Difficult World," reconsiders what it means to be an American citizen at the end of the twentieth century. Pinsky dedicates the poem to his daughter as a personally beloved member of the next generation of Americans—or, as he says in its "Prologue," "If not to you then to my idea of you." *The Figured Wheel: New and Collected Poems, 1966–1996* (New York: Farrar, Straus and Giroux, 1996), 161.

40. I am giving "Dedications" an edgier reading than Rich herself did in an interview with Bill Moyers in *The Language of Life: A Festival of Poets* (New York: Doubleday, 1995), excerpted in Cary Nelson's on-line MAPS project (http://www.english.uiuc.edu/maps/index.htm).

41. Jahan Ramazani, *Poetry of Mourning: The Modern Elegy from Hardy to Heaney* (Chicago: University Chicago Press, 1994).

42. Helen Vendler, *Coming of Age as a Poet: Milton, Keats, Eliot, Plath* (Cambridge, Mass.: Harvard University Press, 2003), 118; 1.

43. Sylvia Plath, "The Colossus," in *The Collected Poems* (New York: Harper and Row, 1981), 129–30 (my emphasis).

44. Leonard M. Scigaj, "The Painterly Plath That Nobody Knows," *Centennial Review*, 32 (1988): 249.

45. Cited in Diane Middlebrook, *Anne Sexton: A Biography* (Boston: Houghton Mifflin, 1991), 199.

46. Middlebrook, *Anne Sexton*, 200; cf. Ramazani, *Poetry of Mourning*, 309.

47. Anne Sexton, "Sylvia's Death," in *The Complete Poems of Anne Sexton, with a Foreword by Maxine Kumin* (Boston: Houghton Mifflin, 1981), 126–28.

48. Sexton, "For John, Who Begs Me Not to Enquire Further," in *The Complete Poems*, 35. I will be discussing this poem at greater length in chapter 1.

49. Gwendolyn Brooks, "when you have forgotten Sunday: the love story," in *A Street in Bronzeville* (New York: Harper, 1945); repr. in *BLACKS* (Chicago: Third World Press, 1987), 36–37.

50. Cf. *Report from Part Two* (Chicago: Third World Press, 1996), 96.

CHAPTER 1

1. The parenthetically cited page numbers for Sexton's poems in this chapter refer to *The Complete Poems of Anne Sexton, with a Foreword by Maxine Kumin* (Boston: Houghton Mifflin, 1981), hereafter abbreviated *The Complete Poems* or *CP*. "The Double Image" is from Sexton's first volume, *To Bedlam and Part Way Back*, which was published in 1960; it begins on page 35 in *The Complete Poems*.

2. In her 1971 volume *Transformations* Sexton introduces herself as "a middle-aged witch . . . tangled on my two great arms, / my face in a book / and my mouth wide, / ready to tell you a story or two" (*The Complete Poems*, 223).

3. Adrienne Rich, "When We Dead Awaken: Writing as Re-Vision," in *On Lies, Secrets, and Silence: Selected Prose 1966–1978* (New York: W. W. Norton, 1979), 44, hereafter abbreviated as *OLSS*.

4. Cf. John Crowe Ransom, "Emily Dickinson: A Poet Restored," *Perspectives (USA)* (Spring 1956), and R. P. Blackmur, "Emily Dickinson's Notation," *Kenyon Review*, 18 (1956); both repr. in *Emily Dickinson: A Collection of Critical Essays*, ed. Richard B. Sewall (Englewood Cliffs, N.J.: Prentice-Hall, 1963). In an even more notorious essay of Ransom's, "The Poet as Woman" (1937), Millay serves as his chief avatar of the woman poet. As Cheryl Walker points out in *Masks Outrageous and Austere: Culture, Psyche and Persona in Modern Women Poets* (Bloomington: Indiana University Press, 1991), Ransom "is condescending in the extreme toward women poets, whom he treats very much as a nineteenth-century anthropologist might treat an elusive tribe of aborigines" (5). Walker notes that Marianne Moore is the one female poet he "exempts from his critique" (7).

5. W. H. Auden, "Foreword" to Adrienne Rich, *A Change of World* (New Haven, Conn.: Yale University Press, 1951), 10; repr. in Barbara Charlesworth Gelpi and Albert Gelpi, eds., *Adrienne Rich's Poetry and Prose: A Norton Critical Edition* (New York: W. W. Norton, 1993), 277–79.

6. "Shakspeare; or, the Poet," in *Representative Men* (1850), repr. in *Ralph Waldo Emerson: Essays and Lectures* (New York: The Library of America, 1983), 710–26. This phrase appears in the essay's opening paragraph.

7. In "Consorting with Angels," a 1963 poem I will be discussing later in this chapter, Sexton pronounces herself "tired of the gender of things."

8. Betty Friedan, *The Feminine Mystique* (New York: W. W. Norton, 1963); see esp. chapter 1: "The Happy Housewife Heroine."

9. Barbara Ehrenreich, *The Hearts of Men: American Dreams and the Flight from Commitment* (New York: Anchor/Doubleday, 1983), 42–51.

10. Robert von Hallberg, *American Poetry and Culture 1945–1980* (Cambridge, Mass.: Harvard University Press, 1985), 30–35. The poem appeared in Hollander's first published volume, *A Crackling of Thorns* (New Haven, Conn.: Yale University Press, 1958), 32–33.

11. Rich, "Autumn Equinox," *The Diamond Cutters* (New York: Harper, 1955); repr. in *Poems Selected and New, 1950–1974* (New York: W. W. Norton, 1975), 22–26.

12. "'To Speak of Woe That Is in Marriage,'" *Life Studies and For the Union Dead* (New York: Farrar, Straus and Giroux, 1964), 88; repr. in *Robert Lowell: Collected Poems*, ed. Frank Bidart and David Gewanter (New York: Farrar, Straus and Giroux, 2003), 190.

13. Judith McDaniel, "Reconstituting the World: The Poetry and Vision of Adrienne Rich" (Argyle, N.Y.: Spinster's Ink, 1978); repr. in Gelpi and Gelpi, *Adrienne Rich's Poetry and Prose*, 314.

14. McDaniel, ibid.

15. Denise Levertov, *The Poet in the World* (New York: New Directions, 1973), 110.

16. Rich, *Poems Selected and New, 1950–1974*, 247.

17. Rich, "When We Dead Awaken," *OLSS*, 40.

18. "For the Conjunction of Two Planets," *A Change of World*, 83 (thus positioned to be the volume's closing poem); repr. in *The Fact of a Doorframe: Poems Selected and New 1950–1984* (New York: W. W. Norton, 1984), 8–9.

19. "Storm Warnings," repr. in *The Fact of a Doorframe: Selected Poems 1950–2001* (New York: W. W. Norton, 2002), 3.

20. Interestingly, both Willard Spiegelman and Deborah Pope construe this speaker's attitude as timid and/or defensive and her gender as female: "In 'Storm Warnings,'" says Spiegelman, "a girl shuns the fluctuations in the external and internal climates." *The Didactic Muse: Scenes of Instruction in Contemporary American Poetry* (Princeton, N.J.: Princeton University Press, 1989), 151. "The 'troubled regions' of *A Change of World* were the poet's struggles to live in the world as a woman," infers Pope in *A Separate Vision: Isolation in Contemporary Women's Poetry* (Baton Rouge: Louisiana State University Press, 1984), 123. I would argue (contra Spiegelman) that this poem's "I" and its "we" are as adult as Rich can make them sound, and (contra Pope) that, as Auden saw, the poem endeavors to stake out territory that is generically human, "the typical experiences of *our* time" (my emphasis).

21. *A Change of World*, 11; Gelpi and Gelpi, *Adrienne Rich's Poetry and Prose*, 278–79.

22. Rich, "When We Dead Awaken," *OLSS*, 44–45.

23. Rich, "Snapshots of a Daughter-in-Law," repr. in *The Fact of a Doorframe: Selected Poems 1950–2001*, 17–21.

24. Claire Keyes, "'The Angels Chiding': *Snapshots of a Daughter-in-Law*," in *Reading Adrienne Rich: Reviews and Re-Visions, 1951–81*, ed. Jane Roberta Cooper (Ann Arbor: University of Michigan Press, 1984), 49. In *The Aesthetics of Power: The Poetry of Adrienne Rich* (Athens: University of Georgia Press, 1986) her book-length study of Rich's career up to 1980, Keyes changed the emphasis in her chapter on this same volume, but I still find her earlier reading persuasive.

25. Rich, *Snapshots of a Daughter-in-Law* (New York: W. W. Norton, 1963), 39.

26. Rich, "A Marriage in the Sixties," repr. in *The Fact of a Doorframe: Poems Selected and New 1950–1984*, 44–45.

27. Rich, "The Roofwalker," repr. in *The Fact of a Doorframe: Selected Poems 1950–2001*, 17–21.

28. Denise Levertov, *Poems 1960–67* (New York: New Directions, 1983), 51–52. At poetry readings, Rich has explained this poem's dedication as an acknowledgment that in the early 1960s she and Levertov were both beginning to try for a looser, freer poetic line.

29. Rich, "Power and Danger: Works of a Common Woman," *OLSS*, 248. This essay was written to introduce *The Work of a Common Woman: The Collected Poetry of Judy Grahn, 1964–1977* (New York: St. Martin's Press, 1978).

30. Rich, "Anne Sexton: 1928–1974," *OLSS*, 121.

31. Sexton, "Music Swims Back to Me," *The Complete Poems*, 6.

32. Alicia Ostriker, *Stealing the Language: The Emergence of Women's Poetry in America* (Boston: Beacon Press, 1986), 205, 209. In *The Cure of Poetry in an Age of Prose: Moral Essays on the Poet's Calling* (Chicago: University of Chicago Press, 1993), Mary Kinzie censures this strategy in the context of pronouncing Sexton to be a very bad poet indeed: "in Sexton," Kinzie observes, "we have a writer . . . whose mask of com-

pulsive confidentiality we are asked to admire" but "whose literary judgment we are never invited to test" (54).

33. Letter from Schopenhauer to Goethe dated 1815, excerpted by Sexton for the epigraph of *To Bedlam and Part Way Back* (*The Complete Poems*, 2).

34. "How It Was: Maxine Kumin on Anne Sexton," *The Complete Poems*, xxiv.

35. Diane Middlebrook, *Anne Sexton: A Biography* (Boston: Houghton Mifflin, 1991), 101.

36. Maxine Kumin, "How It Was," *The Complete Poems*, xxiii.

37. As Susan David Bernstein points out in *Confessional Subjects: Revelations of Gender and Power in Victorian Literature and Culture* (Chapel Hill: University of North Carolina Press, 1997), "confession never occurs outside of particular relationships marked by privilege and dependence, authority and vulnerability" (xi). In her essay on Ted Hughes's *Birthday Letters* for a recently published volume of essays, *Modern Confessional Writing* (London: Routledge, 2006), Jo Gill appositely quotes Foucault's *History of Sexuality, Volume One*: "For Foucault 'one does not confess without the presence (or virtual presence) of a partner who . . . requires the confession, prescribes and appreciates it, and intervenes in order to judge, punish, forgive, console, and reconcile'" (69).

38. Cf. Alicia Ostriker, "Anne Sexton and the Seduction of the Audience," in *Sexton: Selected Criticism*, ed. Diana Hume George (Urbana: University of Illinois Press, 1988), 5. This essay includes the best discussion I have found of Sexton's interlocutory strategy as she used it to get hold of "the complexity of intimate relationships."

39. Sexton, *The Complete Poems*, 15.

40. Sexton, "Said the Poet to the Analyst," *CP*, 12–13.

41. Rich, "An Unsaid Word," *A Change of World*, repr. in *The Fact of a Doorframe: Poems Selected and New 1950–1984*, 5.

42. Ian Hamilton, *Robert Lowell: A Biography* (New York: Random House, 1982), 182.

43. Hamilton, *Robert Lowell*, 80; Linda Gray Sexton, *Searching for Mercy Street* (Boston: Little, Brown, 1994), 44–46, 87–88.

44. Robert Lowell, "91 Revere Street," *Life Studies and For the Union Dead*, 19; repr. in *Robert Lowell: Collected Poems*, 127–28.

45. See esp. Elaine Tyler May, *Homeward Bound: American Families in the Cold War Era* (New York: Basic Books, 1988).

46. Betty Friedan, *The Feminine Mystique, With a New Introduction and Epilogue by the Author* (New York: Dell, 1983), 38.

47. Lowell, "Man and Wife," *Life Studies and For the Union Dead*, 94; repr. in *Collected Poems*, 189.

48. Steven Gould Axelrod, *Robert Lowell: Life and Art* (Princeton, N.J.: Princeton University Press, 1978), 112. Axelrod is quoting Frederick Seidel's interview with Lowell in *The Paris Review*, 25 (1961), repr. in *Collected Prose by Robert Lowell*, ed. Robert Giroux (New York: Farrar, Straus and Giroux, 1987), 235–66 (cf. esp. 247).

49. "Tamed by *Miltown*, we lie on Mother's bed" is the opening line of "Man and Wife"; "the tranquillized *Fifties*" and the quoted phrase "'hardly passionate Marlborough Street'" (which originated either with Henry or William James) are in the immediately preceding poem, "Memories of West Street and Lepke," which begins Part II of *Life Studies*; repr. in *Collected Poems*, 187.

50. "'To Speak of Woe That Is in Marriage,'" *Life Studies and For the Union Dead*, 95; *Collected Poems*, 190.

51. Richard Tillinghast, *Robert Lowell's Life and Work: Damaged Grandeur* (Ann Arbor: University of Michigan Press, 1995), 67.

52. The original wording of the passage Lowell reworked for his epigraph from *The World as Will and Idea* is provided in the Notes to his *Collected Poems*, 1045.

53. Hamilton, *Robert Lowell*, 265, and cf. Terri Witek, *Robert Lowell and Life Studies: Revising the Self* (Columbia, Mo.: University of Missouri Press, 1993), 89–93.

54. Lawrence Kramer, "Freud and the Skunks: Genre and Language in *Life Studies*," in *Robert Lowell: Essays on the Poetry*, ed. Steven Gould Axelrod and Helen Deese (Cambridge: Cambridge University Press, 1986), 82.

55. Lowell, "Grandparents," *Life Studies and For the Union Dead*, 69; *Collected Poems*, 170.

56. "We think of the key, each in his prison, / Thinking of the key, each confirms a prison . . ." "The Waste Land," line 413. *American Poetry: The Twentieth Century* (New York: Penguin Putnam, 2000), 1:755.

57. Lowell, "Dunbarton," *Life Studies and For the Union Dead*, 67; *Collected Poems*, 169.

58. Tillinghast, *Damaged Grandeur*, 8.

59. Brett Millier, *Elizabeth Bishop: Life and the Memory of It* (Berkeley: University of California Press, 1993), 295, ctd. in Tillinghast, *Damaged Grandeur*, 9.

60. Cf. Tillinghast, *Damaged Grandeur*, 9.

61. Ibid., 89.

62. Lawrence Kramer, "Freud and the Skunks," 83.

63. Ibid., 82.

64. Ctd. in Middlebrook, *Anne Sexton: A Biography*, 92. Middlebrook suggests (94) that Lowell "validated" the woman's voice Sexton was developing in such poems as "The Double Image"; she notes, however, that the mostly male-authored poetry Sexton was reading in the seminar made her feel ashamed of having learned how to write poetry in the first place from "minor" poets such as Edna St. Vincent Millay.

65. *The Complete Poems*, 117–18; the poem is dated May 1963.

66. "A Marriage in the Sixties" (dated 1961), originally published in *Snapshots of a Daughter-in Law*; repr. in *The Fact of a Doorframe: Poems Selected and New 1950–1984*, 44–45.

67. Sexton, "The Double Image," *CP*, 35–42.

68. In *Sincerity's Shadow: Self-Consciousness in British Romantic and Mid-Twentieth-Century American Poetry* (Cambridge, Mass.: Harvard University Press, 2004), Deborah Forbes also calls attention to the transgressiveness of this poem's apostrophe: "because we know that Joy is a real person with her own life history, the artificiality of the mode of address here becomes uncomfortably close to reality, with disturbing implications beyond the boundaries of the poem" (142).

69. In *Searching for Mercy Street* (58–60), Linda Gray Sexton recalls a role-reversal game her mother played with her when she was nine: the memory, which is emblematic as well as "real," is of being terrified by her mother's reluctance to end the game and reassume her maternal role.

70. Kramer, "Freud and the Skunks," 82.

71. In "Lyrical Voice in Contemporary Theory: Riffaterre and Jauss," De Man deems it "beyond question that the figure of address is recurrent in lyric poetry, to the point of constituting the generic definition of, at the very least, the ode (which can, in its turn, be seen as paradigmatic for poetry in general)." *Lyric Poetry: Beyond New Criticism*, ed. Chaviva Hosek and Patricia Parker (Ithaca, N.Y.: Cornell University Press, 1985), 61. I have already engaged Culler's version of this argument in my Introduction. In "Reading Lyric," *Yale French Studies*, 69 (1985): 98–106, Culler acknowledges indebtedness to a 1979 essay of De Man's, "Autobiography as De-Facement" (*MLN* 94, no. 5 (1979): 919–30; repr. in *The Rhetoric of Romanticism* [New York: Columbia University Press, 1984], 67–92). Cf. Johnson, "Apostrophe, Animation, and Abortion," in *A World of Difference* (Baltimore, Md.: Johns Hopkins University Press, 1987), 184–99 (also cited in the Introduction).

72. W. D. Snodgrass, *Heart's Needle* (New York: Knopf, 1959), 48; repr. in *Selected*

Poems, 1957–1987 (New York: Soho Press, 1987), 36.

73. Cf. esp. Mary Ann Doane, "Film and the Masquerade: Theorising the Female Spectator," *SCREEN*, 23 (1982): 74–87; repr. in *Feminism and Film*, ed. E. Ann Kaplan (Oxford: Oxford University Press 2000), 418–36.

74. Sexton, "Cinderella," *CP*, 255.

75. Sylvia Plath, *The Collected Poems*, ed. Ted Hughes (New York: Harper and Row, 1981), 129; the poem is dated 1959.

76. Plath, "Electra on Azalea Path," *The Collected Poems*, 117 (this poem is also dated 1959).

77. "Nobody died or withered on that stage" is a line from "Electra on Azalea Path" (*The Collected Poems*, 116); later in the same poem, "The stony actors poise and pause for breath."

78. Rich, "Twenty-One Love Poems," xviii; repr. in *The Fact of a Doorframe: Selected Poems, 1950–2001*, 143.

CHAPTER 2

1. *The Fact of a Doorframe: Selected Poems 1950–2001* (New York: W. W. Norton, 2002), hereafter abbreviated *FD* 2002, will be cited where possible for the poems discussed in this chapter. Poems not included in that volume will be cited from *The Fact of a Doorframe: Poems Selected and New 1950–1984* (New York: W. W. Norton, 1984), hereafter abbreviated *FD* 1984, or from *Poems Selected and New, 1950–1974* (New York: W. W. Norton, 1975). Poems not included in any of these collections will be referred to the volume in which they were originally published.

2. These are the first two lines of Shakespeare's sonnet 22.

3. Cf. Stephen Matterson in his essay on *Life Studies* for the Blackwell *Companion to Twentieth-Century Poetry*, ed. Neil Roberts (Oxford: Blackwell, 2001), 482: "Most significantly in terms of the book's immediate influence, these poems came across as naked representations of personal experiences."

4. This is the title Rich gave to the third of the three sections into which *The Dream of a Common Language: Poems 1974–1977* (New York: W. W. Norton, 1978), is divided; it is also the title of the leadoff poem in that section.

5. For a discussion of the issues raised by a feminist stance of witness that is especially attentive to Rich's goals in this regard and to the relationship between witness and consciousness-raising, see Harriet Davidson, "Poetry, Witness, Feminism," in *Witness and Memory: The Discourse of Trauma*, ed. Ana Douglass and Thomas A. Vogler (New York: Routledge, 2003), 153–72.

6. "Trying to Talk with a Man," dated 1971, was published as the leadoff poem in *Diving into the Wreck* in 1973 (*FD* 2002, 93–94).

7. "Notes toward a Politics of Location," *Blood, Bread, and Poetry: Selected Prose 1979–1985* (New York: W. W. Norton, 1986), 224 (hereafter abbreviated *BBP*). In *The Feminist Poetry Movement* (Jackson, Miss.: University Press of Mississippi, 1996), Kim Whitehead thinks through the politics of voice and address in ways I have found helpful, especially in her chapter on Judy Grahn. Other feminist critics who have done valuable work with these issues include Jan Clausen in *A Movement of Poets: Thoughts on Poetry and Feminism* (Brooklyn, N.Y: Long Haul Press, 1982) and Linda Kinnahan in *Poetics of the Feminine: Authority and Literary Tradition in William Carlos Williams, Mina Loy, Denise Levertov, and Kathleen Fraser* (Cambridge: Cambridge University Press, 1994).

8. Headnote to "Anne Sexton: 1928–1974," in *On Lies, Secrets, and Silence: Selected Prose 1966–1978* (New York: W. W. Norton, 1979), 121 (hereafter cited as *OLSS*).

9. Anne Sexton, *The Complete Poems, with a Foreword by Maxine Kumin* (Boston:

Houghton Mifflin, 1981), 127. This poem's over-the-top deployment of apostrophe was discussed in the Introduction.

10. Sexton, *The Complete Poems*, 15.

11. Sexton, *The Complete Poems*, 77; cf. Diane Wood Middlebrook, *Anne Sexton: A Biography* (Boston: Houghton Mifflin, 1991), 195.

12. Maxine Kumin, "How It Was," in Sexton, *The Complete Poems*, xxviii.

13. *The Complete Poems*, 294–95.

14. Deborah Forbes cites the ending of "Briar Rose" as an example of "the frightening and moving oscillation between poet and persona that makes for [Sexton's] charisma" (149). In *Sincerity's Shadow*, Forbes pairs Sexton and Lord Byron as poets whose "charismatic poetics" refuses to transcend the merely personal, so as to "[imply] that poetry is the irrepressible expression of an unusually intense life" (117).

15. Sexton was the only poet on a panel entitled "The Poet and Extra-literary Criticism" for the New England College English Association in 1962 (cited in Middlebrook, 188).

16. Cf., for example, an apostrophe to Lowell's thirteen-week-old daughter in "Home After Three Months Away" that conjures up the tetrameter couplets of "To His Coy Mistress" to reproach her for "float[ing] my shaving brush / and washcloth in the flush": "Dearest, I cannot loiter here / in lather like a polar bear" (*Collected Poems*, 185).

17. Cf. Plath, "Lady Lazarus," *The Collected Poems*, ed. Ted Hughes (New York: Harper and Row, 1981), 245. "A woman like that" is quoted from "Her Kind" (cf. chapter 1, 35).

18. Middlebrook, 222–23.

19. Interview with Rich, 18 May, 1983, cited in Middlebrook, 296.

20. Letter to Lois Ames dated 30 July, 1968, cited in Middlebrook, 297.

21. A. S. to Joshua Stoller, 25 March, 1970, cited in Middlebrook, 297.

22. Rich's 1971 poem with this title, the leadoff poem in *Diving into the Wreck*, is allegorically situated on a military testing ground (*FD* 2002, 93).

23. Rich, "Sibling Mysteries," *The Dream of a Common Language: Poems 1974–1977* (New York: W. W. Norton, 1978), 52; 49. Cf. "Transcendental Etude," *FD* 1984, 267–68; "Motherhood: The Contemporary Emergency and the Quantum Leap" (1978), *OLSS*, 261; and "Compulsory Heterosexuality and Lesbian Existence" (1980), *BBP*, 32–35.

24. As of the 2002 edition *The Fact of a Doorframe* still includes "Rape" in the selection from *Diving Into the Wreck* that has been chosen to represent this moment in Rich's poetic career. Both Cary Nelson's critique, which I will be citing in some detail, and my own reading of the poem's feminist project can best be weighed by consulting the entire poem at *FD* 2002, 105–6.

25. Helen Vendler, *Part of Nature, Part of Us* (Cambridge, Mass.: Harvard University Press, 1980), 243; Cary Nelson, *Our Last First Poets: Vision and History in Contemporary American Poetry* (Urbana: University of Illinois Press, 1981), 150. Carol Muske recalls in *Women and Poetry: Truth, Autobiography, and the Shape of the Self* (Ann Arbor: University of Michigan Press, 1997) that "Rich was widely attacked by critics" who took the poem to be "an act of linguistic violence against men." Muske argues that "Rich's intent was expository, the revelation of the consciousness of a typical woman, post-sexual trauma" and argues that "statistics bear out [her] portrait of female distrust" (11).

26. Nelson, 153; he is paraphrasing Robert Duncan, whose poetic stance is the subject of *Our Last First Poets'* immediately preceding chapter. The charge of complacency is leveled against Rich's poem on 152.

27. Cf., for example, the study Nelson cites as "an excellent overview of the problems inherent in political poetry," Thomas R. Edwards' *Imagination and Power: A*

Study of Poetry on Public Themes (New York: Oxford University Press, 1971) (cf. Nelson 3, n3). Edwards argues that Yeats's most successful political poem, "Easter 1916," "finds its securest note when it confesses insecurity" (197). Praising a 1953 poem of Lowell's in similar terms, Edwards defines "a serious and responsible mind" in this context as "one which takes public actions . . . as imaginative problems demanding a reflective choice of the self one will adopt to meet the public circumstance" (221).

28. Cf. "Toward a Woman-Centered University" (1973–74), in *OLSS*, 125–56, and esp. "Power and Danger: Works of a Common Woman" (1977), which cites "the mere, immense shift from male to female pronouns" as a transformative act that "lets us hear and see our words in a new dimension" (*OLSS*, 248).

29. For an account of consciousness-raising that is attentive both to its importance for second-wave feminism and to its limitations as a strategy for disclosing the political in the personal, see Hester Eisenstein, *Contemporary Feminist Thought* (Boston: G. K. Hall, 1983), 35–44.

30. "Notes Toward a Politics of Location," *BBP*, 221.

31. Roger Gilbert discusses this poem at some length in "Framing Water: Historical Knowledge in Elizabeth Bishop and Adrienne Rich," *Twentieth Century Literature*, 43 (1997): 144–61. He too finds "Frame" succeeding better than "Rape" with its "language of witness," and suggests that Rich may well have written "Frame" "with criticism of poems like 'Rape' in mind" (n5, 160).

32. An article by Joe Stampleman that appeared on Friday, 4 May, 1990 in the MIT student newspaper, *The Tech*, after Rich had given a poetry reading, speaks of "a well-publicized 1979 court case in which a Boston University student filed charges against police who brutally arrested her for trespassing when she sought shelter from driving snow in one of the university's buildings, while waiting for a bus" (http://www.tech.mit.edu/V110/N24/rich.24a.html).

33. In *Sincerity's Shadow* Deborah Forbes cites "Frame" to exemplify how Rich's poetry often "presents an 'I' that is an almost disembodied self-consciousness about the possibilities and limitations of imaginative sympathy" (20).

34. Harriet Davidson also cites the deictic transgressiveness of this assertion in "I Say I Am There: Siting/Citing the Subject of Feminism and Deconstruction," in *Critical Encounters: Reference and Responsibility in Deconstructive Writing*, ed. Cathy Caruth and Deborah Esch (New Brunswick, N.J.: Rutgers, 1995), but reads its implications differently: see esp. 241–45. Davidson valuably unpacks Rich's usage of the word "location" on 255 ff.

35. *FD* 2002, and cf. Rich's *Notes* to this volume, 315.

36. *What Is Found There: Notebooks on Poetry and Politics* (New York: W. W. Norton, 1993), 33.

37. The first phrase in quotation marks in this sentence is from "North American Time" (dated 1983), a poem whose bitter theme is that the "verbal privilege" accruing to a poet's words can lead to their being (mis)read in the context of subsequent events they had no intention of addressing: "We move but our words stand / become responsible / for more than we intended // and this is verbal privilege" (*FD* 2002, 198).

38. Nick Halpern points out, however, that because Rich has an explicitly prophetic vocation, "too often . . . she seems not like someone who is leading an everyday life but someone who is walking the earth, and the question of the balance between isolation and community will not go away." *Everyday and Prophetic: The Poetry of Lowell, Ammons, Merrill, and Rich* (Madison: University of Wisconsin Press, 2003), 185.

39. Cf. chapter 1 above, n48.

40. Rich, "Caryatid: A Column," *American Poetry Review*, 2 (September–October 1973): 42; repr. as "On *History, For Lizzie and Harriet*, and *The Dolphin*" in *The Criti-*

cal Response to Robert Lowell, ed. Steven Gould Axelrod (Westport, Conn.: Greenwood Press, 1999), 185–87.

41. Lowell, "Dolphin," in *The Dolphin* (1973), *Collected Poems*, ed. Frank Bidart and David Gewanter (New York: Farrar, Straus and Giroux, 2003), 708.

42. Rich, "On *History, For Lizzie and Harriet,* and *The Dolphin*," 186.

43. Wakoski, "The Craft of Carpenters, Plumbers and Mechanics: Column," *American Poetry Review*, 3 (January–February, 1974): 46; repr. as "Reply to Adrienne Rich," in Axelrod, *The Critical Response to Robert Lowell*, 187–88.

44. Tillinghast, *Robert Lowell's Life and Work: Damaged Grandeur* (Ann Arbor: University of Michigan Press, 1995), 54–55. Access to an unpublished earlier manuscript of *The Dolphin* brought David Gewanter to the antithetical conclusion that Lowell cut back on the verbatim use of conversations and letters in order to cause both of his wives "less pain." In "Child of Collaboration: Robert Lowell's *Dolphin*," *Modern Philology* 93, no. 2 (November 1995): 178–203, Gewanter argues that *The Dolphin* was originally conceived as "a postmodernist poetry of multiple voices and authors in the tradition of William Carlos Williams's *Paterson*"; he finds the published version treating Hardwick "more kindly—at the expense of . . . its art" (179).

45. "Sources," *Your Native Land, Your Life: Poems* (New York: W. W. Norton, 1986), 25.

46. "Twenty-One Love Poems," *FD* 2002, 146–47.

47. "Sleepwalking Next to Death," *Time's Power: Poems 1985–88* (New York: W. W. Norton, 1989), 19.

48. In *Of Woman Born: Motherhood as Experience and Institution* (New York: W. W. Norton, 1976), Rich recalls that "once in a while someone used to ask me, 'Don't you ever write poems about your children?'" The reason she gives in 1976 for not doing so is that she experienced poetry writing and caring for young children as activities that were in conflict: "for me, poetry was where I lived as no-one's mother, where I existed as myself" (12).

49. "This" [dated 1985], *Time's Power*, 6.

50. Cf. esp. "When We Dead Awaken: Writing as Re-Vision," in *OLSS*, 40: "But poems are like dreams: in them you put what you don't know you know."

51. "For Memory," *A Wild Patience Has Taken Me This Far: Poems 1978–1981* (New York: W. W. Norton, 1981), 21–22.

52. Jahan Ramazani, *Poetry of Mourning: The Modern Elegy from Hardy to Heaney* (Chicago: University of Chicago Press, 1994), 321.

53. Rich, "Compulsory Heterosexuality and Lesbian Existence," *BBP*, 23. Rich explains in a footnote that the essay was originally written for the "Sexuality" issue of *Signs* in 1978; the Foreword from which my quotations are drawn was added in 1982 when the essay was reprinted in a feminist pamphlet series.

54. Rich, "Vesuvius at Home: The Power of Emily Dickinson," *OLSS*, 157–83.

55. In an interview with Elly Bulkin in 1977, cited by Deborah Pope in *A Separate Vision: Isolation in Contemporary Women's Poetry* (Baton Rouge: Louisiana State University Press, 1984), Rich explains that "Stepping Backward," one of the poems in her first published volume, "is addressed to a woman whom I was close to in my late teens, and whom I really fled from—I fled from my feelings about her" (130, n15). "To Judith, Taking Leave," a 1962 poem that looks from within an ostensibly heterosexual framework ("two women / in love to the nerves' limit / with two men—") toward a time when they "can meet . . . as two eyes in one brow / receiving at one moment / the rainbow of the world," went unpublished until *FD* 1984.

56. In *Stein, Bishop, and Rich: Lyrics of Love, War, and Place* (Chapel Hill: University of North Carolina Press, 1997), Margaret Dickie suggests in her valuable, brief discussion of this poem that "among its multiple meanings" is a necrophilic "nostalgia for all the dead and maimed women she might have loved." Necrophilia "associates

the woman's desire with what is transgressive in desire and unassuageable" (156). Dickie points out that Rich's "most recent poetry has grown out of an appreciation for those mysteries in her own life that she cannot fully fathom" (199).

57. In *The Regenerate Lyric: Theology and Innovation in American Poetry* (Cambridge: Cambridge University Press, 1993), Elisa New argues that "many of the classic American poems are made not of linguistic possibility but of linguistic decision. Honed things, things that end, these poems are vessels of choice" (231).

58. Rich, "Sources," in *Your Native Land, Your Life*, 27.

CHAPTER 3

1. Marjorie Perloff, *The Poetic Art of Robert Lowell* (Ithaca, N.Y.: Cornell University Press, 1973), 181–82. Perloff first developed this account of Plath's poetic stance in "Angst and Animism in the Poetry of Sylvia Plath," *Modern Literature* (1970); repr. in Linda Wagner, ed., *Critical Essays on Sylvia Plath* (Boston, Mass.: G. K. Hall, 1984), 109–24, where she cites Northrop Frye's characterization of a post-Romantic "oracular" stance: "the medium of the oracle . . . is concerned to utter rather than to address, he is turned away from his listener, so to speak, in a state of rapt self-communion." Frye, *Fables of Identity* (New York: Harcourt Brace, 1963), 136. Margaret Dickie Uroff plays Plath off against Lowell and Sexton in similar terms in *Sylvia Plath and Ted Hughes* (Urbana: University of Illinois Press, 1979), 36–39.

2. Parenthetically cited page numbers for Plath's poems in this chapter will refer to *The Collected Poems*, ed. Ted Hughes (New York: Harper and Row, 1981), hereafter abbreviated *CP*. "Kingdom" is from "The Disquieting Muses," which will be discussed below.

3. In her essay on Plath's letters and journals for the *Cambridge Companion to Sylvia Plath*, ed. Jo Gill (Cambridge: Cambridge University Press, 2006), Tracy Brain warns of "a danger . . . of erecting false and overly rigid boundaries between Plath's different types of writings" (142). Brain finds "the talky informality of many of Plath's poems" to be letterlike and thinks they "owe a debt to the direct . . . address that is a feature of letter writing" (ibid.). Perhaps they do, but at their most colloquially "talky" they are also typically calling attention to the difference between what can be said in letters and in poems by way of direct address: "Daddy, I have had to kill you" is not something you'd be saying in a letter, for several reasons!

4. Plath, *Letters Home*, ed. Aurelia Schober Plath (New York: Harper & Row, 1975), 336; ctd. Leonard Scigaj, "The Painterly Plath That Nobody Knows," *Centennial Review*, 32 (1988), 235. Cf. Plath's journal entry of March 20, 1958: "Yesterday sat in the art libe [sic] soaking and seeping in pictures." *The Unabridged Journals of Sylvia Plath, 1950–1962*, ed. Karen V. Kukil (New York: Random House, 2000), 354.

5. Judith Kroll, *Chapters in a Mythology: The Poetry of Sylvia Plath* (New York: Harper & Row, 1976), 22–32. For a more recent discussion of Plath's "de Chiricoesque conceits" cf. Christina Britzolakis, *Sylvia Plath and the Theatre of Mourning* (Oxford: Clarendon, 1999), 61–65.

6. Kroll makes the *Bell Jar* connection in *Chapters in a Mythology*, 25–26.

7. Scigaj, 241. While it is no longer the case in 2007 that "the attention accorded *Ariel* has left Plath's early career in darkness" (Scigaj, 220), her ekphrastic poetry and her "painterliness" as a poet have still received little attention. An earlier version of this chapter was published in *Raritan* in 2001.

8. "Conversation Among the Ruins," an ekphrasis of a painting by de Chirico, is immediately followed in *CP* by "Winter Landscape, with Rooks," a poem that projects its own "landscape of chagrin" in an explicitly painterly way.

9. In the wake of Hughes's publication of *Birthday Letters* (New York: Farrar, Straus and Giroux) in 1998, critics and biographers remain deeply divided as to whether his various writings about Plath are helpful or misleading. Whereas, for example, Susan Bassnett concludes in her second edition of *Sylvia Plath: An Introduction to the Poetry* (Hampshire/New York: Palgrave Macmillan, 2005) that *Birthday Letters* "gives us a version of Plath's life and writings that can truly be described as life-enhancing" (163), Sarah Churchwell, in "'Your Sentence Was Mine Too': Reading Sylvia Plath in Ted Hughes's *Birthday Letters*," finds Hughes using these poems self-interestedly to claim the high ground and have the last word (*Literary Couplings: Writing Couples, Collaborators, and the Construction of Authorship*, ed. Marjorie Stone and Judith Thompson [Madison: University of Wisconsin Press, 2006], 260–87).

10. Diane Wood Middlebrook, *Her Husband: Hughes and Plath—A Marriage* (New York:Viking Penguin, 2003), 278.

11. Ted Hughes, *Birthday Letters*, 3: "Fulbright Scholars."

12. Susan Bassnett points out that "critics have not laid much emphasis on Plath's Americanness, nor is it very evident in her poems" (142). For Hughes, in retrospect, it is hugely significant: "18 Rugby Street," the poem in which he recalls making love with her for the first time, ends with the lines: "So this is America, I marvelled. / Beautiful, beautiful America!" (*Birthday Letters*, 24; cf. Bassnett, 147).

13. *Birthday Letters*, 38: "Your Paris."

14. Ibid., 7: "Visit."

15. Ibid., 15: "St. Botolph's.

16. Sarah Churchwell calls attention to the memory-as-camera trope in "'Your Sentence Was Mine Too': Reading Sylvia Plath in Ted Hughes's *Birthday Letters*." Churchwell's concern is with the way in which Hughes's recourse to this trope acknowledges mediation, thereby compromising his claim to have access to the truth about Sylvia Plath.

17. *Birthday Letters*, 5–6: "Caryatids (2)."

18. Nancy J. Vickers, "Diana Described: Scattered Woman and Scattered Rhyme," *Critical Inquiry*, 7 (Winter 1981): 266.

19. John Berger, *Ways of Seeing* (Harmondsworth, U.K.: Penguin, 1972), 46–47.

20. "She wrote her early poems very slowly, Thesaurus open upon her knee," explains Hughes in "Notes on the Chronological Order of Sylvia Plath's Poems," in *The Art of Sylvia Plath: A Symposium*, ed. Charles Newman (Bloomington: Indiana University Press, 1970), 188.

21. *Unabridged Journals*, 202: entry for February 19. Karen Kukil's note (684) explains that Plath had played the part of a prostitute in the Cambridge Amateur Dramatics Club production of Ben Jonson's *Bartholomew Fair* in the fall of 1955. Plath's journal entry seems to be citing this performance as a way to characterize her social behavior as a "mad poet" at Cambridge.

22. *Unabridged Journals*, 199: entry for February 19. The *Strange Interlude* reference that will be parenthetically cited in the next paragraph is on the same page.

23. *Unabridged Journals*, Appendix 6: Journal Fragment, 31 December 1955–1 January 1956, 548.

24. *Unabridged Journals*, 203: entry for February 20, 1956. Later in the same entry, 205: "Wrote one Good Poem: 'Winter Landscape with Rooks': it moves, and is athletic: a psychic landscape."

25. *Birthday Letters*, 36: "Your Paris,"; 39: "You Hated Spain".

26. Frances McCullough explains in an "Editor's Note" to *The Journals of Sylvia Plath* (New York: Dial Press, 1982) that "there are quite a few nasty bits missing— Plath had a very sharp tongue..." (ix). Before his death in 1998 Hughes released this material for publication in *The Unabridged Journals of Sylvia Plath*.

27. Anne Stevenson, *Bitter Fame: A Life of Sylvia Plath* (Boston: Houghton Mifflin, 1989): illustrations follow page 174. The originals of Plath's sketches of Benidorm are in the Smith College Library Rare Book Room.

28. John Hollander, *The Gazer's Spirit: Poems Speaking to Silent Works of Art* (Chicago: University of Chicago Press, 1995), 4.

29. W. J. T. Mitchell, "Ekphrasis and the Other," *South Atlantic Quarterly* 91, no. 3 (Summer 1992): 695–720; repr. in *Picture Theory: Essays on Verbal and Visual Representation* (Chicago: University of Chicago Press, 1994), 151–82; James Heffernan, *Museum of Words: The Poetics of Ekphrasis from Homer to Ashbery* (Chicago: University of Chicago Press, 1993); Paul Fry, "The Torturer's Horse: What Poems See in Pictures," *A Defense of Poetry* (Stanford: Stanford University Press, 1995), 70–91. Cf. also Grant Scott, "The Rhetoric of Dilation: Ekphrasis and Ideology," *Word and Image* 7 (1991): 301–10.

30. Jean Hagstrum, *The Sister Arts* (Chicago: University of Chicago Press, 1958).

31. Mitchell, "Ekphrasis and the Other," 702.

32. Hollander includes Shelley's poem in his ekphrastic "Gallery" in *The Gazer's Spirit*, 143–44. It was published after his death by Mary Shelley, who, as Hollander notes, "may have collaborated with him on it" (144).

33. "Ekphrasis and the Other," 705–6.

34. Ibid., 717. In "The Torturer's Horse" Paul Fry does attribute to women poets a distinctive set of motives for ekphrastic writing. For a recent version of Fry's theory that puts it in dialogue with Mitchell's, see "The Lamplit Answer? Gjertrud Schnackenberg's Anti-Ekphrases," *In the Frame: Women's Ekphrastic Poetry from Marianne Moore to Susan Wheeler*, ed. Jane Hedley, Nick Halpern, and Willard Spiegelman (Newark, Delaware: University of Delaware Press, 2009).

35. Heffernan, *Museum of Words*, 136–37.

36. Rich, "Mourning Picture," *FD* 2002, 39–40. Heffernan cites Rich's poem as "an exercise in paragonal prosopopoeia, spoken posthumously by a girl whose language strives to outdo the painting" (*Museum of Words*, 136), but he does not credit this "exercise" with a feminist agenda. In Elizabeth Loizeaux, *Twentieth-Century Poetry and the Visual Arts* (Cambridge: Cambridge University Press, 2008), 80–109, this poem receives a more nuanced feminist reading and Rich's affinity for ekphrasis is discussed in fuller detail than I have room for here.

37. "Aunt Jennifer's Tigers," *A Change of World* (New Haven, Conn.: Yale University Press, 1951), 19, repr. in Gelpi and Gelpi, 4; "Mathilde in Normandy," *A Change of World*, 52–53.

38. "Paula Becker to Clara Westhoff," *FD* 1984, 248–50; "Emily Carr," *Your Native Land, Your Life* (New York: W. W. Norton, 1986), 64–65. In "Turning the Wheel" (*FD* 1984, 309), Rich invents a letter from Mary Colter, a woman architect who (as she explains in her Notes on the poem), worked for the Santa Fe railroad at the turn of the twentieth century, supporting her mother and sister with her hotel and restaurant designs (*FD* 1984, 333). Loizeaux discusses an early ekphrastic poem of Rich's "that is not overtly feminist" ("Pictures by Vuillard").

39. In *Sylvia Plath: Confessing the Fictive Self* (New York: Peter Lang, 1992) Toni Saldívar discusses Plath's affinity for Medusa as a "poetic 'death-wish'" that she can be seen to be resisting in many of the poems in *Colossus* (70).

40. John Hollander explains, in "The Gazer's Spirit: Romantic and Later Poetry on Painting and Sculpture," that *Rückfiguren* are "figures seen from behind facing a scene as a surrogate for the viewers of the painting." *The Romantics and Us: Essays on Literature and Culture*, ed. Gene W. Ruoff (New Brunswick, N.J.: Rutgers University Press, 1990), 160. In this case, however, the lady with her back to us is an actor in the drama the painting stages.

41. Leonard Scigaj has suggested that the desolation of both the house and the outdoor landscape may "represent the irretrievable distance between Greek hero and modern counterpart" (225). The image on the wall might indeed be a figment of the lady's imagination or a mirror image of her desire, since there is a strong visual correspondence between her "Grecian tunic" and the togalike garment that drapes its shoulders. I would like to thank Jennifer Hirsh, a specialist in de Chirico, for assisting me to read this painting while she was working on her Ph.D. dissertation at Bryn Mawr in the History of Art.

42. See esp. *Museum of Words*, 3, where Heffernan proposes a definition for ekphrasis that is "simple in form but complex in its implications: *ekphrasis is the verbal representation of visual representation.*"

43. Hughes, "Notes on Poems 1956–1963," *CP,* 275. The likelihood that the poem is an allegory of her nascent relationship with Hughes is strengthened by a verbal coincidence linking the poem's last line to a journal entry from April of 1956 in which Plath seems to have been drafting a letter to Richard Sassoon, the man Hughes supplanted in her erotic imagination: "something very terrifying," she says, "has happened to me . . . and god knows what ceremonies of life or love can patch the havoc wrought" (*Unabridged Journals,* 236).

44. Cf. *Birthday Letters,* 7: "Visit."

45. Hughes explains in his Introduction to *The Collected Poems* that early 1956 "presents itself as a watershed, because from later this year come the earliest poems of her first collection, *The Colossus*" (*CP,* 16).

46. In *The End of the Mind: The Edge of the Intelligible in Hardy, Stevens, Larkin, Plath, and Glück* (London/New York: Routledge, 2005), DeSales Harrison makes a cognate suggestion, that "Plath's interest in representational surfaces (looking glasses, pools, and ultimately poems themselves) derives in part from the way that these surfaces present the looker with a likeness that is also a terrible unlikeness" (165).

47. *Unabridged Journals,* 327–28: entry dated Sunday, February 9.

48. *Unabridged Journals,* 332: entry dated Tuesday noon, February 19.

49. Hughes's note on this poem says they did get rid of the head by leaving it in a tree on the banks of the Cam (*CP,* 275–76); in *Birthday Letters* he recalls that Plath wrote the poem soon afterward to exorcise residual ambivalence, "rhyming yourself into safety / From its orphaned fate" (*Birthday Letters,* 57: "The Earthenware Head").

50. *Unabridged Journals,* 399: entry for Thursday, July 3. In his introduction to *The Collected Poems* Hughes cites these same passages but shortens the (February–July) interval between them to ten weeks (*CP,* 13).

51. *Letters Home,* 468.

52. Scigaj, 243, citing Plath's translation from *The Diaries of Paul Klee: 1898–1918,* ed. Felix Klee (Berkeley: University of California Press, 1964), 160–61. Subsequent quotations are from this same passage.

53. "The Eye-mote" (*CP,* 109) is dated 1959 by Hughes; "Cut" (*CP,* 235) is dated 1962.

54. "The Living Poet," BBC Third Programme, prod. Anthony Thwaite, recorded June 5, 1961, transmitted July 8, 1961; ctd. in Scigaj, 227.

55. *The Well Wrought Urn: Studies in the Structure of Poetry* (New York: Reynal and Hitchcock, 1947), 186. Scigaj (227–28) paraphrases this and other underlined statements, and furnishes the page numbers on which they appear.

56. "The Heresy of Paraphrase" is the title of *The Well Wrought Urn*'s eleventh chapter; " The Intentional Fallacy," of an article by William K. Wimsatt and Monroe Beardsley in the *Sewanee Review* 54 (1946): 468–88, rev. and repr. in *The Verbal Icon: Studies in the Meaning of Poetry* (Lexington: University of Kentucky Press, 1954), 3–18.

57. Scigaj, 228, n17.
58. Cf. *Unabridged Journals*, 507, where Plath says she has written "one good poem [at Yaddo] so far: an imagist piece on the dead snake."
59. In "Sylvia Plath and her Journals," Hughes cites "Medallion" as one of the poems Plath especially valued from this period; but it is in the section of "Poem for a Birthday" subtitled "The Stones," also written at Yaddo, that he suggests we can first hear the voice of her *Ariel* poems. *Ariel Ascending: Writings about Sylvia Plath*, ed. Paul Alexander (New York: Harper & Row, 1985), 158.
60. This is a central theme of "Notes on the Chronological Order of Sylvia Plath's Poems"; cf. esp., in connection with "The Stones": "She had never in her life improvised. The powers that compelled her to write so slowly had always been stronger than she was. But quite suddenly she found herself free to let herself drop, rather than inch over bridges of concepts" (192).
61. Cf. Hughes's note on "Poem for a Birthday," *CP*, 289.
62. Kinzie, "An Informal Checklist of Criticism," in Newman, *The Art of Sylvia Plath*, 283.
63. Dickie, "Sylvia Plath's Narrative Strategies," *Iowa Review*, 13 (1982): 1–14; repr. In Wagner, *Critical Essays on Sylvia Plath*, 171.
64. In "Notes on the Chronological Order," Hughes explains the genesis of the poem. It "depressed [him] greatly," he recalls, while confirming that Plath had finally arrived at her own center of gravity as a poet. "I had no doubt," he says, "that this was a poem, and perhaps a great poem. She insisted that it was an exercise on the theme" (193–94).
65. Cf. Perloff, "Angst and Animism in the Poetry of Sylvia Plath," 110. Cf. also Perloff's reading of "Cut," where "it is immediately not [Plath's] thumb that is bleeding but a new being outside of herself with which she can sympathize" (120).
66. In *Sylvia Plath: A Literary Life*, 2nd rev. ed. (Basingstoke, Hampshire, U.K.: Palgrave Macmillan, 2003), Linda Wagner-Martin's reading of this poem discloses a process of revision that served to enhance the speaker's self-described "emptiness" and lack of agency, as well as reduce our incentive to infer a conventional backstory: thus, for example, the title changed from "Sick Room Tulips" and "Tulips in Hospital" to the single word "Tulips," and "The water I weep . . ." became "The water I taste . . ." in the poem's concluding stanza (cf. Wagner-Martin, 64–65).
67. Perloff reads this poem in similar terms (cf. "Angst and Animism," 118–20).
68. These are the opening lines of "Daddy" (*CP*, 222), "Stopped Dead" (*CP*, 230), and "Lesbos" (*CP*, 227), respectively.
69. "Medusan Imagery in Sylvia Plath," in *Sylvia Plath: New Views on the Poetry*, ed. Gary Lane (Baltimore, Md.: Johns Hopkins University Press, 1979), 97–115. Sister Bernetta's essay begins with an assertion that is also my chapter's theme, albeit differently inflected: "Medusa, though we do not immediately recognize the fact, presides as Muse over Sylvia Plath's poetry . . ." (97).
70. Alfred Alvarez, ["Prologue: Sylvia Plath,"] *The Savage God* (New York: Random House, 1972), 16.
71. Ibid., 17, 27. Hughes objected strongly to Alvarez's having presumed to "explain" Plath's suicide; cf. Janet Malcolm, *The Silent Woman: Sylvia Plath and Ted Hughes* (New York: Knopf/Random House, 2002), 123–30. My interest here is not in the theory of suicide Alvarez used Plath to illustrate but in his firsthand account of Plath performing her own poems for him under the rubric of "light verse."
72. *American Heritage Dictionary of the English Language*, 4th ed. (New York: Houghton Mifflin, 2000).
73. For a reading of "Edge" that takes it to be a thinly concealed suicide note, see Mary Kurtzman, "Plath's 'Ariel' and Tarot," *Centennial Review*, 32 (Summer 1988): 286–95, cited by Wagner-Martin, 104–5. The poem's strategies for achieving a tri-

umph of art over suffering (the enigmatic poise of its central figure, the rigor of its emphasis on illusion and seeming), are shortchanged by this kind of biographical reading, it seems to me.

74. Jacques Lacan, *Four Fundamental Concepts of Psychoanalysis*, ed. Jacques-Alain Miller, trans. Alan Sheridan (New York: W. W. Norton, 1978), 101.

75. For a good recent airing of "the complex relation between the poet in the poem and the poet in the world" as it has played out in biographical and critical accounts of Plath's late poems, cf. Harrison, *The End of the Mind*, 143–45.

76. *Birthday Letters*, 68: "The Blue Flannel Suit."

77. Perloff, "The Two Ariels: The (Re)Making of the Sylvia Plath Canon," *American Poetry Review*, 13 (November 1984): 10–18. Cf. Linda K. Bundtzen, *The Other Ariel* (Amherst: University of Massachusetts Press, 2001), 3: "While it would be an exaggeration to argue that . . . Ted Hughes 'authored' *Ariel*, we know now that it represents his, not Plath's overall narrative intentions."

78. Ostriker, "The Americanization of Sylvia," in Wagner, *Critical Essays on Sylvia Plath*, 97–109; first published in *Language and Style* 1, no. 3 (Summer 1968).

CHAPTER 4

1. Unless otherwise specified, all quotations from Brooks's poems are from *BLACKS* (Chicago: Third World Press, 1987), where this poem appears on page 132.

2. Critics who have looked at how Brooks deploys and extends the role of "mother" include Lesley Wheeler, in *The Poetics of Enclosure* (Knoxville: University of Tennessee Press, 2002) and Betsy Erkkila in *The Wicked Sisters: Women Poets, Literary History and Discord* (Oxford and New York: Oxford University Press, 1992); cf. esp. Erkkila, 197.

3. At age thirteen, according to biographer George Kent, Brooks "published" a handwritten weekly newspaper that sold for 5 cents; at twenty she was putting out a mimeographed "News-Review" with editorials, cartoons, brief biographies of "great Negroes," and reports on local and national events. Cf. *A Life of Gwendolyn Brooks* (Lexington: University Press of Kentucky, 1990), 40–44.

4. The PBS Black Press Web site explains that *The Defender* was smuggled into the South and "read aloud in barbershops and in churches" (http://www.pbs.org/blackpress/news_bios/defender.html, accessed July 2008).

5. Suzanne Juhasz, *Naked and Fiery Forms: Modern American Poetry by Women: A New Tradition* (New York: Harper Colophon, 1976), 150–51.

6. Barbara Jean Bolden, *Urban Rage in Bronzeville: Social Commentary in the Poetry of Gwendolyn Brooks, 1945–1960* (Chicago: Third World Press, 1999), 36 and 174, n15. Bolden once again takes up the suggestion of Juhasz and others that Brooks was not enough of a feminist in her chapter on *Annie Allen*, 77 ff.

7. "when you have forgotten Sunday: the love story," discussed in the Introduction, was obviously written from inside her own marriage to Henry Blakely. At readings Brooks would introduce it with the story of how they met, and talk about the kitchenette apartments they lived in as a young married couple during the 1940s.

8. The question of whom Brooks was writing for at different points in her career will perhaps never be settled to everyone's satisfaction, in spite of her having spoken to it herself a number of times both in interviews and in her own writings. Zofia Burr puts that question front and center in her chapter on Brooks in *Of Women, Poetry, and Power: Strategies of Address in Dickinson, Miles, Brooks, Lorde, and Angelou* (Urbana/Chicago: University of Illinois Press, 2002); in the third section of this chapter I will be in dialogue with her discussion of Brooks's changing posture of address.

9. Abortion was still a risky subject when Anne Sexton published, in her second volume, *All My Pretty Ones* (1962), an abortion poem that is more typically confessional: "The Abortion," (*The Complete Poems of Anne Sexton, with a Foreword by Maxine Kumin* [Boston: Houghton Mifflin, 1981], 61–62).

10. D. H. Melhem, *Gwendolyn Brooks: Poetry and the Heroic Voice* (Lexington: University Press of Kentucky, 1987), 23–24. Joanne V. Gabbin's reading, in "Blooming in the Whirlwind: The Early Poetry of Gwendolyn Brooks," is along the same lines: at first, suggests Gabbin, "the mother attempts to shield herself from the remorse and guilt she feels" by "addressing an indefinite 'you,'" but in the second stanza we find her "confessing and accepting her portion of responsibility." *The Furious Flowering of African American Poetry*, ed. Gabbin (Charlottesville: University Press of Virginia, 1999), 263–64.

11. Brooks, *Report from Part One* (Detroit, Mich.: Broadside Press, 1972), 184 (hereafter cited as *RPO*); also quoted in Melhem, 23.

12. Cf. Barbara Johnson, "Apostrophe, Animation, and Abortion," in *A World of Difference* (Baltimore, Md.: Johns Hopkins University Press, 1987), 189: "The 'you' in the opening lines can be seen as an 'I' that has become alienated, distanced from itself, and combined with a generalized other, which includes and feminizes the reader of the poem." Johnson's is the only reading of this poem I have found that does justice to its complex structure of address.

13. It can equally be said that the poem's speaker is and is not a poet: "I have heard in the wind . . ." is a formulation that evokes the Romantic tradition of "Aeolian" voices. (I would like to thank my colleague, Katherine Rowe, for pointing this out to me.) *A Street in Bronzeville* is full of poems whose relationship to the canonical tradition of the lyric is similarly double-edged: "when you have forgotten Sunday" is discussed in these terms in the Introduction.

14. *A Capsule Course in Black Poetry Writing*, by Gwendolyn Brooks, Keorapetse Kgositsile, Haki R. Madhubuti, and Dudley Randall (Detroit, Mich.: Broadside Press, 1975), 5. The poem she is referring to is "The Womanhood," XV, from *Annie Allen*, *BLACKS*, 139.

15. "Young Heroes–I: To Keorapetse Kgositsile," *BLACKS*, 491.

16. "First person communal voice" is Barbara Jean Bolden's useful coinage (*Urban Rage in Bronzeville*, 16).

17. "Interviews: Summer, 1967," *RPO*, 146.

18. *RPO*, 132.

19. James Weldon Johnson, "The Dilemma of the Negro Author," *American Mercury* 15, no. 60 (December 1928): 481; repr. in *The Politics and Aesthetics of the New Negro Literature*, ed. Cary D. Wintz (New York and London: Garland, 1996), 251. For brief but telling remarks on "the question of audience" for black writers before and after 1960, see Kent, "Aesthetic Values in the Poetry of Gwendolyn Brooks," in Maria K. Mootry and Gary Smith, eds., *A Life Distilled: Gwendolyn Brooks, Her Poetry and Fiction* (Urbana/Chicago: University of Illinois Press, 1987), 38–39.

20. "The Dilemma of the Negro Author," *American Mercury*, 477; *Politics and Aesthetics*, 247. Ironically, a closer look at writing that has been done in a spirit of "strict conformity to the taboos of black America" would reveal, Johnson argues, that its authors were "unconsciously addressing themselves mainly to white America."

21. "The Dilemma of the Negro Author," *American Mercury*, 481; *Politics and Aesthetics*, 251.

22. A. D. Miller, "Some Observations on a Black Aesthetic," in *The Black Aesthetic*, ed. Addison Gayle (Garden City, N.J.: Doubleday, 1971), 402–3.

23. Ibid., 404; my emphasis.

24. Quoted in Kent, *A Life*, 62.

25. Letter from Richard Wright to Edward Aswell, quoted in Kent, *A Life*, 63.

26. *Blackness and the Adventure of Western Culture* (Chicago: Third World Press, 1972), 108. Kent cites Herbert Hill's biographical notes in Hill's 1963 anthology *Soon One Morning* (New York: Knopf, 1963). Melhem plays "The Sundays" off against "Prufrock" (*Gwendolyn Brooks: Poetry and the Heroic Voice*, 34); cf. also Judith P. Saunders, "The Love Song of Satin-Legs Smith: Gwendolyn Brooks Revisits Prufrock's Hell," *Papers on Language and Literature* 36, no. 1 (Winter 2000): 3–18.

27. For a fuller discussion of the voicing of this poem, one that pays special attention to Brooks's use of apostrophe to engage an implied reader who stands in for "the inability of white critics to understand the poetry of black Americans," see Ann Folwell Stanford, "'Like Narrow Banners for Some Gathering War': Readers, Aesthetics, and Gwendolyn Brooks's 'The Sundays of Satin-Legs Smith,'" *College Literature*, 17 (1990): 162–82.

28. Bill Mullen, discussing "The Sundays of Satin-Legs Smith" in *Popular Fronts: Chicago and African American Cultural Politics, 1935–46* (Urbana/Chicago: University of Illinois Press, 1999), 158–67, assumes that its narrator-speaker is addressing herself to upwardly mobile middle-class blacks who are trying to distance themselves from the old neighborhood.

29. *BLACKS*, 48. According to Susan Schweik, Miller's heroism was "noted only grudgingly and belatedly by the Navy and by the white-run media." Schweik suggests that Brooks wrote the poem in response to a call from the editor of a new black literary journal, *Negro Story*, for compensatory attention to the heroism of "the Dorie Millers." *A Gulf So Deeply Cut: American Women Poets and the Second World War* (Madison: University of Wisconsin Press, 1991), 117. "Negro Hero" was originally published in *Common Ground*, in 1945.

30. *BLACKS*, 48. Schweik adduces a disjuncture between the second stanza's image of "the soldier-as-really-a-child" and the third stanza's image of "the soldier-as-Real-Man," and finds that these "two figures of male war-making . . . remain in disconcerting suspension." She takes issue with Harry Shaw's contention (in "Perceptions of Men in the Early Works of Gwendolyn Brooks," in *Black American Poets between Worlds, 1940–1960*, ed. R. Baxter Miller [Knoxville: University of Tennessee Press, 1986], 136–59) that the first of these self-characterizations sarcastically references white readers' assumption that a Negro is not really a man. I see Miller's "of course . . . of course" as rhetorical devices for humanizing the Negro Hero; where Schweik finds competing explanations, I find a self-confident layering of his motives for acting as he did. These differing readings are themselves good evidence for the poem's rhetorical aliveness.

31. Ann Folwell Stanford, "Dialectics of Desire: War and Resistive Voice in Gwendolyn Brooks's 'Negro Hero' and 'Gay Chaps at the Bar,'" *African-American Review* 26, no. 2 (Summer 1992): 201.

32. In his chapter on Brooks in *Blackness and the Adventure of Western Culture*, George Kent credits Brooks with "a legitimate universalism," arguing that her poems do *not* "represent a reach for some pre-existing Western universal to be arrived at by reducing the tensions inherent in the black experience." She gets to the universal, Kent suggests, by "going down deep, not transcending" (112).

33. This is Brooks's own explanation of the thematic motivation for her use of off-rhyme (*RPO*, 156). Cf. also George Kent: "She attacked the sonnet's rigidity by breaking up traditional sentence syntax into punctuated phrases, by emphasizing the colloquial, and by the pressure of her contemporary realism" (*Blackness and the Adventure of Western Culture*, 112).

34. George Kent, *A Life*, 80. Like other Modernist poets, Brooks was accused of willful obscurity by early reviewers: Saunders Redding, in the *Saturday Review of Literature* in 1949 warned that he "[did] not want to see Miss Brooks's fine talents dribble away in the obscure and the too oblique." "Cellini-like Lyrics," repr. in Stephen

Caldwell Wright, ed., *On Gwendolyn Brooks: Reliant Contemplation* (Ann Arbor: University of Michigan Press, 1996), 6–7.

35. One of the "Bronzeville" poems is entitled "the preacher: ruminates behind the sermon" (*BLACKS*, 31).

36. Don L. Lee, "Preface," *RPO*, 17, 19.

37. Margaret Walker, "New Poets," *Phylon* 11, no. 4 (Winter 1950): 354.

38. Ibid., 350.

39. "You often put a burden on the reader that is not commensurate with the rewards," said Elizabeth Lawrence, Brooks's editor at *Harper's*, in a letter that accepted *Annie Allen* for publication with serious reservations (quoted in Kent, *A Life*, 77).

40. "Interviews: Spring, 1971," repr. in *RPO*, 169–70.

41. *Essence* interview, *RPO*, 172, 175.

42. She and her husband separated in 1969, but came back together some years later.

43. It is also expressed in a refusal to give up either the "universalizing" claims Don Lee associates with *"their* rules . . . *their* language" (my emphasis) or the "particularism" that embarrassed Saunders Redding, who doubted that anyone but another Negro could fully appreciate the subtleties of intraracial color prejudice (in Wright, *On Gwendolyn Brooks: Reliant Contemplation*, 7).

44. Hortense Spillers, "Gwendolyn the Terrible: Propositions on Eleven Poems," in Mootry and Smith, *A Life Distilled: Gwendolyn Brooks, Her Poetry and Fiction*, 235. Cf. Claudia Tate, "Anger So Flat: Gwendolyn Brooks's *Annie Allen*," in Mootry and Smith, 140–151, and Bolden, *Urban Rage in Bronzeville*, chapter 4 passim.

45. Cf. esp. Anne Folwell Stanford, "An Epic with a Difference: Sexual Politics in Gwendolyn Brooks's 'The Anniad,'" *American Literature* 67, no. 2 (June 1995): 283–301, and Gertrude Reif Hughes, "Making it *Really* New: Hilda Doolittle, Gwendolyn Brooks, and the Feminist Potential of Modern Poetry," *American Quarterly* 42, no. 3 (September 1990), repr. in Wright, *On Gwendolyn Brooks: Reliant Contemplation*, 186–212.

46. "For Gwen Brooks from Nikki Giovanni," *Essence*, 1 (April 1971): 26; Sonia Sanchez, "Eulogy," *Time*, December 18, 2000, 25. Elizabeth Alexander remembers "The Anniad" giving her permission during the 1980s to make full use of her own powers of language: "If such wild and unexpected curiosities were possible in her language, then anything might be possible for me," Alexander recalls in "Meditations on 'Mecca': Gwendolyn Brooks and the Responsibilities of the Black Poet," in *By Herself: Women Reclaim Poetry*, ed. Molly McQuade (Saint Paul, Minn.: Graywolf Press, 2000), 369–70; repr. in Alexander, *The Black Interior: Essays* (Saint Paul, Minn.: Graywolf Press, 2004).

47. Brooks, *Report from Part Two* (Chicago: Third World Press, 1996), 153 (Brooks's italics). Hereafter cited as *RPT*.

48. Melhem, "Afterword" in Brooks, *RPT*, 157.

49. Brooks had hoped for a poem that would run to two thousand lines—twice as long as the poem she published. D. H. Melhem, who provides a helpful backstory of its lengthy process of gestation in *Gwendolyn Brooks: Poetry and the Heroic Voice*, explains that in the early 1940s she had worked in the Mecca building for the spiritual adviser and purveyor of patent medicines on whom Prophet Williams is loosely based (158).

50. John Bartlow Martin, "The Strangest Place in Chicago," *Harper's*, December 1950, 86–97. In "'A Material Collapse That Is Construction': History and Counter-Memory in Gwendolyn Brooks's *In the Mecca*," *MELUS* 23, no. 3 (Autumn 1998): 3–20, John Lowney calls Martin's description of the Mecca building "dehumanizing" and assimilates the piece to a "racialized discourse of urban decline" that was prevalent by 1950 in the popular press. Lowney finds Brooks intervening to resist this

discourse with an empathetic portrayal of the Mecca residents' individual and collective humanity.

51. Gayl Jones's essay ("Community and Voice: Gwendolyn Brooks's 'In the Mecca,'" in Mootry and Smith, *A Life Distilled*, 193–204) deals especially well with the poem's polyvocality. Jones points out that "the multi-voiced poem has a long tradition in Afro-American poetry" (193).

52. The steel-and-glass structure that replaced it was one that contrived to harbor no "corrupting" shadows: as the centerpiece of the new campus, it epitomized the a-historical modernity of the international style.

53. In Martin's piece for *Harper's* the building's janitor, who fights "a hopeless rearguard action against decay and vandalism," is especially discouraged by the amount of glass that gets broken in the building, some by "Outsiders" and some by children playing in the halls: "The kids gets to playin' and throwin' at one another and first thing you know they break the glass" ("The Strangest Place in Chicago," 90). "Boy Breaking Glass," a stand-alone poem in the "After Mecca" section of *In the Mecca*, will be discussed below.

54. An account of "the Historical Significance of the IIT Campus" on the Web site of the Miës Van der Rohe Society at IIT explained, until 2004, that by the end of the 1970s, in the wake of a decline in student enrollment and a failure to implement a landscaping plan for the immediate neighborhood, "the harsh geometric lines of the buildings . . . conspired . . . to create a barren, inhospitable urban campus. What was once a retreat from urban chaos had become more of a void" (http://mies.iit.edu/significance.html, accessed May 13, 2003). The Web site was subsequently revised to give a more upbeat account of the impact of Van der Rohe's "Master Plan" (http://mies.iit.edu.mies).

55. Brooks has Mecca resident Alfred, whose imagination has been captured by Leopold Senghor's mythic vision of Africa, wonder early in the poem, "When there were all those gods . . . lighting stars and comets and a moon, / what was their one Belief? / what was their joining thing?" (*BLACKS*, 409–10). As Sheila Hassell Hughes points out, "Alfred can only read Africa through Emersonian eyes" ("A Prophet Overheard: A Juxtapositional Reading of Gwendolyn Brooks's 'In the Mecca,'" *African American Review* 38, no. 2 [Summer 2004]: 270).

56. During the more than thirty years since *The Dialogic Imagination* was published in English, a number of critics have pointed out that poems as well as novels can and sometimes do foreground heteroglossia. See esp. David H. Richter, "Dialogism and Poetry," *Studies in the Literary Imagination* 23, no. 1 (1990): 9–27.

57. Henry Taylor deals especially well with the "unobtrusive anachronism" involved here in "Gwendolyn Brooks: An Essential Sanity," first published in the *Kenyon Review* in the fall of 1991 and reprinted in Wright, *On Gwendolyn Brooks: Reliant Contemplation*, 254–75.

58. This is Gertrude Reif Hughes's reading in "Making it *Really* New: Hilda Doolittle, Gwendolyn Brooks, and the Feminist Potential of Modern Poetry," in Wright, *On Gwendolyn Brooks: Reliant Contemplation*, 204–5. But surely we are to infer that the poet "saw" this happen also, since the description is mediated by an omniscient narratorial discourse.

59. Wikipedia, drawing from the *Encyclopedia Britannica*, 11th edition, translates the Greek word "turning away" and defines it as "an exclamatory rhetorical figure of speech, when a speaker or writer breaks off and directs speech to an imaginary person or abstract quality or idea" (http://en.wikipedia.org/wiki/Apostrophe, accessed July 2008).

60. Addison Gayle, Jr., "Gwendolyn Brooks: Poet of the Whirlwind," in Mari Evans, ed. *Black Women Writers (1950–1980): A Critical Evaluation* (Garden City, N.Y.:

Anchor Doubleday, 1984), 82; Don L. Lee, "Preface: Gwendolyn Brooks: Beyond the Word Maker—The Making of an African Poet," *RPO*, 22–23.

61. The poem's account of Way-Out Morgan's revolutionary project is also laced with potential ironies that in Lee's introduction go unremarked. Whereas he finds Blackness beautiful as a political abstraction, Morgan is less inclined to do so in the context of private domestic arrangements: thus he "postpones a *yellow woman* in his bed (my emphasis), postpones / wetnesses and little cries and stomachings—to consider Ruin." The verbal echo that links this passage to the poem's closing description of "she whose little stomach fought the world" suggests that Pepita is a casualty not only of Jamaican Edward's predatory pedophilia but also, indirectly, of Amos's and Way-Out Morgan's single-minded fantasies of revenge.

62. In the poem's account of how Pepita's sister Melodie Mary looks at the world, "other importances" refers to the Mecca building's rats and roaches, whose deaths don't make the headlines but are easier for her to pity than the deaths of children in China (*BLACKS*, 412).

63. Walter Kalaidjian, in *Languages of Liberation: The Social Text in Contemporary American Poetry* (New York: Columbia University Press, 1989), likens Alfred to T. S. Eliot's Teiresias in his capacity as "'spectator' to *The Waste Land*'s unfolding action" (192). Kalaidjian finds Brooks "ultimately" siding "more with the poems' embittered extremists," Amos and Way-Out Morgan. I am suggesting that the question, "How many care, Pepita?" finds them, like the other Mecca residents, too preoccupied with the fantasy of another life somewhere else to care for the child in their midst.

64. "Poets Who Are Negroes," *Phylon* 11, no. 4 (1950): 312. The essay is just a page long.

65. In "The Black Poet as Cultural Sign," in *The Second Black Renaissance: Essays in Black Literature* (Westport, Conn.: Greenwood Press, 1980), 257–301, C. W. E. Bigsby gives a nuanced account of the shifts in attitude and aspiration that are discernible in black artists' negotiations with a European poetic tradition whose hallmarks were importantly formal—beginning with Phillis Wheatley's use of heroic couplets.

66. Phillip Brian Harper, "Nationalism and Social Division in Black Arts Poetry of the 1960s," *Critical Inquiry* 19, no. 2 (Winter 1993); repr. in *Are We Not Men?: Masculine Anxiety and the Problem of African-American Identity* (New York: Oxford University Press, 1996), 53. Brooks is a good example from Harper's perspective because she "built her reputation on her expertly crafted lyrics of the 1940s and 1950s."

67. Ibid. This lack of a specified objective, Harper suggests, presaged "fundamental difficulties in the nationalist agenda of the Black Arts poets."

68. Imamu Amiri Baraka, "SOS," in *Black Magic Poetry, 1961–1967* (New York: Bobbs-Merrill, 1969), 3. The poem is quoted here in its entirety.

69. Brooks cites this "Websterian" definition from the dictionary: "1. opposite to white; . . . 2. dark-complexioned; 3. Negro; 4. without light . . . ; 5. dirty . . . ; 6. evil; wicked [etc.]" (*RPO*, 83).

70. Jeffrey Walker, "The View from Halicarnassus: Aristotelianism and the Rhetoric of Epideictic Song," in *New Definitions of Lyric: Theory, Technology, and Culture*, ed. Mark Jeffreys (New York and London: Garland, 1998), 27. Walker cites the contemporary rhetorician Chaim Perelman for a broader understanding of epideictic along these same lines.

71. Lawrence W. Rosenfield, "The Practical Celebration of Epideictic," in *Rhetoric in Transition: Studies in the Nature and Uses of Rhetoric*, ed. Eugene E. White (University Park: Penn State University Press, 1998), 133 (cited in Wikipedia [http://en.wikipedia.org/wiki/Epideictic] in 2007).

72. That is what Pindar was doing, for instance, at a moment of political transition in ancient Greece from one kind of political regime to another. In this connection

Walker cites Leslie Kurke's discussion of Pindar's poems in *The Traffic in Praise: Pindar and the Poetics of Social Economy* (Ithaca, N.Y.: Cornell University Press, 1991).

73. *A Capsule Course in Black Poetry Writing* was a collaborative publication: it includes essays by Keorapetse Kgositsile, Haki R. Madhubuti (formerly Don L. Lee), and Dudley Randall. Randall explains in his brief Introduction that the volume was Brooks's idea and that "each writer's section is divided into six topics suggested by Miss Brooks" (1).

74. Brooks, *RPT*, 96. Burr reads Brooks's public assertions of a radical change in her poetic stance as "strategic speech-acts" aimed at "chang[ing] the terms of her reception." "What she was seeking to repudiate in talking of a 'turn' in her career . . . was the critical tradition that . . . spoke of her as a 'true,' 'universal,' and 'genuine' poet in an effort to discipline other black poets who placed politics ahead of art" (142). Burr's point is well taken, but I do hear Brooks speaking in *Report from Part One* of a conversion experience, and I see her poetic practice changing "after Mecca" in order to engage with Blackness differently from before.

75. Burr cites a reading at Ithaca College in 1992 at which she herself was present, where in choosing to read "To Those of My Sisters Who Kept Their Naturals" Brooks gave a mostly non-black audience the experience of *not* being addressed. One of this poem's meanings, for that audience on that occasion, was that "a gesture of solidarity is inextricable from a gesture of exclusivity" (Burr, *Of Women, Poetry, and Power*, 145). D. H. Melhem's counterpart recollection, from a reading at City College in 1971, is of a poet less problematically in dialogue with her audience, "almost as if a brilliant friend—or mother—had come to visit students at their school" ("Afterword," *RPT*, 155).

76. When Sanchez reads her recent work she builds in sounds that are not also words, thereby calling attention to her medium of expression as a medium of "sounded" speech. Brooks expressed great admiration for Sanchez, Shange, and others who have taken this direction, both in interviews and in the support she gave them during her term as poetry consultant to the Library of Congress.

77. Brooks, *Winnie* (Chicago: Third World Press, 1988), repr. as "Winnie" and "Song of Winnie" in *In Montgomery and Other Poems* (Chicago: Third World Press, 2003), 47.

78. The Greek verb "ekphrasein" literally means "to speak out."

79. *BLACKS*, 331; originally published in *The Bean Eaters* in 1960. In a 1972 interview with Gloria Hull, Brooks aspires to write more poems that can speak to ordinary black people as successfully as this one had done (Gloria Hull and Posey Gallagher, "Update on *Part One:* An Interview with Gwendolyn Brooks" *College Language Journal*, 21 [1977]: 19–40; repr. in *Conversations with Gwendolyn Brooks*, ed. Gloria Wade Gales. Jackson: University Press of Mississippi, 2003, 85–103.

80. *RPO*, 156 (Interview with George Stavros for *Contemporary Literature*, March 28, 1969).

81. "The Colossus" counts as such an image, and so do "Medusa" and "Edge." In "Daddy," the lines "You stand at the blackboard, Daddy, / In the picture I have of you . . ." provide a literal starting point, midway through the poem, for the funhouse mirror image of a "ghastly statue with one grey toe / Big as a Frisco seal" with which the poem begins.

82. *BLACKS*, 482–89; originally published in *Family Pictures* in 1970.

83. For a long time, as a white reader of this poem, I took from it an implicit message that with this kind of start in life, Lincoln West was headed for juvenile delinquency. Why did I not credit him instead with a capacity for making lemonade out of lemons—because his "ugliness" frightened me a little?

84. D. H. Melhem suggests, in her Afterword to *Report from Part Two*, that the "coherent impulse" underlying all of Brooks's work is *caritas*, nourished by a . . . vivid

sense of the Black Nation as an extension of the Black family" ("Afterword," 150).

85. *BLACKS*, 444. This poem is part of a diptych entitled "Two Dedications" that was published in the "After Mecca" section of *In the Mecca* in 1968.

86. Malcolm himself, in an interview published in *Life* magazine March 20, 1964, entitled "The Ominous Malcolm X Exits from the Muslims," suggested that every Negro should own a gun so that if attacked, he would be prepared to "die like a man." "Malcolm expects for the present," says the article, "to find his financial and political base in Harlem where, he contends, 'ninety percent of the people feel as I do, admit it or not.'" Article cited in *Reporting Civil Rights: American Journalism 1963–1973* (http://reportingcivilrights.org, accessed July 2008).

87. Soon after these poems were published, Don Lee became Haki Madhubuti.

88. D. H. Melhem points out that this title refers not only to the relative youth of its subjects but also to their status as "leadership exemplars . . . for black youth" (*Poetry and the Heroic Voice*, 203). Melhem suggests that together these poems present a conception of heroism that is threefold or three-dimensional: artistic, spiritual, and practical.

89. Cf. Melhem, who finds Brooks shifting from a conventionally lyric into a conspicuously heroic mode for this poem (*Poetry and the Heroic Voice*, 204).

90. "To Don at Salaam" does not entirely dispense with pronouncements that are publicly hero-izing: "Your voice is the listened-for music. / Your act is the consolidation." But the main purpose of the poem seems to be to emphasize that a man does not need to be always playing the hero in order to qualify for herohood.

91. In *BLACKS, RIOT* begins on page 470.

92. "The Third Sermon on the Warpland" ends inconclusively with a valedictory section that includes the lines "Lies are told and legends made. / Phoenix rises unafraid" (*BLACKS*, 478). The reference to "ice and fire" in the third section's title invokes Robert Frost's professed uncertainty as to whether it will be love or hate that brings the world to an end.

93. Walter Kalaidjian finds Brooks using Cabot's destruction to herald "the liberation of blacks from the cultural domination of consumer capitalism" (*Languages of Liberation*, 197). In "Killing John Cabot and Publishing Black: Gwendolyn Brooks's *Riot*," *African American Review* 36, no. 4 (Winter 2002), James D. Sullivan points out that she has chosen for this purpose "one of the most prestigious forms in the English tradition: blank verse" (565).

94. The hardcover edition of *RIOT*, published in 1970, includes a dated, handwritten version of "An Aspect of Love" that is signed by Brooks and dated "March 17/18, 1968."

95. At the end of the novel Maud Martha is stuck in a very conventional marriage to a man who would rather she weren't so "black." Brooks said in an interview while she was planning a sequel to the novel that she intended to kill off Maud Martha's husband, since it was "obvious he wasn't going to change."

96. Both Gloria Hull and Betsy Erkkila (Hull in Gloria Hull and Posey Gallagher, "Update on *Part One*," 91, in 1977 and Erkkila in her chapter on Brooks in *The Wicked Sisters*) have taken Brooks to task for not paying as much attention to Black womanhood after Fisk as before; both infer that she accepted, more or less uncritically, the Black Power movement's emphasis on empowering "the Black Male." In relation to this poem, however, that charge seems misplaced, since its purpose is not only to envision a new kind of black man but also to speak as his female counterpart, thereby putting black men and women on a different footing than before.

97. Cf. Melhem, 200. We might also think of "Break of Day," an aubade of Donne's that is in a woman's voice.

98. L. M. Findlay reminds us, in a 1985 riposte to Jonathan Culler's essay on "apostrophe" in *The Pursuit of Signs*, that the device itself is closely linked to the

lyric's invocation of a "timeless present." "Culler and Byron on Apostrophe and Lyric Time," *Studies in Romanticism*, 24 (Fall 1985): 336.

99. As Bonnie Costello points out in *Shifting Ground: Reinventing Landscape in Modern American Poetry* (Cambridge, Mass.: Harvard University Press, 2003), "diverse critics of lyric . . . tend to agree that lyric time involves a resistance to, suspension of, or transcendence of experiential and historical time" (40). Cf. esp. Sharon Cameron, *Lyric Time: Emily Dickinson and the Limits of Genre* (Baltimore, Md.: Johns Hopkins University Press, 1979).

CODA

1. Louise Glück, "Education of the Poet," in *Proofs and Theories: Essays on Poetry* (Hopewell, N.J.: Ecco Press, 1994), 4. In the Introduction, Glück's *Ararat* sequence was used to exemplify poetry that addresses its readers directly. "Addressivity" is a term I encountered first in Zofia Burr's discussion of Gwendolyn Brooks's strategies of address, with which this study engages in chapter 4.

2. For a study of the lyric that captures the potential as well as actual complexities of lyric "audience" unusually well, see Heather Dubrow, *The Challenges of Orpheus: Lyric Poetry and Early Modern England* (Baltimore, Md.: Johns Hopkins University Press, 2008), especially chapter 2 (54–105).

3. Helen Vendler, *Invisible Listeners: Lyric Intimacy in Herbert, Whitman, and Ashbery* (Princeton, N.J.: Princeton University Press, 2005).

4. Both of the phrases in quotation marks are cited in chapter 1.

5. Cf. my discussion of Plath's poem "Medusa" in chapter 3.

6. Cf. "And this is the kingdom you bore me to, / Mother, mother . . ." in "The Disquieting Muses," *The Collected Poems*, ed. Ted Hughes (New York: Harper and Row, 1992), 76.

7. Rich, "Notes toward a Politics of Location," *Blood, Bread, and Poetry*, 224.

8. Brooks, *Report from Part One* (Detroit, Mich., Broadside Press, 1972), 183.

9. In the headnote to her 1973 essay, "Teaching Language in Open Admissions" (*On Lies, Secrets, and Silence: Selected Prose 1966–1978* [New York: W. W. Norton, 1979], 51), Rich names Brooks as one of the poets whose work she "came to know and put on my reading lists" in the SEEK program at City College from 1968–72, even though "few books by black women writers were available" at that time. During the 1970s, however, the African American poets with whom Rich was in dialogue around issues of sexism and racism were Audre Lorde and June Jordan, not Brooks.

10. Plath, "Electra on Azalea Path," *The Collected Poems*, 117.

11. Adrienne Rich, *Telephone Ringing in the Labyrinth* (New York: W. W. Norton, 2007), hereafter cited as *Telephone*.

12. That Rich has been headed in this direction ever since *Dark Fields of the Republic* in 1995 is suggested by Ann Keniston's discussion of how figures of address are used throughout that volume to affirm "the simultaneous necessity and fictionality of intimate address." See Keniston, "'To feel with a human stranger': Adrienne Rich's Post-Holocaust Confession and the Limits of Identification," in Jo Gill, ed., *Modern Confessional Writing: New Critical Essays* (London and New York: Routledge, 2006), 50–66.

13. In paraphrasing this section of the poem I have had recourse to the pronoun "I," but Rich avoids using it, in part by attributing greater agency to a "green glass bowl" than to a speaker whose "hand slipped" while rinsing it.

14. The jacket blurb for *Telephone* cites "the dialogic urgencies of the title poem" as being deeply characteristic of Rich's poetic "sensibility."

15. I have put quotation marks around "locate" here to allude to Rich's advocacy during the 1980s of a "politics of location" (discussed at greater length in chapter 2).

16. Insofar as Tory Dent wrote movingly of her own impending death during an almost twenty-year-long struggle with AIDS, the voice Rich's poem conjures up is itself already a poetic construct as well as the actual, remembered voice of a friend. Dent died in December of 2005; Rich's poem is dated 2006.

17. Christopher MacGowan, *Twentieth-Century American Poetry* (London: Blackwell Publishing, 2004), 28.

18. Maxine Kumin, "Itinerary of an Obsession," in *Selected Poems 1960–1990* (New York: W. W. Norton, 1997), 184. This poem was originally published in *Our Ground Time Here Will Be Brief* (New York: Penguin Books, 1982).

BIBLIOGRAPHY

PRIMARY TEXTS

Baraka, Imamu Amiri. *Black Magic: Poetry, 1961–1967*. New York: Bobbs-Merrill, 1969.
Brooks, Gwendolyn. *Annie Allen*. New York: Harper Perennial, 1999.
———. *BLACKS*. Chicago: Third World Press, 1987.
———. *Conversations with Gwendolyn Brooks*. Edited by Gloria Wade Gayles. Jackson: University Press of Mississippi, 2003.
———. *In Montgomery and Other Poems*. Chicago: Third World Press, 2003.
———. "Poets Who Are Negroes." *Phylon* 11, no. 4 (1950): 312.
———. *Report from Part One*. Detroit, Mich.: Broadside Press, 1972.
———. *Report from Part Two*. Afterword by D. H. Melhem. Chicago: Third World Press, 1996.
Brooks, Gwendolyn, Keorapetse Kgositsile, Haki R. Madhubuti, and Dudley Randall. *A Capsule Course in Black Poetry Writing*. Detroit, Mich.: Broadside Press, 1975.
Friedan, Betty. *The Feminine Mystique*. New York: W. W. Norton, 1963.
Glück, Louise. *Ararat*. Hopewell, N.J.: Ecco Press, 1990.
———. "Education of the Poet." In *Proofs and Theories: Essays on Poetry*. Hopewell, N.J.: Ecco Press, 1994.
Hollander, John. *A Crackling of Thorns*. New Haven, Conn.: Yale University Press, 1958.
Hughes, Ted. *Birthday Letters*. New York: Farrar, Straus and Giroux, 1998.
Kumin, Maxine. "Itinerary of an Obsession." *Selected Poems 1960–1990*. New York: W. W. Norton, 1997. 182–84.
Levertov, Denise. *Poems 1960–67*. New York: New Directions, 1983.
———. *The Poet in the World*. New York: New Directions, 1973.

Lowell, Robert. *Collected Poems*. Edited by Frank Bidart and David Gewanter. New York: Farrar, Straus and Giroux, 2003.
———. *Collected Prose by Robert Lowell*. Edited by Robert Giroux. New York: Farrar, Straus and Giroux, 1987.
Martin, John Bartlow. "The Strangest Place in Chicago." *Harper's*, December 1950, 86–97.
Orr, Peter, ed. *The Poet Speaks: Interviews with Contemporary Poets*. London: Routledge, 1966.
Pinsky, Robert. *The Figured Wheel: New and Collected Poems, 1966–1996*. New York: Farrar, Straus and Giroux, 1996.
Plath, Sylvia. *The Collected Poems*. Edited by Ted Hughes. New York: Harper and Row, 1981.
———. *The Journals of Sylvia Plath*. Edited by Frances McCullough; consulting editor Ted Hughes. New York: Dial Press, 1982.
———. *Letters Home*. Edited by Aurelia Schober Plath. New York: Harper & Row, 1975.
———. *The Unabridged Journals of Sylvia Plath, 1950–1962*. Edited by Karen V. Kukil. New York: Anchor Books, 2000.
Rich, Adrienne. *Blood, Bread, and Poetry: Selected Prose, 1979–1985*. New York: W. W. Norton, 1986.
———. *A Change of World*. Foreword by W. H. Auden. New Haven, Conn.: Yale University Press, 1951.
———. *The Dream of a Common Language: Poems 1974–1977*. New York: W. W. Norton, 1978.
———. *The Fact of a Doorframe: Poems Selected and New 1950–1984*. New York: W. W. Norton, 1984.
———. *The Fact of a Doorframe: Selected Poems 1950–2001*. New York: W. W. Norton, 2002.
———. *Of Woman Born: Motherhood as Experience and Institution*. New York: W. W. Norton, 1976.
———. *On Lies, Secrets, and Silence: Selected Prose 1966–1978*. New York: W. W. Norton, 1979.
———. *Poems Selected and New, 1950–1974*. New York: W. W. Norton, 1975.
———. *Snapshots of a Daughter-in-Law*. New York: W. W. Norton, 1963.
———. *Telephone Ringing in the Labyrinth: Poems 2004–2006*. New York: W. W. Norton, 2007.
———. *Time's Power: Poems 1985–1988*. New York: W. W. Norton, 1989.
———. *What Is Found There: Notebooks on Poetry and Politics*. New York: W. W. Norton, 1993.
———. *A Wild Patience Has Taken Me This Far: Poems 1978–1981*. New York: W. W. Norton, 1981.
———. *Your Native Land, Your Life: Poems*. New York: W. W. Norton, 1986.
Sexton, Anne. *The Complete Poems of Anne Sexton, with a Foreword by Maxine Kumin*. Boston: Houghton Mifflin, 1981.
Snodgrass, W. D. *Heart's Needle*. New York: Knopf, 1959. Repr. in *Selected Poems, 1957–1987* (New York: Soho Press, 1987).

CRITICAL, BIOGRAPHICAL, THEORETICAL

Altieri, Charles. *Canons and Consequences: Reflections on the Ethical Force of Imaginative Ideals*. Evanston, Ill.: Northwestern University Press, 1990.
Alexander, Elizabeth. "Meditations on 'Mecca': Gwendolyn Brooks and the Respon-

sibilities of the Black Poet." In *By Herself: Women Reclaim Poetry*, edited by Molly McQuade. Saint Paul, Minn.: Graywolf Press, 2000. 368-79. Repr. in Alexander, *The Black Interior: Essays*. St. Paul: Minn.: Graywolf Press, 2004. 43-58.
Alvarez, Alfred. *The Savage God*. New York: Random House, 1972.
Axelrod, Steven Gould, ed. *The Critical Response to Robert Lowell*. Westport, Conn.: Greenwood Press, 1999.
———. *Robert Lowell: Life and Art*. Princeton, N.J.: Princeton University Press, 1978.
Baker, Houston A. "The Florescence of Nationalism in the 1960s and 1970s." In Wright, *On Gwendolyn Brooks: Reliant Contemplation*, 116-23.
Bassnett, Susan. *Sylvia Plath: An Introduction to the Poetry*. 2nd ed. Hampshire/New York: Palgrave Macmillan, 2005.
Berger, John. *Ways of Seeing*. Harmondsworth, U.K.: Penguin, 1972.
Bernstein, Susan David. *Confessional Subjects: Revelations of Gender and Power in Victorian Literature and Culture*. Chapel Hill: University of North Carolina Press, 1997.
Bigsby, C. W. E. "The Black Poet as Cultural Sign." In *The Second Black Renaissance: Essays in Black Literature*. Westport, Conn.: Greenwood Press, 1980. 257-301.
Bixler, Francis, ed. *Original Essays on the Poetry of Anne Sexton*. Conway, Ark.: University of Central Arkansas Press, 1988.
Black American Poets Between Worlds, 1940-1960. Edited by R. Baxter Miller. Knoxville: University of Tennessee Press, 1986.
Bolden, Barbara Jean. *Urban Rage in Bronzeville: Social Commentary in the Poetry of Gwendolyn Brooks, 1945-1960*. Chicago: Third World Press, 1999.
Brain, Tracy. "Sylvia Plath's Letters and Journals." In *The Cambridge Companion to Sylvia Plath*, edited by Jo Gill. Cambridge: Cambridge University Press, 2006. 139-55.
Breslin, James E. B. *From Modern to Contemporary: American Poetry, 1945-1965*. Chicago: University of Chicago Press, 1984.
Britzolakis, Christina. *Sylvia Plath and the Theatre of Mourning*. Oxford: Clarendon, 1999.
Brooks, Cleanth. *The Well Wrought Urn: Studies in the Structure of Poetry*. New York: Reynal and Hitchcock, 1947.
Bundtzen, Linda K. *The Other Ariel*. Amherst: University of Massachusetts Press, 2001.
Burns, Michael. "Confession as Sacrament." In Bixler, *Original Essays on the Poetry of Anne Sexton*, 130-37.
Burr, Zofia. *Of Women, Poetry, and Power: Strategies of Address in Dickinson, Miles, Brooks, Lorde, and Angelou*. Urbana/Chicago: University of Illinois Press, 2002.
Cameron, Sharon. *Lyric Time: Emily Dickinson and the Limits of Genre*. Baltimore, Md.: Johns Hopkins University Press, 1979.
Capo, Kay E. "'I Have Been Her Kind': Anne Sexton's Communal Voice." In Bixler, *Original Essays on the Poetry of Anne Sexton*, 22-45.
Churchwell, Sarah. "'Your sentence was mine too': Reading Sylvia Plath in Ted Hughes's *Birthday Letters*." In *Literary Couplings: Writing Couples, Collaborators, and the Construction of Authorship*, edited by Marjorie Stone and Judith Thompson. Madison: University of Wisconsin Press, 2006. 260-87.
Clausen, Jan. *A Movement of Poets: Thoughts on Poetry and Feminism*. Brooklyn, N.Y.: Long Haul Press, 1982.
Costello, Bonnie. *Shifting Ground: Reinventing Landscape in Modern American Poetry*. Cambridge, Mass.: Harvard University Press, 2003.
Culler, Jonathan. "Apostrophe." In *The Pursuit of Signs*. Ithaca, N.Y.: Cornell University Press, 1981. 135-44.
———. "Reading Lyric." *Yale French Studies*, 69 (1985): 98-106.

Davidson, Harriet. "'In the Wake of Home': Adrienne Rich's Politics and Poetics of Location." In Easthope and Thompson, *Contemporary Poetry Meets Modern Theory*, 166–76.

———. "I Say I Am There: Siting/Citing the Subject of Feminism and Deconstruction." In *Critical Encounters: Reference and Responsibility in Deconstructive Writing*, edited by Cathy Caruth and Deborah Esch. New Brunswick, N.J.: Rutgers, 1995. 241–61.

———. "Poetry, Witness, Feminism." In *Witness and Memory: The Discourse of Trauma*, edited by Ana Douglass and Thomas A. Vogler. New York: Routledge, 2003. 153–72.

De Man, Paul. "Autobiography as De-Facement." *MLN* 94, no. 5 (1979): 919–30. Repr. in *The Rhetoric of Romanticism*. New York: Columbia University Press, 1984. 67–92.

———. "Lyrical Voice in Contemporary Theory: Riffaterre and Jauss." In Hosek and Parker, *Lyric Poetry: Beyond New Criticism*, 55–72.

Dennis, Helen M. "Adrienne Rich: Consciousness Raising as Poetic Method." In Easthope and Thompson, *Contemporary Poetry Meets Modern Theory*, 177–94.

Dickie, Margaret. *Stein, Bishop, and Rich: Lyrics of Love, War, and Place*. Chapel Hill: University of North Carolina Press, 1997.

———. "Sylvia Plath's Narrative Strategies." *Iowa Review* 13 (1982): 1–14. Repr. in Wagner, *Critical Essays on Sylvia Plath*, 170–82.

Diehl, Joanne Feit. *Women Poets and the American Sublime*. Bloomington: Indiana University Press, 1990.

Doane, Mary Ann. "Film and the Masquerade: Theorising the Female Spectator." *SCREEN* 23 (1982): 74–87. Repr. in *Feminism and Film*, edited by E. Ann Kaplan. Oxford/New York: Oxford University Press, 2000. 418–36.

Dodd, Elizabeth. *The Veiled Mirror and the Woman Poet: H.D., Louise Bogan, Elizabeth Bishop, and Louise Glück*. Columbia: University of Missouri Press, 1992.

Dubrow, Heather. *The Challenges of Orpheus: Lyric Poetry and Early Modern England*. Baltimore, Md.: Johns Hopkins University Press, 2008.

Easthope, Anthony, and John O. Thompson, eds. *Contemporary Poetry Meets Modern Theory*. Toronto: University of Toronto Press, 1991.

Edwards, Thomas R. *Imagination and Power: A Study of Poetry on Public Themes*. New York: Oxford University Press, 1971.

Eisenstein, Hester. *Contemporary Feminist Thought*. Boston: G. K. Hall, 1983.

Ehrenreich, Barbara. *The Hearts of Men: American Dreams and the Flight from Commitment*. New York: Anchor/Doubleday, 1983.

Eliot, T. S. *The Three Voices of Poetry*. New York: Cambridge University Press, 1954.

Erkkila, Betsy. *The Wicked Sisters: Women Poets, Literary History and Discord*. Oxford and New York: Oxford University Press, 1992.

Evans, Mari, ed. *Black Women Writers (1950–1980): A Critical Evaluation*. Garden City, N.Y.: Anchor Doubleday, 1984.

Findlay, L. M. "Culler and Byron on Apostrophe and Lyric Time." *Studies in Romanticism*, 24 (Fall 1985): 335–53.

Forbes. Deborah. *Sincerity's Shadow: Self-Consciousness in British Romantic and Mid-Twentieth-Century American Poetry*. Cambridge, Mass.: Harvard University Press, 2004.

Ford, Karen. *Gender and the Poetics of Excess: Moments of Brocade*. Jackson: University of Mississippi Press, 1997.

Friedan, Betty. *The Feminine Mystique, With a New Introduction and Epilogue by the Author*. New York: Dell, 1983.

Fry, Paul. "The Lamplit Answer?" Gjertrud Schnackenberg's Anti-Ekphrases." In *In the Frame: Women's Ekphrastic Poetry from Marianne Moore to Susan Wheeler*, edited by

Jane Hedley, Nick Halpern, and Willard Spiegelman. Newark, Del.: University of Delaware Press, 2009.
———. "The Torturer's Horse: What Poems See in Pictures." In *A Defense of Poetry*. Stanford: Stanford University Press: 1995. 70–91.
Frye, Northrop. *Anatomy of Criticism*. Princeton, N.J.: Princeton University Press, 1957.
Gabbin, Joanne V. "Blooming in the Whirlwind: The Early Poetry of Gwendolyn Brooks." In *The Furious Flowering of African American Poetry*, ed. Joanne V. Gabbin. Charlottesville: University Press of Virginia, 1999. 252–73.
Gayle, Addison, Jr. "Gwendolyn Brooks: Poet of the Whirlwind." In Evans, *Black Women Writers (1950–1980): A Critical Evaluation*, 79–87.
———, ed. *The Black Aesthetic*. New York: Doubleday, 1971.
Gelpi, Barbara Charlesworth, and Robert Gelpi, eds. *Adrienne Rich's Poetry and Prose: A Norton Critical Edition*. New York: W. W. Norton, 1993.
George, Diana Hume. *Oedipus Anne: The Poetry of Anne Sexton*. Urbana: University of Illinois Press, 1987.
Gewanter, David. "Child of Collaboration: Robert Lowell's *Dolphin*." *Modern Philology* 93, no. 2 (November 1995): 178–203.
Gilbert, Roger. "Framing Water: Historical Knowledge in Elizabeth Bishop and Adrienne Rich." *Twentieth Century Literature*, 43 (1997): 144–61.
Gilbert, Sandra, and Susan Gubar. *No Man's Land: The Place of the Woman Writer in the Twentieth Century*. Vol. 1, *The War of the Words*. New Haven, Conn.: Yale University Press, 1980.
Gill, Jo. "'Your story. My story': Confessional Writing and the Case of *Birthday Letters*." In Gill, *Modern Confessional Writing: New Critical Essays*, 67–83.
———, ed. *Modern Confessional Writing: New Critical Essays*. London: Routledge, 2006.
Giovanni, Nikki. "To Gwen Brooks from Nikki Giovanni." *Essence*, 1 (April 1971): 26.
Gray, Richard. *American Poetry of the Twentieth Century*. New York: Longman, 1990.
Hagstrum, Jean. *The Sister Arts*. Chicago: University of Chicago Press, 1958.
Halpern, Nick. *Everyday and Prophetic: The Poetry of Lowell, Ammons, Merrill, and Rich*. Madison: University of Wisconsin Press, 2003.
Hamilton, Ian. *Robert Lowell: A Biography*. New York: Random House, 1982.
Harper, Philip Brian. *Are We Not Men?: Masculine Anxiety and the Problem of African-American Identity*. New York: Oxford University Press, 1996.
Harrison, DeSales. *The End of the Mind: The Edge of the Intelligible in Hardy, Stevens, Larkin, Plath, and Glück*. London/New York: Routledge, 2005.
Heffernan, James. *Museum of Words: The Poetics of Ekphrasis from Homer to Ashbery*. Chicago: University of Chicago Press, 1993.
Hogue, Cynthia. *Scheming Women: Poetry, Privilege, and the Politics of Subjectivity*. Albany, N.Y.: SUNY Press, 1995.
Holden, Jonathan. *The Rhetoric of the Contemporary Lyric*. Bloomington: Indiana University Press, 1980.
Hollander, John. *The Gazer's Spirit: Poems Speaking to Silent Works of Art*. Chicago: University of Chicago Press, 1995.
———. "The Gazer's Spirit: Romantic and Later Poetry on Painting and Sculpture." In *The Romantics and Us: Essays on Literature and Culture*, edited by Gene W. Ruoff. New Brunswick, N.J.: Rutgers University Press, 1990. 130–67.
Homans, Margaret. *Women Writers and Poetic Identity: Dorothy Wordsworth, Emily Brontë and Emily Dickinson*. Princeton, N.J.: Princeton University Press, 1980.
Horvath, Brooke Kenton. "The Satisfactions of What's Difficult in Gwendolyn Brooks's Poetry." In Wright, *On Gwendolyn Brooks: Reliant Contemplation*, 213–23.

Hosek, Chaviva, and Patricia Parker, eds. *Lyric Poetry: Beyond New Criticism*. Ithaca, N.Y.: Cornell University Press, 1985.

Hughes, Gertrude Reif. "Making it *Really* New: Hilda Doolittle, Gwendolyn Brooks, and the Feminist Potential of Modern Poetry." *American Quarterly* 42, no. 3 (September 1990). Repr. in Wright, *On Gwendolyn Brooks: Reliant Contemplation*, 186–212.

Hughes, Sheila Hassell. "A Prophet Overheard: A Juxtapositional Reading of Gwendolyn Brooks's 'In the Mecca.'" *African American Review* 38, no. 2 (Summer 2004): 257–79.

Hughes, Ted. "Notes on the Chronological Order of Sylvia Plath's Poems." In Newman, *The Art of Sylvia Plath: A Symposium*, 187–95.

———. "Sylvia Plath and her Journals." In *Ariel Ascending: Writings about Sylvia Plath*, edited by Paul Alexander. New York: Harper & Row, 1985. 152–64.

Hull, Gloria, and Posey Gallagher. "Update on *Part One*: An Interview with Gwendolyn Brooks." *College Language Journal*, 21 (1977): 19–40. Repr. in *Conversations with Gwendolyn Brooks*, ed. Gloria Wade Gayles. 85–103.

Jackson, Virginia. "Dickinson's Figure of Address." In *Dickinson and Audience*, edited by Martin Orzeck and Robert Weisbuch. Ann Arbor: University of Michigan Press, 1996. 77–104.

Jacobs, Joshua S. "'An Atlas of the Difficult World': Adrienne Rich's Countermonument." *Contemporary Literature* 42, no. 4 (Winter 2001): 727–49.

Jakobson, Roman. *Selected Writings*. The Hague: Mouton, 1981.

Johnson, Barbara. "Apostrophe, Animation, and Abortion." In *A World of Difference*. Baltimore, Md.: Johns Hopkins University Press, 1987. 184–99.

Johnson, James Weldon. "The Dilemma of the Negro Author." *American Mercury* 15, no. 60 (December 1928). Repr. in *The Politics and Aesthetics of the New Negro Literature*, edited by Cary D. Wintz. New York and London: Garland, 1996. 247–53.

Johnson, W. R. *The Idea of Lyric: Lyric Modes in Ancient and Modern Poetry*. Berkeley: University of California Press, 1982.

Jones, Gayl. "Community and Voice: Gwendolyn Brooks's 'In the Mecca.'" In Mootry and Smith, *A Life Distilled*, 193–204.

Juhasz, Suzanne. *Naked and Fiery Forms: Modern American Poetry by Women: A New Tradition*. New York: Harper Colophon, 1976.

Kalaidjian, Walter B. *Languages of Liberation: The Social Text in Contemporary American Poetry*. New York: Columbia University Press, 1989.

Keniston, Ann. "'The Fluidity of Damaged Form': Apostrophe and Desire in Nineties Lyric." *Contemporary Literature* 42, no. 2 (Summer 2001): 294–324.

———. *Overheard Voices: Address and Subjectivity in Postmodern American Poetry*. New York: Routledge, 2006.

———. "'To feel with a human stranger': Adrienne Rich's Post-Holocaust Confession and the Limits of Identification." In Gill, *Modern Confessional Writing: New Critical Essays*, 50–66.

Kent, George E. "Aesthetic Values in the Poetry of Gwendolyn Brooks." In Mootry and Smith, *A Life Distilled*, 30–47.

———. *Blackness and the Adventure of Western Culture*. Chicago: Third World Press, 1972.

———. *A Life of Gwendolyn Brooks*. Lexington: University Press of Kentucky, 1990.

———. "The Poetry of Gwendolyn Brooks." In Wright, *On Gwendolyn Brooks: Reliant Contemplation*, 66–80.

Keyes, Claire. *The Aesthetics of Power: The Poetry of Adrienne Rich*. Athens: University of Georgia Press, 1986.

———. "'The Angels Chiding': *Snapshots of a Daughter-in-Law*." In *Reading Adrienne*

Rich: Reviews and Re-Visions, 1951–81, edited by Jane Roberta Cooper. Ann Arbor: University of Michigan Press, 1984. 30–50.

Kinnahan, Linda A. *Poetics of the Feminine: Authority and Literary Tradition in William Carlos Williams, Mina Loy, Denise Levertov, and Kathleen Fraser*. Cambridge: Cambridge University Press, 1994.

Kinzie, Mary. *The Cure of Poetry in an Age of Prose: Moral Essays on the Poet's Calling*. Chicago: University of Chicago Press, 1993.

———. "An Informal Checklist of Criticism." In Newman, *The Art of Sylvia Plath*, 283–319.

Kramer, Lawrence. "Freud and the Skunks: Genre and Language in *Life Studies*." In *Robert Lowell: Essays on the Poetry*, edited by Steven Gould Axelrod and Helen Deese. Cambridge: Cambridge University Press, 1986. 80–96.

Kroll, Judith. *Chapters in a Mythology: The Poetry of Sylvia Plath*. New York: Harper & Row, 1976.

Kumin, Maxine. "How It Was: Maxine Kumin on Anne Sexton." In Sexton, *The Complete Poems of Anne Sexton*, xix–xxxiv.

Lacan, Jacques. *Four Fundamental Concepts of Psychoanalysis*. Edited by Jacques-Alain Miller, translated by Alan Sheridan. New York: W. W. Norton, 1978.

Lee, Don L. "Preface: Gwendolyn Brooks: Beyond the Word Maker—The Making of an African Poet." In Brooks, *Report from Part One*, 13–30.

Loizeaux, Elizabeth Bergmann. *Twentieth-Century Poetry and the Visual Arts*. Cambridge: Cambridge University Press, 2008.

Lowney, John. "'A Material Collapse That Is Construction': History and Counter-Memory in Gwendolyn Brooks's *In the Mecca*." *MELUS* 23, no. 3 (Autumn 1998): 3–20.

MacGowan, Christopher. *Twentieth-Century American Poetry*. London: Blackwell Publishing, 2004.

Malcolm, Janet. *The Silent Woman: Sylvia Plath and Ted Hughes*. New York: Knopf/Random House, 2002.

Matterson, Stephen. "Robert Lowell: *Life Studies*." In *A Companion to Twentieth-Century Poetry*, edited by Neil Roberts. Oxford: Blackwell, 2001.

May, Elaine Tyler. *Homeward Bound: American Families in the Cold War Era*. New York: Basic Books, 1988.

McDaniel, Judith. "Reconstituting the World: The Poetry and Vision of Adrienne Rich." Argyle, N.Y.: Spinster's Ink, 1978. Repr. in Gelpi and Gelpi, *Adrienne Rich's Poetry and Prose: A Norton Critical Edition*, 310–21.

Melhem, D. H. *Gwendolyn Brooks: Poetry and the Heroic Voice*. Lexington: University Press of Kentucky, 1987.

Michie, Helena. *Sororophobia: Differences among Women in Literature and Culture*. New York: Oxford University Press, 1992.

Middlebrook, Diane Wood. *Anne Sexton: A Biography*. Boston: Houghton Mifflin, 1991.

———. *Her Husband: Hughes and Plath—A Marriage*. New York: Viking Penguin, 2003.

———. "'I Tapped My Own Head': The Apprenticeship of Anne Sexton." In *Coming to Light: American Women Poets in the Twentieth Century*, edited by Diane Wood Middlebrook and Marilyn Yalom. Ann Arbor: University of Michigan Press, 1985. 195–213.

———. "What Was Confessional Poetry?" In *The Columbia History of American Poetry*, edited by Jay Parini and Brett C. Millier. New York: Columbia University Press, 1993. 642–49.

Mill, John Stuart. "What Is Poetry?" In *Essays on Poetry*, edited by F. Parvin Sharpless. Columbia: University of South Carolina Press, 1976. 3–22.

Miller, A. D. "Some Observations on a Black Aesthetic." In *The Black Aesthetic*, edited by Addison Gayle. Garden City, N.J.: Doubleday, 1971. 374–80.

Miller, R. Baxter. "'Define . . . the Whirlwind'": Gwendolyn Brooks's Epic Sign for a Generation." In Wright, *On Gwendolyn Brooks: Reliant Contemplation*, 146–60.

Millier, Brett. *Elizabeth Bishop: Life and the Memory of It*. Berkeley: University of California Press, 1993.

Mitchell, W. J. T. *Picture Theory: Essays on Verbal and Visual Representation*. Chicago: University of Chicago Press, 1994.

Montefiore, Jan. *Feminism and Poetry: Language, Experience, Identity in Women's Writing*. London/New York: Pandora, 1987.

Mootry, Maria K., and Gary Smith, eds. *A Life Distilled: Gwendolyn Brooks, Her Poetry and Fiction*. Urbana/Chicago: University of Illinois Press, 1987.

Mullen, Bill. *Popular Fronts: Chicago and African American Cultural Politics, 1935–46*. Urbana/Chicago: University of Illinois Press, 1999.

Muske, Carol. *Women and Poetry: Truth, Autobiography, and the Shape of the Self*. Ann Arbor: University of Michigan Press, 1997.

Nelson, Cary. *Our Last First Poets: Vision and History in Contemporary American Poetry*. Urbana: University of Illinois Press, 1981.

New, Elisa. *The Regenerate Lyric: Theology and Innovation in American Poetry*. Cambridge: Cambridge University Press, 1993.

Newman, Charles, ed. *The Art of Sylvia Plath: A Symposium*. Bloomington: Indiana University Press, 1970.

Ostriker, Alicia. "The Americanization of Sylvia." In Wagner, *Critical Essays on Sylvia Plath*, 97–109.

———. "Anne Sexton and the Seduction of the Audience." In *Sexton: Selected Criticism*, edited by Diana Hume George. Urbana: University of Illinois Press, 1988. 3–18.

———. *Stealing the Language: The Emergence of Women's Poetry in America*. Boston: Beacon Press, 1986.

Perloff, Marjorie. "Angst and Animism in the Poetry of Sylvia Plath." In Wagner, *Critical Essays on Sylvia Plath*, 109–24.

———. *The Poetic Art of Robert Lowell*. Ithaca, N.Y.: Cornell University Press, 1973.

———. "The Two Ariels: The (Re)Making of the Sylvia Plath Canon." *American Poetry Review*, 13 (November 1984): 10–18.

Pope, Deborah. *A Separate Vision: Isolation in Contemporary Women's Poetry*. Baton Rouge: Louisiana State University Press, 1984.

Quinn, Sister Bernetta. "Medusan Imagery in Sylvia Plath." In *Sylvia Plath: New Views on the Poetry*, edited by Gary Lane. Baltimore, Md.: Johns Hopkins University Press, 1979. 97–115.

Ramazani, Jahan. *Poetry of Mourning: The Modern Elegy from Hardy to Heaney*. Chicago: University of Chicago Press, 1994.

Redding, Saunders. "Cellini-like Lyrics." Repr. in Wright, *On Gwendolyn Brooks: Reliant Contemplation*, 6–7.

Richter, David H. "Dialogism and Poetry." *Studies in the Literary Imagination* 23, no. 1 (1990): 9–27.

Rogers, William Elford. *The Three Genres and the Interpretation of Lyric*. Princeton, N.J.: Princeton University Press, 1983.

Rosenthal, M. L. *The New Poets*. New York: Oxford University Press, 1967.

Saldívar, Toni. *Sylvia Plath: Confessing the Fictive Self*. New York: Peter Lang, 1992.

Sanchez, Sonia. "Eulogy." *Time*, December 18, 2000, 25.

Saunders, Judith P. "The Love Song of Satin-Legs Smith: Gwendolyn Brooks Revisits Prufrock's Hell." *Papers on Language and Literature* 36, no. 1 (Winter 2000): 3–18.

Schweik, Susan. *A Gulf So Deeply Cut: American Women Poets and the Second World War.* Madison: University of Wisconsin Press, 1991.
Scigaj, Leonard. "The Painterly Plath That Nobody Knows." *Centennial Review,* 32 (1988): 220-49.
Sexton, Linda Gray. *Searching for Mercy Street.* Boston: Little, Brown, 1994.
Spiegelman, Willard. *The Didactic Muse: Scenes of Instruction in Contemporary American Poetry.* Princeton, N.J.: Princeton University Press, 1989.
Spillers, Hortense. "Gwendolyn the Terrible: Propositions on Eleven Poems." In Mootry and Smith, *A Life Distilled,* 224-35.
Stanford, Ann Folwell. "Dialectics of Desire: War and the Resistive Voice in Gwendolyn Brooks's 'Negro Hero' and 'Gay Chaps at the Bar.'" *African American Review* 26, no. 2 (Summer 1992): 197-211.
———. "An Epic with a Difference: Sexual Politics in Gwendolyn Brooks's 'The Anniad.'" *American Literature* 67, no. 2 (June 1995): 283-301.
———. "'Like Narrow Banners for Some Gathering War': Readers, Aesthetics, and Gwendolyn Brooks's 'The Sundays of Satin-Legs Smith.'" *College Literature,* 17 (1990): 162-82.
Stevenson, Anne. *Bitter Fame: A Life of Sylvia Plath.* Boston: Houghton Mifflin, 1989.
Stewart, Susan. "Lyric Possession." *Critical Inquiry,* 22 (Autumn 1995): 34-63.
Sullivan, James D. "Killing John Cabot and Publishing Black: Gwendolyn Brooks's *Riot.*" *African American Review* 36, no. 4 (Winter 2002): 557-69.
Tate, Claudia. "Anger So Flat: Gwendolyn Brooks's *Annie Allen.*" In Mootry and Smith, *A Life Distilled,* 140-52.
Taylor, Henry. "Gwendolyn Brooks: An Essential Sanity." In Wright, *On Gwendolyn Brooks: Reliant Contemplation,* 254-75.
Templeton, Alice. *The Dream and the Dialogue: Adrienne Rich's Feminist Poetics.* Knoxville: University of Tennessee Press, 1994.
Tillinghast, Richard. *Robert Lowell's Life and Work: Damaged Grandeur.* Ann Arbor: University of Michigan Press, 1995.
Tucker, Herbert. "Dramatic Monologue and the Overhearing of Lyric." In Hosek and Parker, *Lyric Poetry: Beyond New Criticism,* 226-43.
Uroff, Margaret Dickie. *Sylvia Plath and Ted Hughes.* Urbana: University of Illinois Press, 1979.
Vendler, Helen. *Coming of Age as a Poet: Milton, Keats, Eliot, Plath.* Cambridge, Mass.: Harvard University Press, 2003.
———. *Invisible Listeners: Lyric Intimacy in Herbert, Whitman, and Ashbery.* Princeton, N.J.: Princeton University Press, 2005.
———. *Part of Nature, Part of Us.* Cambridge, Mass.: Harvard University Press, 1980.
———. *Poems, Poets, Poetry: An Introduction and Anthology.* Boston: St. Martin's Press, 1997.
Vickers, Nancy J. "Diana Described: Scattered Woman and Scattered Rhyme." *Critical Inquiry,* 7 (Winter 1981): 265-79.
von Hallberg, Robert. *American Poetry and Culture: 1945-1980.* Cambridge, Mass.: Harvard University Press, 1985.
Wagner, Linda, ed. *Critical Essays on Sylvia Plath.* Boston, Mass.: G. K. Hall, 1984.
Wagner-Martin, Linda. *Sylvia Plath: A Literary Life.* 2nd rev. ed. Basingstoke, Hampshire, U.K.: Palgrave Macmillan, 2003.
Walker, Cheryl. *Masks Outrageous and Austere: Culture, Psyche and Persona in Modern Women Poets.* Bloomington: Indiana University Press, 1991.
Walker, Jeffrey. "The View from Halicarnassus: Aristotelianism and the Rhetoric of Epideictic Song." In *New Definitions of Lyric: Theory, Technology, and Culture,* edited by Mark Jeffreys. New York and London: Garland, 1998. 17-48.

———. *Rhetoric and Poetics in Antiquity.* New York: Oxford University Press, 2000.
Walker, Margaret. "New Poets." *Phylon* 11, no. 4 (Winter 1950): 349–54.
Waters, William. *Poetry's Touch: On Lyric Address.* Ithaca, N.Y.: Cornell University Press, 2003.
Wheeler, Lesley. *The Poetics of Enclosure.* Knoxville: University Press of Tennessee, 2002.
Whitehead, Kim. *The Feminist Poetry Movement.* Jackson: University of Mississippi Press, 1996.
Wimsatt, William K., and Monroe Beardsley. "The Intentional Fallacy." In *The Verbal Icon: Studies in the Meaning of Poetry.* Lexington: University of Kentucky Press, 1954. 3–18.
Witek, Terri. *Robert Lowell and Life Studies: Revising the Self.* Columbia, Miss.: University of Missouri Press, 1993.
Wright, Stephen Caldwell, ed. *On Gwendolyn Brooks: Reliant Contemplation.* Ann Arbor: University of Michigan Press, 1996.
Yorke, Liz. *Impertinent Voices: Subversive Strategies in Contemporary Women's Poetry.* London and New York: Routledge, 1991.

INDEX

Page numbers in italics refer to figures.

A

abortion, 106–9, 169nn9–10
"The Abortion" (Sexton), 169n9
Alexander, Elizabeth, 171n46
allegory, 22, 82, 84, 166n43
All My Pretty Ones (Sexton), 169n9
Altieri, Charles, 6, 153n22
Alvarez, Alfred, 2, 73, 98, 167n71
American Mercury, 110
Ames, Lois, 53
anger, 121–23, 128
Angle, Paul, 109
"The Anniad" (Brooks): comparison to "In the Mecca," 124; and power of language, 121–22, 171n46; strategies of address in, 118–24
Annie Allen (Brooks): audience of, 119; Brooks on, 120; chronology, 151n5; publication, 109, 118; subject, 2–3, 103. *See also* "The Anniad" (Brooks)
apostrophe: Baraka's use of, 133; Brooks's use of, 20–23, 107, 108, 112, 115, 118–19, 127, 139, 140, 142, 143, 170n27; in confessional poetry, 49; definition, 172n59; in elegies, 16–20; Lowell's use of, 28, 39–40, 63–64, 160n16; in lyric discourse, 6, 8, 9, 44, 143, 158n71, 175n98; Plath's use of, 97–98, 146; purpose of, 4, 5, 152n13; Rich's use of, 14, 15, 16, 62, 64–65; Sexton's use of, 43–45, 158n68. *See also* lyric discourse; rhetorical structures
Ararat (Glück), 11–13, 176n1
Ariel poems (Plath), 101–2, 151n1, 167n59, 168n77
art. *See* ekphrastic poetry
Art News, 72, 81, 87
The Art of Sylvia Plath (Newman), 79
"An Aspect of Love, Alive in the Ice and Fire" (Brooks), 140–43, 175n94
Astrophil and Stella (Sidney), 10
"An Atlas of the Difficult World" (Rich), 14, 62, 70, 154n39
aubade, 39, 142, 143, 175n97
Auden, W. H., 26, 30, 156n20

189

"Aunt Jennifer's Tigers" (Rich), 29, 31
Axelrod, Steven, 39

B

Bakhtin, Mikhail, 125
"ballad of chocolate mabbie" (Brooks), 133
Bambara, Toni Cade, 134
Baraka, Imamu Amiri, 108, 132–33, 136
Bassnett, Susan, 164n9, 164n12
Baudelaire, Charles, 31
The Bean Eaters (Brooks), 174n79
"Behind the Motel" (Rich), 148
The Bell Jar (Plath), 73, 95
Benjamin, Walter, 154n35
Benn, Gottfried, 5, 153n26
Berger, John, 76, 100
Bernstein, Susan David, 157n37
Bigsby, C. W. E., 173n65
"the birth in a narrow room" (Brooks): placement in *Annie Allen*, 3, 151n5; publication, 2–3, 151n5; structure, 118, 119
Birthday Letters (Hughes), 73–79, 84, 94, 101, 149, 164n9
Bishop, Elizabeth, 26, 41
Bitter Fame (Stevenson), 79
Black Arts movement, 108–9, 111, 122, 126, 146
Black Expression, 140
Blackmur, R. P., 26
Blackness: and apostrophe, 23; and Brooks's poetic stance, 134, 146, 174n74; definition, 133, 173n69; in "In the Mecca," 125, 128; personification of, 132–43; and quasi-ekphrastic poetry, 102, 135–36; and women, 175n96. *See also* blacks; race
blacks: as Brooks's audience, 3, 22–23, 105, 106, 109–12, 134–35, 169n20, 174n75; as family, 137, 174n84; humanity of, 3, 107, 108, 112, 116, 118, 123, 125, 126, 130, 172n50; portrayal of urban life of, 111–13, 124–31, 141; as writers, 131–32, 173nn65–67, 176n9. *See also* Blackness; race
BLACKS (Brooks), 104–5, 107–8, 112–17, 120, 122, 124, 127–31, 138–42, 155n43, 168n1, 169n14, 169n15, 170n29, 170n30, 171n35, 172n55, 173n62, 174nn79, 174n82, 175n85, 175n91, 175n92
Blakely, Henry, 121, 168n7
blank verse, 175n93
Blasing, Mutlu Konuk, 153n24
"Blood, Bread and Poetry" (Rich), 60
Blood, Bread and Poetry (Rich), 58–59. *See also* "Notes toward a Politics of Location" (Rich)
"Blooming in the Whirlwind" (Gabbin), 169n10
Bolden, Barbara Jean, 105, 106, 118, 121, 169n16
Bond, Bruce, 153n31
Boston, MA, 63. *See also* Boston University
Boston University, 18, 59–61, 161n32. *See also* Boston, MA
"Boy Breaking Glass" (Brooks), 137, 138
Bradford, Walter, 138–40
Brain, Tracy, 163n3
"Break of Day" (Donne), 175n97
Brecht, Bertolt, 62
Breslin, James, 152n7
"Briar Rose" (Sexton), 51, 160n14
Broadside Press, 137
Brooks, Cleanth, 93, 94
Brooks, Gwendolyn: call to black people, 132–33, 173n66; endurance, 150; hero poems, 138–40; identity, 2–3; influences on, 3, 110, 112, 117, 151n6; journalistic quality, 104–5, 123, 126, 128–30; lyric discourse, 10, 12; marriage, 121, 168n7, 171n42; motherhood, 104–9, 115, 169n10; newspaper, 104, 168n3; obscurity in, 118, 120, 170n34; personification of Blackness, 132–43; poetic stance, 4, 5, 20–23, 111–12, 121–23, 134–35, 145–46; quasi-ekphrastic poetry of, 23, 102, 135–36, 139; poetry consultant to the Library of Congress, 174n76; and Rich, 176n9; strategies of address, 106, 168n8, 176n1; on technique, 131–32; "Teller" in, 103–4, 114, 123, 126, 130
Brooks, Raymond, 114, 116
Brown, Sterling, 146–47

INDEX

Page numbers in italics refer to figures.

A

abortion, 106–9, 169nn9–10
"The Abortion" (Sexton), 169n9
Alexander, Elizabeth, 171n46
allegory, 22, 82, 84, 166n43
All My Pretty Ones (Sexton), 169n9
Altieri, Charles, 6, 153n22
Alvarez, Alfred, 2, 73, 98, 167n71
American Mercury, 110
Ames, Lois, 53
anger, 121–23, 128
Angle, Paul, 109
"The Anniad" (Brooks): comparison to "In the Mecca," 124; and power of language, 121–22, 171n46; strategies of address in, 118–24
Annie Allen (Brooks): audience of, 119; Brooks on, 120; chronology, 151n5; publication, 109, 118; subject, 2–3, 103. *See also* "The Anniad" (Brooks)
apostrophe: Baraka's use of, 133; Brooks's use of, 20–23, 107, 108, 112, 115, 118–19, 127, 139, 140, 142, 143, 170n27; in confessional poetry, 49; definition, 172n59; in elegies, 16–20; Lowell's use of, 28, 39–40, 63–64, 160n16; in lyric discourse, 6, 8, 9, 44, 143, 158n71, 175n98; Plath's use of, 97–98, 146; purpose of, 4, 5, 152n13; Rich's use of, 14, 15, 16, 62, 64–65; Sexton's use of, 43–45, 158n68. *See also* lyric discourse; rhetorical structures
Ararat (Glück), 11–13, 176n1
Ariel poems (Plath), 101–2, 151n1, 167n59, 168n77
art. *See* ekphrastic poetry
Art News, 72, 81, 87
The Art of Sylvia Plath (Newman), 79
"An Aspect of Love, Alive in the Ice and Fire" (Brooks), 140–43, 175n94
Astrophil and Stella (Sidney), 10
"An Atlas of the Difficult World" (Rich), 14, 62, 70, 154n39
aubade, 39, 142, 143, 175n97
Auden, W. H., 26, 30, 156n20

"Aunt Jennifer's Tigers" (Rich), 29, 31
Axelrod, Steven, 39

B

Bakhtin, Mikhail, 125
"ballad of chocolate mabbie" (Brooks), 133
Bambara, Toni Cade, 134
Baraka, Imamu Amiri, 108, 132–33, 136
Bassnett, Susan, 164n9, 164n12
Baudelaire, Charles, 31
The Bean Eaters (Brooks), 174n79
"Behind the Motel" (Rich), 148
The Bell Jar (Plath), 73, 95
Benjamin, Walter, 154n35
Benn, Gottfried, 5, 153n26
Berger, John, 76, 100
Bernstein, Susan David, 157n37
Bigsby, C. W. E., 173n65
"the birth in a narrow room" (Brooks): placement in *Annie Allen*, 3, 151n5; publication, 2–3, 151n5; structure, 118, 119
Birthday Letters (Hughes), 73–79, 84, 94, 101, 149, 164n9
Bishop, Elizabeth, 26, 41
Bitter Fame (Stevenson), 79
Black Arts movement, 108–9, 111, 122, 126, 146
Black Expression, 140
Blackmur, R. P., 26
Blackness: and apostrophe, 23; and Brooks's poetic stance, 134, 146, 174n74; definition, 133, 173n69; in "In the Mecca," 125, 128; personification of, 132–43; and quasi-ekphrastic poetry, 102, 135–36; and women, 175n96. *See also* blacks; race
blacks: as Brooks's audience, 3, 22–23, 105, 106, 109–12, 134–35, 169n20, 174n75; as family, 137, 174n84; humanity of, 3, 107, 108, 112, 116, 118, 123, 125, 126, 130, 172n50; portrayal of urban life of, 111–13, 124–31, 141; as writers, 131–32, 173nn65–67, 176n9. *See also* Blackness; race
BLACKS (Brooks), 104–5, 107–8, 112–17, 120, 122, 124, 127–31, 138–42, 155n43, 168n1, 169n14, 169n15, 170n29, 170n30, 171n35, 172n55, 173n62, 174nn79, 174n82, 175n85, 175n91, 175n92
Blakely, Henry, 121, 168n7
blank verse, 175n93
Blasing, Mutlu Konuk, 153n24
"Blood, Bread and Poetry" (Rich), 60
Blood, Bread and Poetry (Rich), 58–59. *See also* "Notes toward a Politics of Location" (Rich)
"Blooming in the Whirlwind" (Gabbin), 169n10
Bolden, Barbara Jean, 105, 106, 118, 121, 169n16
Bond, Bruce, 153n31
Boston, MA, 63. *See also* Boston University
Boston University, 18, 59–61, 161n32. *See also* Boston, MA
"Boy Breaking Glass" (Brooks), 137, 138
Bradford, Walter, 138–40
Brain, Tracy, 163n3
"Break of Day" (Donne), 175n97
Brecht, Bertolt, 62
Breslin, James, 152n7
"Briar Rose" (Sexton), 51, 160n14
Broadside Press, 137
Brooks, Cleanth, 93, 94
Brooks, Gwendolyn: call to black people, 132–33, 173n66; endurance, 150; hero poems, 138–40; identity, 2–3; influences on, 3, 110, 112, 117, 151n6; journalistic quality, 104–5, 123, 126, 128–30; lyric discourse, 10, 12; marriage, 121, 168n7, 171n42; motherhood, 104–9, 115, 169n10; newspaper, 104, 168n3; obscurity in, 118, 120, 170n34; personification of Blackness, 132–43; poetic stance, 4, 5, 20–23, 111–12, 121–23, 134–35, 145–46; quasi-ekphrastic poetry of, 23, 102, 135–36, 139; poetry consultant to the Library of Congress, 174n76; and Rich, 176n9; strategies of address, 106, 168n8, 176n1; on technique, 131–32; "Teller" in, 103–4, 114, 123, 126, 130
Brooks, Raymond, 114, 116
Brown, Sterling, 146–47

Browning, Elizabeth Barrett, 2
Bulkin, Elly, 162n55
Burr, Zofia, 23, 134–35, 174nn74–75, 176n1
Byron, Lord, 160n14

C

"Calibrations" (Rich), 148
Cambridge University, 75–78, 84, 164n21
The Canterbury Tales (Chaucer), 76. See also Chaucer's Wife of Bath
A Capsule Course in Black Poetry Writing (Brooks), 108, 134, 174n73
Carr, Emily, 81
A Change of World (Rich), 2, 26, 29, 30, 36, 156n20
"Chaucer" (Hughes), 76
Chaucer's Wife of Bath, 28, 39, 40
Chicago, 3, 104, 140–41, 146. See also *A Street in Bronzeville* (Brooks)
The Chicago Defender, 104, 168n4
Churchwell, Sarah, 164n9, 164n16
City College, New York, 50, 52, 174n75, 176n9
class, 26–27, 47, 59, 112, 125, 146
Clausen, Jan, 159n7
Cold War period, 26–28, 38, 47, 59, 119
Coleridge, Samuel Taylor, 44
Collected Poems (Plath): content and organization, 73, 84, 94, 99, 101, 164n8, 166n45; ekphrastic poetry in, 81–82, 84, 90; and Plath's antinarrative bias, 96; Ted Hughes and, 73, 84, 99, 101–2
"The Colossus" (Plath), 16–19, 71, 95, 174n81
The Colossus (Plath), 2, 165n39, 166n45
Colter, Mary, 165n38
Coming of Age as a Poet (Vendler), 16
Common Ground, 170n29
Complete Poems (Sexton), 33, 53–54, 154nn47–48, 159n9, 169n9
confession: in 1960s, 20; and authority, 34–35, 157n37; and Brooks, 105–8; in Cold War period, 27; and Lowell, 28, 36, 38–41, 46–47, 49, 51–52, 64, 70, 162n44; in lyric discourse, 13; and Plath, 52, 71, 87, 95–102; and political poetry, 56–57, 160n27; and Rich, 31, 47, 52, 57, 63–68, 70, 105; and Sexton, 25–26, 28, 33–35, 43, 46–51. See also "I"; personal experience
Confessional Subjects (Bernstein), 157n37
Confessions (St. Augustine), 48
"Consorting with Angels" (Sexton), 46
Conversation Among the Ruins (de Chirico), 81–84, 83, 166nn40–41
"Conversation among the Ruins" (Plath), 82–84, 87, 99, 100
Costello, Bonnie, 176n99
Crane, Hart, 63
Culler, Jonathan, 4, 6, 7, 9, 10, 44, 175n98
The Cure of Poetry in an Age of Prose (Kinzie), 156n32
"Cut" (Plath), 167n65

D

"Daddy" (Plath): ekphrasis in, 174n81; and New Critical poetics, 18, 95; and "Perseus," 87, 92; and Plath's legacy, 149–50; speaker, 71, 97, 98; writing of, 151n1
Dark Fields of the Republic (Rich), 61–62, 176n12
death, 94–95, 99–100, 116–17, 124. See also elegies
de Chirico, Giorgio, 72, 73, 81–84, 166nn40–41
"Dedications" (Rich), 14–16, 62, 154n38
"Defence of Poetry (Shelley), 5
De Man, Paul, 44, 158n71
Dent, Tory, 149, 177n16
detachment, 58, 70, 123
The Dialogic Imagination (Bakhtin), 172n56
The Diamond Cutters (Rich), 29, 32
Dickie, Margaret, 96, 162n56, 163n1
Dickinson, Emily, 1–3, 2, 26, 68
"The Dilemma of the Negro Author" (Johnson), 110
"The Disquieting Muses" (Plath), 71–73, 87, 100
Diving into the Wreck (Rich), 50, 160n22, 160n24
The Dolphin (Lowell), 63–64, 70, 162n44

Donne, John, 52, 142, 175n97
"The Double Image" (Sexton), 4, 25, 43–46, 48, 65, 107, 158n64, 158n68
"Drawing" (Hughes), 78–79
The Dream of a Common Language (Rich), 32
Duncan, Robert, 160n26

E

"The Earthenware Head" (Plath). *See* "The Lady and the Earthenware Head (Plath)"
"Easter 1916" (Yeats), 160n27
"Eavesdropper" (Plath), 96
"Edge" (Plath), 99–101, 167n73, 174n81
"The Education of the Poet" (Glück), 144, 153n31, 176n1
Edwards, Thomas, 161n27
Ehrenreich, Barbara, 27
"18 Rugby Street" (Hughes), 164n12
ekphrastic poetry: of Brooks, 23, 102, 135–36, 139; definition, 166n42, 174n78; of Plath, 72, 73, 78–79, 87–93, 99–102, 174n81; of Rich, 81, 165n36, 165n38; theory, 79–84
elegies, 16–20, 137, 150, 151n5. *See also* death; "Sylvia's Death" (Sexton); "A Woman Dead in her Forties" (Rich)
Eliot, T. S., 5–8, 26, 31, 41, 42, 111–12, 126, 153n22, 173n63
Elmer, Edwin Romanzo, 81
Emerson, Ralph Waldo, 26, 63
emotion, 97, 98, 121–23. *See also* anger
epic poems, 22, 105. *See also* "In the Mecca" (Brooks); "The Anniad" (Brooks)
epideictic poetry, 23, 134, 173n70
Erkkila, Betsy, 151n4, 175n96
Essence magazine, 121
ethics, 13–14, 65, 68, 70, 107, 115
"Even Then Maybe" (Rich), 147
Evers, Medgar, 137–38
"The Exorcists" (Sexton), 35
"An Explanation of America" (Pinsky), 154n39

F

The Fact of a Doorframe (Rich), 3–5, 63, 66, 160n24
Family Pictures (Brooks), 137
The Feminine Mystique (Friedan), 38, 51
feminism, 38, 55, 58–60, 64, 66–68, 105, 122, 160n24
feminist critics, 152n10, 159n7
Findlay, L. M., 175n98
first-person communal voice, 109, 169n16. *See also* "we"
Fisk University, 133, 142
Forbes, Deborah, 158n68, 160n14, 161n33
"For Both of You, The Divorce Being Final" (Hollander), 27
"For John, Who Begs Me Not to Enquire Further" (Sexton), 32, 33–35, 46, 48, 54
"For Memory" (Rich), 66
For the Union Dead (Lowell), 64
Foucault, Michel, 157n37
"Frame" (Rich), 59–61, 161n31, 161n33
"Framing Water" (Gilbert), 161n31
Friedan, Betty, 26–27, 38
"From the Roof" (Levertov), 32
"Frost at Midnight" (Coleridge), 44
Fry, Paul, 79, 165n34
Frye, Northrop, 5–7, 13, 163n1

G

Gabbin, Joanne V., 169n10
Gadamer, Hans-Georg, 153n23
Gauguin, Paul, 81
"Gay Chaps at the Bar" (Brooks), 113–14, 116–18, 143
Gayle, Addison, Jr., 128
The Gazer's Spirit (Hollander), 79
gender: and Black Power movement, 175n96; in Cold War period, 26–28; and ekphrastic poetry, 80–84; and identity, 3–4; in Lowell, 42, 46–47; and lyric discourse, 149; and Plath–Hughes partnership, 73–77; and poetic stance, 13, 25, 145; in Rich, 2, 26, 27, 29–32, 35–36, 53–55, 57–61, 66–70; in Sexton, 2, 25–26, 32–36, 42, 44,

46–49, 53–55, 145, 158n64; stereotypes, 28–29. *See also* women
Gewanter, David, 162n44
Gilbert, Roger, 161n31
Gill, Jo, 157n37
Giovanni, Nikki, 122
"The Girlhood" (Brooks), 120
Glück, Louise, 11–13, 16, 144, 153n31, 176n1
Grahn, Judy, 159n7
Greek poetry, 8, 9, 17
Gwendolyn Brooks (Melhem), 171n49

H

Hagstrum, Jean, 79
Halpern, Nick, 161n38
Hamilton, Ian, 36
Hardwick, Elizabeth, 28, 38–40, 63, 64, 162n44
Harper and Brothers, 110, 111
Harper, Phillip Brian, 132, 173nn66–67
Harper's, 124, 172n53
Harrison, DeSales, 166n46, 168n75
Harvard University, 52–53, 95
"Heart's Needle" (Snodgrass), 44–45
Heffernan, James, 79–82, 165n36
"Her Kind" (Sexton), 35, 51
heroic couplets, 173n65
heroism. *See* mock-heroic discourse; "YOUNG HEROES" series (Brooks)
heteroglossia, 125, 172n56. *See also* language, poetic function of
Hill, Herbert, 170n26
History of Sexuality, Volume One (Foucault), 157n37
Holden, Jonathan, 13
Hollander, John, 27, 79, 80, 99, 165n32, 165n40
Holmes, John, 34
"Home After Three Months Away" (Lowell), 160n16
"Housewife" (Sexton), 51
"Hubble Photographs" (Rich), 147
Hughes, Sheila Hassell, 172n55
Hughes, Ted, 91; and *Ariel* poems, 101, 168n77; and arrangement of *Collected Poems*, 73, 84, 99, 101–2, 166n45; and "Conversation Among the Ruins," 84; early memories of Path, 73–79, 164n9, 164n12; on "The Earthenware Head," 85, 166n49; on "Medallion," 94, 167n59; on "The Moon and the Yew Tree," 167n64; and "Perseus," 90; on Plath's ekphrastic poetry, 72; and Plath's legacy, 149; and Plath's poetic stance, 20, 96, 97; on Plath's suicide, 167n71; on Plath's work habits, 94–95; publication of Plath's journals, 165n26; use of memory-as-camera trope, 75, 164n16
Hull, Gloria, 174n79, 175n96

I

"I": in Brooks, 106, 107, 114–16, 118, 142–43, 169n12; and feminist consciousness, 105; in "For John, Who Begs Me Not to Enquire Further," 48; and poetic stance, 3–4, 144, 146, 153n23, 153n24; Rich's use of, 59, 60, 70, 146–48, 156n20, 161n33, 176n13. *See also* confession; lyric discourse
Illinois Institute of Technology, 124, 172n52, 172n54
Imagination and Power (Edwards), 161n27
"In the Mecca" (Brooks), 123–31; Blackness in, 137; length, 123, 171n49; poetic stance, 127, 128; polyvocality of, 124, 172n51; reportage in, 105, 123
"In Those Years" (Rich), 14, 154n35
Invisible Listeners (Vendler), 144–45
Ithaca College, 135, 174n75

J

Jackson, Virginia, 6, 153n22
Jakobson, Roman, 152n12
Johnson, Barbara, 10, 11, 44, 169n12
Johnson, James Weldon, 110–11, 169n20
Johnson, W. R., 4, 8–10, 13, 14, 20, 22, 153n26
Jones, Gayl, 172n51
Jordan, June, 176n9
The Journals of Sylvia Plath (Plath),

164n26. See also *Unabridged Journals* (Plath)
Juhasz, Suzanne, 105

K

Kalaidjian, Walter, 173n63, 175n93
Keats, John, 9, 49, 80, 111
Keniston, Ann, 6, 13, 153n22, 154n35, 176n12
Kent, George, 106, 111–13, 118, 168n3, 170n26, 170n32
Keyes, Claire, 31
Kgositsile, Keorapetse, 138–40, 174n73
King, Martin Luther, Jr., 140
Kinnahan, Linda, 159n7
Kinzie, Mary, 95, 156n32
Klee, Paul, 73, 81, 87–93, 89
Kramer, Lawrence, 40–42, 44
Kroll, Judith, 72
Kukil, Karen, 164n21
Kumin, Maxine, 34, 51, 150
Kuumba dance troupe, 137

L

Lacan, Jacques, 34, 100–101
The Ladies' Home Journal, 27, 77
"The Lady and the Earthenware Head" (Plath), 85–86, 97, 166n49
"Lady Lazarus" (Plath), 18, 52, 75, 87, 92, 95, 98, 149, 151n1
language: poetic function of, 4, 150, 152n12, 153n24; power of, 121–22, 171n43, 171n46. *See also* heteroglossia
Lee, Don, 119, 126, 128, 138–40, 171n43, 173n61, 174n73, 175n87
lesbian existence, 68, 162n53
"Lesbos" (Plath), 95, 96
"Letters Censored, Shredded, Returned to Sender, or Judged Unfit to Send" (Rich), 147
Levertov, Denise, 28–29, 32, 156n28
Lewis, Ida, 121
"The Life of Lincoln West" (Brooks), 137, 174n83
Life magazine, 31, 175n86
Life Studies (Lowell): confessional intimacy of, 36, 40–43, 49, 51–52; gender identity in, 37–39; and Lowell's poetic stance, 63; on marriage, 28, 38–41
"Linguistics and Poetics" (Jakobson), 152n12
"Little Girl, My Stringbean, My Lovely Woman" (Sexton), 52–54
Lord Weary's Castle (Lowell), 36
Lorde, Audre, 176n9
love poetry, 21–22, 140–43, 168n7
"The Love Song of J. Alfred Prufrock" (Eliot), 7, 111, 170n26
Lowell, Amy, 2, 26, 37
Lowell, Charlotte, 36–38, 40
Lowell, Robert: apostrophe in, 28, 39–40, 63–64, 160n16; poetic authority of, 41–43; comparison to Plath, 71, 73, 96, 163n1; confessional intimacy, 28, 36, 38–41, 46–47, 49, 51–52, 64, 70, 162n44; and gendered perspectives, 42, 145, 158n64; legacy, 149; on marriage, 27–28, 35–41; poetic stance, 13, 63; political poetry of, 161n27; as teacher, 18, 50, 95
Lowney, John, 172n50
"Lycidas" (Milton), 16
lyric discourse: "addressivity" of, 144, 176n1; apostrophe in, 6, 8, 9, 44, 143, 158n71, 175n98; in Brooks, 22, 105, 121, 134, 142, 143, 169n13, 173n66; of confessional poets, 49–50; as "I-you" poems, 4–17, 152n13; language of, 153n24; legacy of, 146–50; meaning of, 4–5; and time, 143, 176n99. *See also* apostrophe
Lyric Poetry (Blasing), 153n24

M

MacGowan, Christopher, 149
Madhubuti, Haki R. *See* Lee, Don
Malcolm X, 137–38, 175n86
Mallarmé, Stéphane, 8, 153n26
"Man and Wife" (Lowell), 36, 39–41, 42–43
"Man and Wife" (Sexton), 42–43
marriage, 27–28, 42–43, 68, 73–79, 84–85, 121, 168n7, 171n42
"A Marriage in the Sixties" (Rich), 31, 43
Martin, John Bartlow, 124, 171n50, 172n53

Marvell, Andrew, 18, 52, 95, 160n16
Masks Outrageous and Austere (Walker), 155n4
Maud Martha (Brooks), 142, 175n95
McCullough, Frances, 164n26
McDaniel, Judith, 28, 29
McNamara, Robert, 52
Mecca building, 123–24, 171n49, 171n50, 172n53. *See also* "In the Mecca" (Brooks)
"Medallion" (Plath), 94–95, 167n59
Medusa, Plath's affinity for, 74, 75, 86–88, 90, 92, 95, 98, 102, 165n39, 167n69
"Medusa" (Plath), 18, 92, 95, 97–98, 174n81
Medusan theories of ekphrasis, 80–81
Melhem, D. H., 106, 123, 142, 143, 169n10, 170n26, 171n49, 174n75, 174n84, 175n88
memory-as-camera trope, 75, 164n16
metaphors, 122–23, 130, 133, 140
Middlebrook, Diane, 18, 34, 53, 54, 73, 158n64
Mill, John Stuart, 5–7, 152n14, 153n22
Millay, Edna St. Vincent, 2, 26, 155n4, 158n64
Miller, Brett, 41, 42
Miller, Dorie, 114, 170n29, 170n30. *See also* "Negro Hero" (Brooks)
Millier, A. D., 111
The Mills of the Kavanaughs (Lowell), 36, 64
Milton, John, 16
Mitchell, W. J. T., 79–81
mock-heroic discourse, 120
Modersohn-Becker, Paula, 81
"The Moon and the Yew Tree" (Plath), 96–97, 167n64
Moore, Marianne, 2, 26, 155n4
Morison, Emily, 110, 112, 117
"the mother" (Brooks), 106–9, 115, 169nn12–13
motherhood, 43–46, 48, 53–55, 65, 98–100, 104–9, 158n69, 162n48. *See also* patriarchy; women
"Mourning Picture" (Rich), 81, 165n36
A Movement of Poets (Clausen), 159n7
Mullen, Bill, 170n28
Museum of Words (Heffernan), 80
"Music Swims Back to Me" (Sexton), 35, 46

Muske, Carol, 2, 160n25
"My Last Afternoon with Uncle Devereux Winslow" (Lowell), 36
My Name Is Afrika (Kgositsile), 138–39

N

necrophilia, 163n56
"Negro Hero" (Brooks), 113–18, 128, 170nn29–30
Negro Story magazine, 170n29
Nelson, Cary, 55–57, 62, 107, 160n24, 160n26, 161n27
New Critics, 17–18, 49, 81, 92–95
New, Elisa, 163n57
"91 Revere Street" (Lowell), 36–41, 73
"North American Time" (Rich), 161n37
"Notes from the Childhood and the Girlhood" (Brooks), 118
"Notes on the Chronological Order of Sylvia Plath's Poems" (Hughes), 94, 101, 167n64
"Notes toward a Politics of Location" (Rich), 50, 59, 159n7

O

"Observations on a Black Aesthetic" (Miller), 111
ode, 158n71
"Ode on a Grecian Urn" (Keats), 49, 80, 111
Oedipus, 34, 35
off-rhyme sonnet sequence, 113–18, 143, 170n33
Of Woman Born (Rich), 162n48
"the old marrieds" (Brooks), 109, 118
Olsen, Tillie, 51
"On the Medusa of Leonardo da Vinci" (Shelley), 165n32
oral presentation, 23, 134–36, 138, 140–43, 174nn74–76
Ostriker, Alicia, 33, 102, 151n3, 156n32
Our Last First Poets (Nelson), 55–56, 160n26

P

Paterson (Williams), 162n44
patriarchy, 59, 100. *See also* motherhood

"Paul Robeson" (Brooks), 137
Pearl Harbor, 116
Perelman, Chaim, 173n70
Perloff, Marjorie, 96; on the *Ariel* volume, 101, on Plath's "I," 71, 86, 163n1, 167n65
Perseus (Klee), 87–93, 89
"Perseus: The Triumph of Wit Over Suffering" (Plath), 87–92, 136
personal experience, 26–28, 33, 59, 105, 111–12, 168n7. *See also* confession; selfhood
Petrarchan blazon, 76
Phylon, 119, 131–32, 137, 140, 141
Pindar, 173n72
Pinsky, Robert, 154n39
Plath, Aurelia, 98
Plath, Sylvia, *91*; Americanness, 74, 164n12; boundedness of poems, 93–95; comparison to Brooks, 136; and confessional poetry, 52, 71, 87, 95–102; Electra complex, 17, 47; and elegies, 16–20; Hughes's early memories of, 73–79, 164n9, 164n12; journal entries, 78–79, 85–87, 90, 92, 164n26; legacy, 149–50; lyric discourse, 10; poetic stance, 5, 20, 47, 71–73, 86–87, 95–102, 145, 146, 163n1, 163n3; and representational surfaces, 85, 166n46; Rich on suicide of, 50; rivalry of, 2, 151n4; work habits, 93–95, 167n60
Playboy magazine, 27
"Poem for a Birthday" (Plath), 95, 167n59
Poems, Poets, Poetry (Vendler), 7
Poems Selected and New (Rich), 29
"The Poet as Woman" (Ransom), 155n4
"The Poet in the World" (Levertov), 28–29
Poetics of the Feminine (Kinnahan), 159n7
poets: and gender identity, 1–3, 26, 43, 50–51, 151n3, 155n4; generational studies of, 152n7; Plath on techniques of, 93; power of language, 121–22, 171n43, 171n46; Rich's conception of, 63, 70, 161n38; rivalry among, 2, 18, 19–20, 50, 151n4; stereotypes, 28–29; "Poets Who Are Negroes" (Brooks), 131–32, 137, 140
politics: in Brooks, 106, 107, 110, 115, 122, 143; and confessional poetry, 56–57, 161n27; and personal experience, 59; and poetic stance, 13–14, 63, 146; of race, 3; in Rich, 61–63, 66, 68. *See also* Cold War period; Vietnam War
Pope, Deborah, 156n20
"Portrait of a Lady" (Eliot), 111
"Portraits" (Hughes), 94
Poulet, George, 153n23
prophets, 63, 101, 104–5, 123, 126, 161n38
Prouty, Olive Higgins, 77
Prufrock and Other Observations (Eliot), 111

Q

Quinn, Sister Bernetta, 98, 167n69

R

race: in Brooks's *Annie Allen* poems, 118–24; and Brooks's Bronzeville poems, 106–18; and Brooks's poetic stance, 3, 22–23, 104, 134–35, 146, 174n75; in Rich, 59–61, 146. *See also* Blackness; blacks
Radcliffe Institute, 51
Ramazani, Jahan, 16, 18–20, 68
Randall, Dudley, 174n73
Ransom, John Crowe, 26, 155n4
"Rape" (Rich), 55–59, 106, 107, 160nn25–26, 161n31
"Readings of History" (Rich), 31
Redding, Saunders, 171n34, 171n43
The Regenerate Lyric (New), 163n57
relationships, intimate, 66–70. *See also* marriage; motherhood
religion, 34, 126–27
Report from Part One (Brooks), 106–7, 109–10, 121, 133, 141–42, 174n74
Report from Part Two (Brooks), 137, 174n84
rhetorical structures: in Brooks, 21, 106, 108, 109, 115, 116, 119, 129, 132, 134, 140, 170n30; in Plath, 20, 47, 84, 87, 99, 102; in Rich, 15, 31, 50, 56, 58, 60, 62, 69–70,

163n57; in Sexton, 4, 18, 28, 33, 42, 44; in sonnets, 21. *See also* apostrophe
"Rhyme" (Rich), 148–49
Rich, Adrienne: on African American poets, 176n9; comparison to Brooks, 106, 107; and confessional poetry, 31, 47, 52, 57, 63–68, 70, 105; ekphrastic poetry of, 81, 165n36, 165n38; endurance, 150; and "Frame," 59–61; and gender identity, 2, 26, 27, 29–32, 35–36, 53–55, 57–61, 66–70; on "Little Girl, My Stringbean," 52–53; location in, 61, 62, 148, 161n34, 177n15; lyric discourse, 10, 146–47, 176n12, 176n14, 177n16; on marriage, 43; memorial tribute to Sexton, 50–52, 57; on motherhood, 65, 162n48; on personal experience, 33; poetic stance, 4–5, 13–15, 16, 49–50, 70, 145–49; and "Rape," 55–59; and "Roofwalker" dedication, 32, 156n28; witness in, 60, 161n31
"RIOT" (Brooks), 140–43; aubade in, 143
Roethke, Theodore, 95
Rogers, William Elford, 153n23
Roget's Thesaurus, 77
Roman poetry, 8
Romantic poets, 4–6, 9, 44, 49, 63
"The Roofwalker" (Rich), 32, 156n28
Rosenfield, Lawrence, 134
Rosenthal, M. L., 95
Rossetti, Christina, 2
Rousseau, Henri, 73, 81
Rückfiguren, 82, 165n40

S

"Said the Poet to the Analyst" (Sexton), 32, 46
Saldívar, Toni, 165n39
Sanchez, Sonia, 122, 135, 174n76
Sappho, 2, 8
Saturday Review of Literature, 171n34
Schopenhauer, Arthur, 34, 40
Schwartz, Delmore, 40
Schweik, Susan, 170nn29–30
Scigaj, Leonard, 17–18, 73, 87, 88, 92–94, 166n41
SEEK program, 176n9

"self-focused," 4, 152n12
selfhood: and Brooks, 106, 115, 134–35, 137, 142, 146; and lyric discourse, 9–13; and Plath, 76–78, 85–92, 95; Rich on, 67–69; and Sexton, 43. *See also* personal experience
Senghor, Leopold, 130, 172n55
Sexton, Anne: charisma, 160n14; comparison to Brooks, 107, 169n9; comparison to Plath, 71, 73, 163n1; dramatization of self, 43; and gender identity, 2, 25–26, 32–36, 42, 44, 46–49, 53–55, 145, 158n64; and language, 153n24; legacy, 149, 150; lyric discourse, 10; on marriage, 35–36, 42–43; and Plath, 1–2, 18–20, 95, 101; poetic stance, 4, 5, 13, 20, 32, 63, 146, 156n32; Rich on death of, 50–52, 55, 57
Sexton, Linda Gray, 36, 44, 46, 52–54, 158n69
sexuality, 53–55, 68–69, 121–23, 162n53, 162n55
Shakespeare, William, 9, 21, 52
Shange, Ntozake, 135, 174n76
Shaw, Harry, 170n30
Shelley, Mary, 165n32
Shelley, Percy Bysshe, 4, 5, 9, 49, 63, 80, 165n32
Shifting Ground (Costello), 176n99
"Sibling Mysteries" (Rich), 54–55
Sidney, Philip, 9–10, 49
Signs, 68, 162n53
Sincerity's Shadow (Forbes), 158n68, 160n14
The Sister Arts (Hagstrum), 79
Sitwell, Edith, 2
Smith College, 72, 78, 94
Smith, Satin-Legs, 137. *See also* "The Sundays of Satin-Legs Smith" (Brooks)
"Snapshots of a Daughter-in-Law" (Rich), 30–31
Snodgrass, W. D., 42, 44–45, 95, 149
"Song of Myself" (Whitman), 108
sonnets, 9, 21, 81–82, 113–18, 143, 170n33
Sonnets (Shakespeare), 9
Soon One Morning (Hill), 170n26
Sophocles, 34, 90
"SOS" (Baraka), 132–33, 136

"Sources" (Rich), 65, 70
Spiegelman, Willard, 156n20
Spillers, Hortense, 121–22
Stampleman, Joe, 161n32
Stanford, Ann Folwell, 116
Starbuck, George, 18, 19
St. Augustine, 48
St. Botolph's Review, 76, 77
Stavros, George, 120
Stealing the Language (Ostriker), 151n3
"Stepping Backward" (Rich), 162n55
Stevenson, Anne, 79
Stewart, Susan, 152n13
"The Stones" (Plath), 167nn59–60
"Storm Warnings" (Rich), 30, 156n20
A Street in Bronzeville (Brooks), 106–18; Blackness in, 133; content and organization, 109, 110; strategies of address in, 20–22, 106, 112, 118–19, 169n13. See also "Gay Chaps at the Bar" (Brooks); "Negro Hero" (Brooks); "The Sundays of Satin-Legs Smith" (Brooks); "when you have forgotten Sunday: the love story" (Brooks)
"Strumpet Song" (Plath), 77
Sullivan, James D., 175n93
"The Sun Rising" (Donne), 142
"The Sundays of Satin-Legs Smith" (Brooks), 111–13; audience, 112, 117, 170nn27–28; comparison to hero poems, 114; humanity in, 125; and "The Love Song of J. Alfred Prufrock," 170n26; protagonist, 121, 127. See also Smith, Satin-Legs
Sylvia Plath (Bassnett), 164n9
"Sylvia's Death" (Sexton), 18–20, 50

T

Tate, Claudia, 121, 122
"Teaching Language in Open Admissions" (Rich), 176n2
Telephone Ringing in the Labyrinth (Rich), 146–49, 176n14
third-person narrative, 60–61, 109, 115
"The Third Sermon on the Warpland" (Brooks), 140, 175n92
"this" (Rich), 65, 162nn48–49

The Three Voices of Poetry (Eliot), 5
Tillinghast, Richard, 40, 41, 64
"Tintern Abbey" (Wordsworth), 44, 49
To Bedlam and Part Way Back (Sexton), 25, 33–35
"To Don at Salaam" (Brooks), 139, 140, 175n90
"To His Coy Mistress" (Marvell), 160n16
"To Judith, Taking Leave" (Rich), 162n55
"To Keorapetse Kgositsile" (Brooks), 139–40
"To Speak of Woe That Is in Marriage" (Lowell), 28, 40
"To Those of My Sisters Who Kept Their Naturals" (Brooks), 174n75
"tone of the center," 27, 30
"The Torturer's Horse" (Fry), 165n34
"The Tour" (Plath), 96
"The Tourist and the Town" (Rich), 29, 31
Transformations (Sexton), 46, 47, 51
Travisano, Thomas, 152n7
truth: in Brooks, 103–4, 106, 111, 123, 131, 132; Glück on, 11, 13; in Plath, 95; in Rich, 67–68, 70; in Sexton, 36, 48
"Trying to Talk with a Man" (Rich), 53, 160n22
Tucker, Herbert, 152n14
"Tulips" (Plath), 97, 167n66
Twentieth-Century American Poetry (MacGowan), 149
"Twenty-One Love Poems" (Rich), 65, 70

U

Unabridged Journals (Plath), 149. See also *The Journals of Sylvia Plath* (Plath)
Understanding Poetry (Brooks and Warren), 94
universality, 26, 109, 117, 119, 145, 170n32, 171n43, 174n74
"The University Reopens as the Floods Recede" (Rich), 148
"An Unsaid Word" (Rich), 35–36
Uroff, Margaret Dickie. See Dickie, Margaret
"The Untrustworthy" (Glück), 13

V

Van der Rohe, Miës, 124, 125, 128, 172n54
Vaughan, Henry, 8
Vendler, Helen: on "The Colossus," 16, 17; on lyric discourse, 7, 9–10, 12, 16, 144–45, 153n22, 153n23, 153n24, 153n30; on poetic stance, 4, 5; on "Rape," 55
"verbal privilege," 63, 161n37
"Via Insomnia" (Rich), 149
Vickers, Nancy, 76
Vietnam War, 52–53, 56–57
von Hallberg, Robert, 27
"Voyage to the Denouement" (Rich), 148

W

Wagner-Martin, Linda, 167n66
Wakoski, Diane, 64
Walker, Cheryl, 155n4
Walker, Margaret, 119
"The Wall" (Brooks), 137, 175n85
"Walter Bradford" (Brooks), 139, 140
Ward, Val Gray, 137
"The Waste Land" (Eliot), 31, 41, 111, 126, 173n63
Waters, William, 4, 152n12
Ways of Seeing (Berger), 76
"we": Brooks's use of, 109, 114–15, 136, 142–43; Rich's use of, 14, 15, 29–30, 57, 59, 62, 63, 145–46, 156n20; Sexton's use of, 42, 53. *See also* first-person communal voice
"we real cool" (Brooks), 136, 174n79
The Well Wrought Urn (Brooks), 93, 94
West, Lincoln, 137. *See also* "The Life of Lincoln West" (Brooks)
"western" poetry, 3, 23, 118–21
What Is Found There (Rich), 62
"What Kind of Times Are These" (Rich), 61–62
Wheatley, Phillis, 173n65
"when you have forgotten Sunday: the love story" (Brooks), 21–22, 168n7, 169n13
Whitehead, Kim, 159n7
Whitman, Walt, 61, 108, 109
The Wicked Sisters (Erkkila), 151n4
Wilbur, Richard, 4
Williams, William Carlos, 8, 162n44
"Winnie" (Brooks), 135–36
"Winter Landscape, with Rooks" (Plath), 164n8
"A Woman Dead in her Forties" (Rich), 67–70, 162n56
"The Womanhood" (Brooks), 108, 169n14
women: and Black Power movement, 175n96; desire to be looked at, 76; and ekphrastic writing, 80, 165n34; in Plath's poetry, 99–101; poetry about, 105. *See also* gender; motherhood
Women and Poetry (Muske), 160n25
Wordsworth, William, 44, 49
Wright, Richard, 106, 111

Y

Yeats, William Butler, 8, 153n30, 161n27
"you": in Brooks, 106, 107, 115, 129, 139, 169n10, 169n12; and poetic stance, 4; in Rich, 56–58, 61–63, 67, 70, 146–49; in Sexton, 25, 34, 48, 53. *See also* lyric discourse
"You, Doctor Martin" (Sexton), 32, 35, 46
"YOUNG HEROES" series (Brooks), 137–40, 175nn88–90
"Your Paris" (Hughes), 78
"'Your Sentence Was Mine Too'" (Churchwell), 164n9, 164n16